Avant-Garde

Leonard Cabell Pronko

Avant-Garde: The Experimental Theater in France

GREENWOOD PRESS, PUBLISHERS
WESTPORT, CONNECTICUT

Library of Congress Cataloging in Publication Data

Pronko, Leonard Cabell.
     Avant-garde : the experimental theater in France.

     Reprint of the ed. published by University of
California Press, Berkeley.
     Bibliography: p.
     1. French drama--20th century--History and
criticism. 2. Avant-garde (Aesthetics). I. Title.
[PQ558.P7 1978]   842'.9'1409   77-26017
ISBN 0-313-20096-3

© 1962 by The Regents of the University of California

Reprinted with the permission of The University of California
Press

Reprinted in 1978 by Greenwood Press, Inc.
51 Riverside Avenue, Westport, CT 06880

Printed in the United States of America

To My Students

"After the performance the audience is not supposed to have well digested their dinner and to be thoroughly entertained, but rather they are supposed to go home, their mind full of questions, and think!"

(FROM A TEST PAPER ON THE AVANT-GARDE.)

"Les sots croient que plaisanter, c'est ne pas être sérieux."

P. VALÉRY

Preface

THIS BOOK is intended for the intelligent lover of theater and not for the specialist in French literature or the theoretician of drama. I have not attempted to prove anything: any drama must ultimately stand on its own. The duty of the critic is to understand (and consequently to appreciate), and then to help others to understand. Where others see nonsense and confusion, he must find meaning and patterns, provided they are present, in however unfamiliar a form. To do this he must both enter into the world of the artist and examine it from without. His views will necessarily reflect his own background, preferences and sensibilities. If each man is a solitude, then we may profit through a "sharing of solitudes."

I have included all the avant-garde dramatists of importance, and several who strike me (but not everyone) as distinctly minor figures. Where plays exist in English translation I have used the English title. Plays not well-known in English or as yet untranslated I have preferred to refer to by French title.

I owe an immense debt of gratitude to Mrs. Barbara Bray and the British Broadcasting Corporation for permission to use the scripts of several pertinent "Art-Anti-Art" programs, and to Mr. Jacques Brunius, author of the scripts, for his kindness in allowing me to quote from them and for the wealth of supplementary information he furnished me. I am also indebted to Professor Lloyd J. Lanich, Jr. and Professor Ruby Cohn for reading my manuscript and making many valuable suggestions. Any omissions or ineptitudes are, of course, due to my own obstinacy. It is a particular pleasure to express here my appreciation to Mrs. Cohn for many hours of inspiring conversation, for constant encouragement, and for the benefit of her brilliant critical insight.

I wish to thank also the Research Committee of the Claremont Colleges for a grant which enabled me to have secretarial help at certain points, and to obtain the photographs which illustrate this book; the editors of the *French Review* and of *Modern Drama* for their kind permission to use material from articles on Schehadé and Ionesco which had previously appeared in their publications; the editors of Gallimard for permission to quote from Tardieu's *Théâtre de Chambre* (copyright Librairie Gallimard, 1955), Ghelderode's *Théâtre,* volumes III (copyright Librairie Gallimard, 1953) and IV (copyright Librairie Gallimard, 1955), Audiberti's *Théâtre,* volume III (copyright Librairie Gallimard, 1956), Schehadé's *Monsieur Bob'le* (copyright Librairie Gallimard, 1951), and *La Soirée des proverbes* (copyright Librairie Gallimard, 1954); and the editors of Grove Press for permission to quote from their translations of Artaud's *The Theater and Its Double* (copyright Grove Press, 1958), Beckett's *Waiting for Godot* (copyright Grove Press, 1954) and *Endgame* (copyright Grove Press, 1958), and Ionesco's *Four Plays* (copyright Grove Press, 1958), *Three Plays* (copyright John Calder, 1958), *The Killer and Other Plays* (copyright John Calder, 1960), and *Rhinoceros and Other Plays* (copyright John Calder, 1960).

A word regarding the genesis of this study, lest the reader be deceived by the dedication. This book did not grow out of a course, but was fully written in first draft before being used as background reading for a course on the avant-garde drama. I consider my students, or some

viii

of them at least, to be intelligent lovers of theater, and it is to the *amateur* that this work is addressed, not the student as such.

LEONARD C. PRONKO

Claremont, California
December, 1961

Contents

Illustrations

1

Many Avant-Gardes

AFTER A silent pregnancy of almost twenty years, the French theater at mid-twentieth century gave healthy birth to a type of drama that had been conceived, and briefly drew breath, as early as 1896 when Alfred Jarry shocked the placid audience at the Théâtre de l'Oeuvre with Père Ubu's resounding "Merdre!" Jarry's revolt against bourgeois morality and prevalent theater values, drawing inspiration from the romanticism and bohemianism of the nineteenth century, led in the theater to the more organized revolt of Apollinaire's *Les Mamelles de Tirésias*, and the few dramatic efforts of dada and surrealism. By 1930, however, despite the efforts of Antonin Artaud, the lineage of Jarry seemed extinct, and it was only in 1950, with the performance of Ionesco's *Bald Soprano*, and three years later with Beckett's *Waiting for Godot*, that it became clear that the spirit of the avant-garde was still alive in the theater.

When we speak of Beckett, Ionesco, Adamov, or Genêt as members of the avant-garde, it is partly a matter of convenience, and partly in deference to common usage which has found this particular tag to apply to the experimental theater in France from 1950 to 1960. Avant-garde is, of course, a military term denoting the vanguard that precedes the main body of an army and prepares the terrain. In a very physical sense, then, the avant-garde is what the beat generation would

1

call "way out." The literary use of the word apparently came into being about the end of the nineteenth century, and was popular by the middle of the second decade of the twentieth, when it was used to describe those imaginative and talented *bons vivants* of the *belle époque* who scandalized the settled world of the middle class and brought about a revolution in the arts. It expressed what Roger Shattuck, in his brilliant evocation of the period, calls "a 'tradition' of heterodoxy and opposition which defied civilized values in the name of individual consciousness."[1] Eccentric behavior, the desire to shock and the pursuit of newness for its own sake are characteristic of the avant-garde of the "Banquet Years," and the decade following. On these grounds at least we must make a clear distinction between the early avant-garde, and the dramatists with whom we are concerned in this book, for the theaters we are about to investigate reveal a fundamentally serious attitude toward life and toward the art of the theater. Such critics as Jean-Jacques Gautier notwithstanding, the drama of a Ionesco or a Beckett is a great deal more than a game compounded of tricks, scandal, nonsense, charlatanism, and newness at any cost. It may even be noted with some regret that the picturesque behavior of such characters as Alfred Jarry is lacking today. On the other hand, this may indicate that today's avant-garde is first of all interested in effecting a revolution in the theater. The criticism of prevailing social attitudes is if not secondary, at any rate to be expressed through the theater, rather than through that exuberant, adolescent (but most often ineffective) personal revolt which was typical of the earlier avant-garde. Today the personal defiance seems to have been channeled more exclusively into artistic efforts. I do not wish to suggest that today's drama is a purely artistic undertaking, for the avant-garde is seriously concerned with the meaning of man's existence, and even of his role in society. But this concern is expressed through artistic achievements rather than through personal idiosyncrasies.

It should be clear by now that there is no single avant-garde. There are only certain characteristics that we may associate with any achievement so classified. "Every avant-garde," says Bernard Dort, "is first of all a breaking away from the bulk of the troop, and a refusal of accepted discipline and behavior."[2] This general definition is, it seems to me, about as specific as we can become and still include all the groups which have been dubbed with this name. The essence of avant-gardism is that it is never satisfied with accepted standards and is constantly searching. In its most distinguished manifestations it is not only a revolt, but a renewal. In an essay entitled, "There Is No Avant-Garde Theater,"[3] Ionesco rejects the idea that the avant-garde theater is transitional, for *all* theater is transitional. Instead he sees the avant-garde as a restoration, a return. It constitutes a rediscovery of the fundamental models of theater, a return in some respects to primitive theater, and a return to man, rather than society, as the center of the dramatic universe. Its "object is to rediscover the timeless truth and to reintegrate it with our time."

The writers, groups, or movements which have been called avant-garde are legion. Eric Bentley suggests that Sartre is a writer of the avant-garde,[4] while Georges Pillement, writing at almost the same time, claims "there is no longer an avant-garde theatre,"[5] but lists in his volume devoted to that group such dramatists as Jules Romains, Charles Vildrac, Marcel Achard, Stève Passeur, and Jean Anouilh. He points out in his introduction that many of these writers who began as avant-garde authors have ended up on the boulevards in the popular commercial theaters. Ionesco, whose right to the name is probably unchallenged, not only rejects Sartre (with the exception of *Huis clos*), but claims that he himself is "not at all what people call an avant-garde author."[6] Jacques Copeau, the great director and founder of the Théâtre du Vieux Colombier, has also received baptism, along with the four directors commonly grouped together as Le Cartel des Quatre: Dullin, Jouvet, Baty, and Pitoëff, for each of these men contributed in his own way to the renewal of the French theater in the first half of the twentieth century. With this in mind, we may also reach back to 1887 in order to include Antoine and his Théâtre Libre, responsible to a great degree for the founding of the little theater movements not only in France but throughout Europe and America. Without the little theaters, the small houses of Paris such as the Huchette and the Babylone, and the Off-Broadway theaters of New York, one might well wonder where today's avant-garde plays would have found their public.

The men who interest us chiefly here are those who have contributed in varying ways to the possibility of the experimental theater which today is enjoying a success it has never known before.

With *Ubu roi,* Alfred Jarry may be said to have founded the avant-garde drama, for it is the first modern play reflecting the anarchy of the author's double revolt against the society in which he lived and the more or less set forms of the realistic and naturalistic drama favored by the Théâtre libre. The center of the play and its *raison d'être* is the preposterous and monstrous figure of Père Ubu himself, the embodiment of what Catulle Mendès called "eternal imbecility, eternal lust, eternal gluttony, the baseness of instinct become tyrannical; of the modesty, virtues, patriotism and ideals of people who have dined well."

The play originated as a schoolboy project parodying an incompetent professor of physics at the lycée in Rennes, a certain Monsieur Hébert, whose name was changed to Hébé, and finally to Ubu. The first performance took place in 1888 in a marionette theater, and indications of its guignolesque nature survive in the present version, particularly in the oversimplification of the characters, the grossness of the farce, and the slapstick

4

elements employed. Jarry had also suggested to Lugné-Poë, his director at the Théâtre de l'Oeuvre in 1896, that he avoid scene changes by using placards to indicate the settings, as was customarily done in puppet shows. The anti-realistic nature of the play was further stressed by Jarry's desire to have Ubu wear a mask and speak in a "special" tone of voice, to use cardboard horses hanging around the actors' necks for the equestrian scenes, to use one character to represent a crowd, and to use costumes which possessed no local color in order to "render better the idea of something eternal."

The mock Middle French epigraph on the dedicatory page of *Ubu roi*, with its play on words, its pseudo-learned cadence, its reference to Shakespeare's tragedies, and its obvious absurdity, sets the tone for the play that follows:

> Adonc le Père Ubu hoscha la poire, dont fut depuis nommé par les Anglois Shakespeare, et avez de lui sous ce nom maintes belles tragoedies par escript.

> Then Father Ubu shook his pear [slang for head], whence he was thereafter called by the English Shakespeare, and you have by him, under this name, many a beautiful tragedy in writing.

The epic of Père Ubu, spurred on by his ambitious wife to murder King Venceslas and become King of Poland himself, parodies *Macbeth*. Defeated finally by his own vices and by the only surviving son of Venceslas, Bougrelas, Ubu finds refuge in a cavern where like Richard III he has a dream in which he is visited by the specters of his victims. Finally he flees with Mère Ubu to France. The sequel, *Ubu enchaîné*, whose title is an obvious parody of Aeschylus' *Prometheus Bound*, known in French as *Prométhée enchaîné*, shows how Ubu, now in the country of liberty, decides to become a slave. After showing himself capable of obeying orders in a country where everyone systematically disobeys, he becomes shoeshine boy, servant, prisoner, and finally galley slave. In the upside-down world created in *Ubu enchaîné,* where liberty is slavery and slavery liberty, all free men revolt and become slaves, and once again Ubu sails away to new adventures in unknown lands.

André Breton has called *Ubu* "the great prophetic avenging play of modern times." Avenging, because Jarry depicted, exaggerated beyond belief, the viciousness, the avidity and cowardice, the gluttony and pettiness of man. "When the curtain rose," wrote Jarry,

> I wanted the stage to be before the audience like a mirror . . . in which the vicious one would see himself with the horns of a bull and the body of a dragon, according to the exaggeration of his vices; and it is not surprising that the public was stupefied at the sight of its ignoble reflection which had not yet been completely presented to it.

A prophetic play not only because it looks forward to the senseless carnage of the twentieth century and the topsy-turvy world of today in which values have lost all absolute meaning so that upside down may very well be right side up, but prophetic also in a sense of which Breton was unaware when he made his statement, for the *Ubu* plays point straight forward to the works of today's avant-garde in France, and particularly to the theater of Ionesco. The immense verve of Jarry's work, the grotesqueness of his exaggeration, the simplicity of characterization, his deep-cutting social satire, and his free linguistic invention all herald plays like *The Bald Soprano, Jack,* and *The Chairs.*

"Recounting comprehensible things," Jarry once said to his friend Jean Saltas, "only serves to make heavy the spirit and to warp the memory, whereas the absurd exercises the spirit and makes memory work." The vision of the absurd which Jarry reveals through his truculent creations is an essential part of the view propounded by the major writers of today's new French theater, and is as important to the form of both theaters as it is to the substance. The disregard for verisimilitude in charac-

6

ter, setting or action, the looseness of structures (which in Jarry does not, however, reach the illogicality and extreme laxity of an Adamov—or a Strindberg dream play, for that matter) reflect on a formal level the chaotic, the anarchic, point of view expressed through the very substance of the play. The apprehensive laughter which Ubu elicits is the same laughter which explodes today in the theaters where *Waiting for Godot* and *The Lesson* are performed. Nevertheless, there is an added dimension in the more recent plays. *Ubu* is essentially a social (and, if you will, a political) satire. The anarchy it reveals is made by man and may presumably be corrected by man. Similarly, the absurd language is indicative of an exuberant imagination, and underlines the earthy aspects of Ubu, but it does not suggest that language has lost its meaning and no longer serves as communication. On the contrary, the characters in *Ubu roi* understand each other almost too well, and beat each other as unmercifully with words as they do with sticks and feet. Ubu is fundamentally optimistic, a gross bourgeois who is master of his fate at least to the extent that he can silence his conscience (which he keeps in a box), using it always to his own wicked ends, and finally sail off to new adventures. He constitutes a savage commentary on man in relationship to himself and to other men, but unlike the characters of today's avant-garde theater, he suggests very little of an ontological nature.

People may have been scandalized by *Ubu roi*, but few would contest Jarry's assertion that it "has the advantage of being accessible to the majority of the audience." Apollinaire's *Les Mamelles de Tirésias* (*The Breasts of Tiresias*), on the other hand, was charged with obscurity and confused symbolism. First written in 1903, but not performed until 1917, Apollinaire's "surrealist" drama uses many of Jarry's devices, and in addition several new ones of a decidedly anti-realistic cast, such as an animated décor, characters who enter through

7

the auditorium or the prompter's box, and a megaphone to address the audience. No wonder that these, and other marvels like the blue-painted face of Thérèse (who becomes Tirésias when she calmly removes her breasts which turn out to be large balloons) threw the public into confusion. The reaction was scarcely different when thirty years later the play was performed at the Opéra-Comique, set to the rollicking music of Poulenc.

Les Mamelles de Tirésias is even less human, less realistic, less logical than *Ubu*, for it is closer to dada and surrealism, movements in which Apollinaire played an important role as precursor and impresario. In fact, it was in the preface to his play that Apollinaire coined the word "surrealism," and defined it as a return to nature without imitating her photographically: "When man wished to imitate walking, he created the wheel which does not resemble a leg. He was thus engaging in surrealism without knowing it." If *Les Mamelles de Tirésias,* which Apollinaire claimed was propaganda in favor of a rising birth rate, is obscure at points, it is also irrepressibly gay, and forms part of an organized personal revolt against the drab realistic drama of the era. Jarry had stated in the epigraph to *Ubu enchaîné* that he was tearing down in order to build a handsome new edifice. In the preface to Apollinaire's play, and in the prologue spoken by the Director before the curtain, there is a positive program for infusing the theater with a new spirit, at once joyous and modern, blending, without necessarily logical ties, all the arts:

Sounds gestures colors cries noises
Music dance acrobatics poetry painting
Choruses actions and multiple décors

A mingling of the pathetic with the burlesque will be encouraged, as well as the "reasonable usage of the improbable. . . . For the theater should not be the art of *trompe-l'oeil* [illusion]." The dramatist, according to

Apollinaire, has total liberty, he is creator and lord of
his universe:

> It is just that he should make crowds of inanimate
>   objects speak
> If he wish
> And that he disregard time
> As well as space
> His universe is his play
> Inside of which he is god the creator
> Who disposes at will
> The sounds and gestures the movement the masses
>   of colors
> Not with the sole end
> Of photographing what is called a slice of life
> But in order to bring forth life itself in all its truth
> For the play should be a complete universe
> With its creator
> That is to say nature itself
> And not only the representation of a small piece
> Of what surrounds us or what happened once.

Today's experimental dramatists in France recognize
Apollinaire as one of the most instrumental in clearing
the ground for the kind of writing they are doing. In
an interview for the BBC's Third Programme (Jan. 5,
1960), Ionesco mentioned *Les Mamelles de Tirésias*
as one of the works that had most impressed him, for it
represents a style and a mentality of an entire epoch in
its forthright rejection of fixed forms and ideas. And
this is surely one of the aspects of surrealism and the
avant-garde of the "Banquet Years" which most appeals to the experimental dramatists of today.

The dramas of Jarry, Apollinaire, the dadaists, and
the surrealists, however, did not enjoy a wide popularity, particularly after the first hubbub of the 1920's
had subsided. Ionesco ascribes this to the fact that their
theater was not spontaneous (and he is speaking particularly of the dadaist and surrealist groups proper),

9

but was a theater with intellectual pretensions, artificial, cerebral, and studied. These are rather strange adjectives to associate with a movement whose major efforts were directed against the intellectual and in favor of the irrational. Yet one cannot help feeling that some of this criticism is warranted when one reads so "cute" a play as Tristan Tzara's *Coeur à gaz* (*Gas Heart*), in which the characters are Mouth, Eyebrow, Ear, Neck, Eye, and Nose.

In the script of a BBC broadcast made the day following the interview with Ionesco, and devoted to the theaters of dada and surrealism, Jacques Brunius asserts that

> during seven years of Dada and over thirty years of Surrealism, the impact of their ideas on the stage has been almost negligible. Their influence on poetry and painting was immediate in the twenties: poetry and painting will never be the same. On the stage we had to wait until 1950 to see Eugène Ionesco gather the loose ends left dangling by Dada and Surrealism and accomplish what his predecessors had failed to achieve.

The plays written by dadaists and surrealists are few and far between. Brunius mentions only thirteen,[7] chiefly short works by men whose major attention was directed to poetry or the novel, and he ascribes their failure at least partly to the cavalier attitude adopted by the writers, their detachment, their insolence and desire to shock. In concluding, Brunius adds:

> Surely the relevant factor must have been the paucity of talented dramatists in the Dada and Surrealist groups. The denunciation of literature and art by Dada and Surrealism would have been less striking if the Dadaists and the Surrealists had been writers and painters of mediocre talent. Their self-denial when they renounced the use of traditional techniques could then have been taken as mere spite. They refused to consider literature or art

10

as an *end*, nevertheless when they condescended to use them as *means*, they were fully conversant with the techniques, and they could pretend to despise it. They did not know the technique of the theatre and did not seem inclined to learn it. This is, I think, the main reason why this particular medium turned out to be less efficient than expected.

The two most successful surrealist dramatists, Roger Vitrac and Raymond Roussel, were rather on the fringe of the group, but they were the only ones who made the theater their career. Before the advent of Ionesco, Vitrac could be called "the most direct heir of Alfred Jarry in the contemporary avant-garde theater." But Vitrac lacks the grotesque fancy and savage originality of Jarry, and despite his satire of bourgeois life and language, with its commonplaces, its banality, and ugliness, *Victor ou les Enfants au pouvoir* (*Victor or The Children in Power*, performed in 1928 by Artaud at his Théâtre Alfred Jarry) and his later plays remind us more of the run-of-the-mill productions in commercial theaters than they do of the rebellious efforts of Jarry and Apollinaire. His first play, *Les Mystères de l'amour* (1924), however, is more clearly a product of the dada and surrealist movements, for it attempts to reveal in a dreamlike atmosphere, the inner workings of the minds of two lovers, and recalls many of the experimental films of the period (and the so-called experimental films still being turned out thirty years later).

Raymond Roussel, whom Ionesco also mentioned in the interview referred to above, was actually detached from any movement of his time, and his plays are virtually unclassifiable. A very wealthy man, he hired actors and theaters to perform his plays, which were ridiculed by most of the audience and widly applauded by the devotees of dada and surrealism. His complete disregard for the most elementary rules of stagecraft results in plays that have extremely complex plots but no real action. Instead, the indistinguishable characters stand around and talk about what has happened or is happening, using the most stilted of literary styles. In *La Poussière de soleils (The Dust of Suns*, 1926) a certain Blache sets out to find a treasure hidden by a misanthropic uncle, and to which clues have been concealed along the way in books, idols, skulls, and paintings. Through five acts and twenty-five tableaux, vaguely reminiscent of a Jules Vernes adventure story, we follow Blache and his friends in their pursuit. Most often, however, they talk about their pursuit, and by the strangest of coincidences always fall upon precisely the right detail to send them off to the next clue in their search. There are two related subplots treated in rather romantic exaggerated style, but one is not certain whether Roussel was taking himself seriously or not. It is easy to see that the absurdity of comic detail and coincidence, the absolute freedom from conventional dramatic techniques, and the charming ingenuousness of the tale, would appeal to a dramatist like Ionesco. The use of magic, incantation, and exoticism—we are in French Guiana—would also account for a considerable part of the admiration accorded Roussel by the surrealists and by Cocteau.

Cocteau himself had earlier contributed to the avant-garde theater in his ballets *Parade* (1917) and *Le Boeuf sur le toit* (1920) in which he introduced the clowns and acrobats of fair, circus, and music hall into the theater proper, and in his play *Les Mariés de la Tour Eiffel (The Newlyweds of the Eiffel Tower*, 1921) in which phonographs speak in place of the actors, and a marvelous photographer's camera gives birth to an ostrich, a lion, a baby, and a bathing beauty. The play, which shows a wedding party on the Eiffel Tower, is once again a satire of bourgeois life. Furthermore, this rather disconcerting work, Neal Oxenhandler assures us in his study of Cocteau's theater,

is trying to awaken in us a sense of the marvelous. [Cocteau] is saying that dance and gesture are in themselves a kind of moral attitude, and that the absurdity of bourgeois life must be relieved by poetry and this sense of the marvelous or fantastic. Even a commonplace lunch on the Eiffel Tower can become a ballet, can be lifted, that is, to the dignity and mystery of art.

The waking of the spectator to an awareness of the marvelous, the unusual, the *insolite* that is a part of our everyday existence, is one of the functions of today's avant-garde and of course reaches back as far as Apollinare and Jarry, and beyond to symbolism and romanticism.

One of Cocteau's major contributions to avant-garde theater has been his stress on the visual aspects of the performance, what, in his famous 1922 preface to *Les Mariés de la Tour Eiffel*, he calls "poésie de théâtre":

> The action of my play is adorned with images whereas the text is not. I am attempting therefore to substitute a "poetry of the theatre" for "poetry in the theatre." Poetry in the theatre is a delicate lace impossible to see from a distance. Poetry of the theatre would be a thick lace; a lace of ropes, a ship upon the sea.

I am not convinced that what he is describing is poetry of any kind, but nevertheless Cocteau makes it clear that poetry as such is not dramatic and does not suffice in itself to make successful poetic drama. He helps at least partly to account for the failure of the symbolist poets in their incursion into the theatrical genre, and reminds us, as Artaud will ten or fifteen years later, that a play is to be seen as well as heard. The development of this particular streak in Cocteau (which becomes one of Artaud's major tenets) finds its happiest realization in the theaters of Beckett and Ionesco, and in certain plays of Adamov, where both dialogue and the visible space on the stage are taken into account.

Artaud's weakness, as is so often true in men of genius, was precisely what made his strength: he was apparently incapable of moderation, and once he had found what he believed to be the answer to the ills of western theater, he vigorously rejected the psychological, realistic theater of dialogue which prevails in our century, and preached the virtues of magic, metaphysics, and *mise en scène* (literally, the "putting on the stage" of a play). These three words sum up the credo of Antonin Artaud as it is reflected in his essays on the theater gathered together under the title *Le Théâtre et son Double* (*The Theater and Its Double,* 1938), a rich storehouse of suggestions, insights, hopes, and dreams, which will no doubt continue to influence the theater in subtle ways for many years to come. "*The Theater and Its Double,*" affirms Jean-Louis Barrault, "is indisputably the most important thing written on the theatre in the twentieth century."[8] Through his activities with the surrealists, his work with the short-lived Théâtre Alfred Jarry, which he founded with Roger Vitrac, and particularly through his association with the company of Charles Dullin, Artaud came into close contact with many young writers, actors, and directors who have since then stepped into the first rank: Barrault, Vilar, Blin, and Adamov, for example.

Magic, metaphysics, and *mise en scène.* The object of the theater, according to Artaud,

> is not to resolve social or psychological conflicts, to serve as battlefield for moral passions, but to express objectively certain secret truths, to bring into the light of day by means of active gestures certain aspects of truth that have been buried under forms in their encounters with Becoming.

Through the creation of myths, the dramatist may reveal truth to the spectator, reawaken in him an awareness of the chaos that underlies life, the void that constantly threatens. "We are not free. And the sky can still fall on our heads. And the theater has been created to teach us that first of all." The theater's task is a metaphysical one that goes far beyond the psychological, moral, or social limits set by conventional drama. This is what

Artaud meant by the Theater of Cruelty, a theater that would teach us the precariousness of our position and reveal the secrets of the unconscious. "Without an element of cruelty at the root of every spectacle, the theatre is not possible. In our present state of degeneration it is through the skin that metaphysics must be made to re-enter our minds."

Dialogue, Artaud believes, can scarcely serve the purposes of metaphysics, for speech as it is commonly used defeats anything deeper than mere representation, reducing mystery to matter and meaning to logic. Most often Artaud rejects language and sets the *mise en scène* in its place. Occasionally, however, he is willing to recognize the utility of language if it is used in a special way. In a passage that conjures up Mallarmé and another search for the Absolute, Artaud states:

> To make metaphysics out of a spoken language is to make the language express what it does not ordinarily express: to make use of it in a new, exceptional, and unaccustomed fashion; to reveal its possibilities for producing physical shock; . . . to turn against language and its basely utilitarian, one could say alimentary, sources, against its trapped-beast origins; and finally, to consider language as the form of *Incantation*.

For everything in the theater must have an incantatory, a magical power, to evoke and suggest what is beyond the realm of logic and words. For this reason Artaud, always fascinated by the esoteric practices of the tarot cards, the kabala, yoga, and primitive magic, turned to the popular ceremonial theater of Bali as the embodiment of his ideal, pure theater.

> The spectacle of the Balinese theater, which draws upon dance, song, pantomime—and a little of the theater as we understand it in the Occident—restores the theater, by means of ceremonies of indubitable age and well-tried efficacy, to its original destiny which it presents as a combination of

15

all these elements fused together in a perspective of hallucination and fear.

The theater of Bali speaks a language that is specifically a stage language, nonverbal, and composed of the various elements of the spectacle, movement, gesture, costume, decoration, music, light, and so on. The actor-dancers are "animated hieroglyphs," who have a precise spiritual meaning that cannot, however, be translated into discursive language, but still strike us at a deep level with sufficient violence to leave a scar. For the theatrical experience must be a physical one, addressed to all the senses.

Artaud's theater would give the stage its autonomy, and free it from what he considers the dictatorship of the written word. In his ideal theater he plans to present Elizabethan plays but freed from the script, retaining only situations, characters, and actions. Since the theater "is above all a space to fill and a place where something happens," the major creator in the theater will be not the dramatist, who is simply a manipulator of paralyzing words, but the *metteur en scène*—the director who welds together all the aspects of the production, and who in Artaud's ideal theater would be author as well, supreme magician, priest, maker of myths, and manipulator of signs and hieroglyphs.

The ambitious—and probably impossible—theater envisioned by Artaud never became a reality. The failure of his Renaissance play, *Les Cenci,* in 1935 dashed his hopes to the ground. After spending nine years in asylums for the insane, Artaud was released in 1946 and continued vainly to try to present a spectacle that would conform to his idea of a Theater of Cruelty. "I will do what I have dreamed, or I will do nothing," Artaud had written in 1933. A martyr to the Absolute, he may well have died believing he had failed. And yet it is impossible to read *The Theater and Its Double* today without realizing the immense influence Artaud has exercised on

16

the living writers and directors of France. Time and again, a phrase or a paragraph on the solidification of language, the encroachment of the inanimate universe on man, the importance of visual symbols, the meaning of gesture, the metaphysical function of theater, will point directly to a realization of Ionesco, Adamov, or Beckett. Artaud's book is so rich in suggestions and insights that one is willing to overlook his exaggerations, or rather one relishes them as a reflection of the enthusiasm which is largely responsible for the liberating view of theater which he espoused.

The period from 1930 to 1950 produced no outstanding avant-garde drama, but the work of Copeau and of that group of devoted theater craftsmen known as Le Cartel des Quatre (Dullin, Pitoëff, Jouvet, and Baty) had begun to bear fruit. Their revolt against commercialism raised the artistic standards of the French theater. Their experimentalism educated the public for nonrealistic drama, and during the 'thirties and early 'forties the plays of Giraudoux, presented by Jouvet, showed that an intellectual, poetic dramatist with something to say and an unusual way of saying it, could enjoy popularity. The total theater of Gaston Baty, like the theories of Artaud, stressed again the nonverbal aspects of drama. Following the example of their master Copeau, the directors of the Cartel opened their doors to foreign dramatists, and a strong draft of international air freshened the Paris halls. Three foreign influences are particularly significant for their enormous impact on dramatic literature in France, or on the concept of life which we associate with the avant-garde: Pirandello, Kafka, and Brecht.

Pitoëff first introduced Pirandello to France in 1923, and was followed a few years later by Dullin. Pirandello's acceptance of the stage as a stage, his wry mingling of the comic and the tragic, his revolt against the binding forms of naturalism, and his obsession with the

17

theme of appearance and reality, have all been taken up by the various writers of today's avant-garde and used to stress their own preoccupations.

Franz Kafka, presented in dramatic form by Dullin's disciple Barrault, in the Gide adaptation of *The Trial* (1947), evokes a nightmare world resembling that of Beckett, Ionesco, or Adamov, in which we find ourselves helpless, confronted by inexplicable and frustrating experiences that are strangely similar to everyday life.

The influence of Brecht, immense in France for the past ten years and largely fostered by Jean Vilar (another heir of the Cartel), stresses once again the awareness of the play as a play and of the characters as actors on a stage. His famous "alienation" effect results in something like the objectivity we sometimes feel while viewing a play of Adamov or Ionesco. A measure of Brecht's importance is found not only in the popularity of his plays in France today, and in the allegiance paid him by such dramatists as Adamov, but also in the vehemence with which he has been denounced on more than one occasion by Ionesco.

The years of war and occupation were instrumental in orienting the minds of writers in France, and in most of Europe, towards a serious consideration of man's role not only as a social animal, but as the inhabitant of a universe whose meaning and structure were crumbling. The most noteworthy manifestation of this outlook during the 'thirties and 'forties lies in the writings of the existentialists, and particularly of Jean-Paul Sartre who is, of course, not only the outstanding philosopher of the atheistic branch of that school, but a very gifted dramatist as well. It is, however, as a thinker that Sartre most interests us here, for his drama is based upon the accepted formulas of theater and in no way constitutes a revolution. Since about 1935, the theater in France had been turning more and more to the problems of man's condition, without rejecting traditional attitudes toward plot, character, theme, or language. The major playwrights of the period, Anouilh, Sartre, Camus, Montherlant, and Salacrou, deal with serious and even metaphysical problems, but do not wander too far afield from the realistic conceptions of theater, although now and then symbol or thought overshadows character or plot and seems to lead it.

I am not prepared to discuss the intricacies of existential philosophy—which would be irrelevant here—but I should like to point out three or four attitudes that were popularized and "codified" by the existentialists and have been embraced by most of the avant-garde dramatists today. I do not mean to suggest that Beckett, Ionesco, or Adamov are existentialists, or would even acknowledge a debt to existentialism. It is simply that the school of Sartre sums up a certain attitude that prevailed in France in the 'forties and continues, in certain respects, to prevail today. Here are four principles of existentialism which are reflected in one or more of the major avant-garde writers today. (1) Absurdity is the underlying fabric of man's existence. Man, in his moments of honesty and lucidity, is aware that his life has no absolute meaning, that he must live as in a void. Nonexistence constantly threatens him. (2) Man may become bogged down in his physical being, attached to a pattern, a fixed idea of good, a conception of himself, which denies his humanity. He ceases to change, to become, is turned into a thing. The overabundance of things is nauseating, for it limits our freedom. (3) Just as man and his values may congeal through habit, so may language become dead and inoperative, paralyzing our thoughts. With such an instrument no communication is possible. Each man is a solitude. (4) There is no human nature. Man is only what he makes of himself; therefore there is no such thing as a fixed character in the usual sense. Man is an existent in a situation.

At mid-twentieth century the writers of the avant-garde theater in France fell heir to a rich tradition of anarchy, compounded of revolt against the conformity and banality of bourgeois life and ideals. A purely theatrical rebellion against the hampering forms of realism and naturalism in the drama, expressed with an irrepressible *élan;* an exploitation of the peripheral theater arts of fair, circus, and music hall; an emphasis upon the visual aspects of the theater; symbolism, futurism, dada, surrealism, expressionism, and cosmopolitanism—all of these helped to make possible the kind of theater that is being written in France today. Such antecedents and aims, however, do not explain the success that the avant-garde has enjoyed in the past few years, a limited success to be sure, but one that far outstrips that of earlier efforts in the same direction. Certainly today's avant-garde is more exclusively devoted to the theater and has developed a skill in theatrical expression which is unapproached by its forerunners. But talent and skill alone are not responsible. Today's public—or a segment of it—is better prepared to accept the revolutionary ideas of theater exemplified by Ionesco and Beckett. Fifty years of exposure to fresh approaches in painting, poetry, and music, two world wars, and the popularization of a philosophy of absurdity have perhaps broken down resistance to a theater that for the first time reflects the modern spirit in both substance and form.

Most of the dramatists we are about to explore began writing for the theater around 1950. For some time their efforts remained isolated. It was *En Attendant Godot* (*Waiting for Godot*) that first attracted world-wide attention to the new dramatists and the new kind of drama being written in France. As a matter of fact, these writers do not form a group except insofar as they are all experimenting with new ways of expression, some in one direction, some in another. In fact, there· is no school of new writers, there are no rules, no principles observed by one or more among them. Indeed, what is perhaps most typical of these writers is their refusal to codify their practice, to restrain their inspiration. This is essentially what Ionesco meant when he said that "there is no avant-garde theater." The heterogeneity of these dramatists is adumbrated by their diversity of national background: Irish (Beckett), Rumanian (Ionesco), Russian (Adamov), Lebanese (Schehadé).

Various designations have been applied to them. "The School of Paris" suggests too organized a group, while "The Generation of 1950" would require a very loose interpretation when we recall that Beckett began to publish in the early 'thirties and Ghelderode produced a play before 1920. "The Theater of the Absurd" is pertinent, but seems to exclude a writer like Schehadé and at the same time to stress too close a rapport with existentialism. I have chosen "avant-garde" as being the most general (and most ambiguous no doubt), and at the same time suggestive of a certain continuity with the writers we have already mentioned.

Today Beckett and Ionesco stand out quite clearly as the most important—as well as the most popular—dramatists of the avant-garde. Consequently I have centered my study on them. Adamov serves as an illustration of anti-theater, and Genêt of ritual theater. In the final chapter I have grouped together a number of disparate writers under the signs of Babel and Eden, realizing full well that Beckett, Ionesco, Genêt, and Adamov might equally well have found places there. With the exception of Ghelderode, the writers in the last chapter are virtually unknown to English-speaking audiences. In my discussion I have attempted to give a general view that will serve as an introduction to them.

2

Samuel Beckett

WAITING FOR GODOT burst upon the Parisian theatrical scene, in January, 1953, very much like a bombshell, and its author was famous almost overnight. The people attending the première, unprepared for such a radically different kind of play, were either perplexed, disgruntled, or deeply thrilled. The disgruntled left after the first act, the thrilled remained to applaud wildly at the end of the performance and the perplexed sat on in puzzled silence. At the intermission, the struggle between support and opposition was symbolically represented by a fist fight in the lobby.

By the time two weeks had elapsed, word had gone around, people were forewarned, and the audience at the Théâtre Babylone was prepared for something "astonishing, and at the limits of the endurable." Critics greeted the play with anathema or rapture, as incomprehensible confusion or as lucid revelation, as the complete absence of drama or as the epitome of dramatic economy. But of its originality there was no doubt. *Waiting for Godot* marks a date in the modern theater, and, in the words of Anouilh, "has the importance of the first Pirandello presented in Paris by Pitoëff in 1923." The feeling of surprise, the sense of newness it inspired could be matched only by the revelation of the "old Sicilian magician's" *Six Characters in Search of an Author* thirty years before.

22

Godot enjoyed more than three hundred performances in Paris, was received enthusiastically in Frankfort, Rome, and Helsinki. In London it played for sixteen months. Since then it has been translated into many languages, including Japanese, and has been presented all over the world. Its American *première* in January, 1956, at Miami was a fiasco, with over half of the audience walking out after the first act. "*Variety* and Walter Winchell," comments Kenneth Rexroth, "instantly recognizing themselves as two of the leading characters in the play turned on it with a savagery remarkable even for them."[1] The pleasure-seekers of Miami Beach were scarcely the audience for this stark but amusing play, and the producer, Michael Myerberg took it to New York, where he advertized, "Wanted: 70,000 Playgoing Intellectuals." Apparently the intellectuals turned out, —or at any rate the curious and the snobbish—as well as the readers of *Newsweek* whose reviewer had advised them to "Go ahead and take a chance; it's fun, anyway." The limited run was extended. Tennessee Williams, Thornton Wilder, and William Saroyan joined the chorus of praise, and pronounced *Waiting for Godot* one of the significant plays of the century. Who, people asked, was this puzzling dramatist who had come to light so suddenly?

Samuel Beckett was born in Dublin in 1906, and studied at Trinity College, where he received his Bachelor's degree in French and Italian in 1927. He made his first trip to Paris in 1926, and returned two years later as an exchange lecturer in English at the École Normale Supérieure. Following this he was appointed assistant to the Professor of French in Dublin, but resigned after four terms. "I didn't like teaching. I couldn't settle down to the work," he explained in an interview published in the *New York Times*. "I didn't like living in Ireland. You know the kind of thing—theocracy, censorship of books, that kind of thing. I preferred to live abroad. In 1936, I came back to Paris and lived in a hotel for a time and then decided to settle down and make my life here."

Before this he had already published several works in English: a brief poem entitled *Whoroscope,* in 1930, whose title suggests both the unhappy world view he was to reveal later, and his interest in language as such; in 1931 a brief literary study of Proust which has been pronounced one of the finest examples of literary criticism of our day; and a collection of short stories in 1934, *More Pricks than Kicks.*

His first novel, *Murphy,* appeared in 1938 (to be translated into French by the author nine years later). In 1945 he finished *Watt,* his last novel to be written in English, and turned to writing in French: "Just felt like it," he is reported as saying. "It was a different experience from writing in English. It was more exciting for me." Between 1946 and 1950 he wrote the greater part of his French work: a novelistic trilogy, *Molloy, Malone meurt (Malone Dies),* and *L'Innommable (The Unnamable);* three tales, the *Textes pour rien (Texts for Nothing);* and *Godot.* This spurt of creative energy seems to have left Beckett demoralized and shattered, for in 1956 he admitted, "Since then [1950] I haven't written anything. Or at least nothing that has seemed to me valid. The French work brought me to the point where I felt I was saying the same thing over and over again. For some authors writing gets easier the more they write. For me it gets more and more difficult. For me the area of possibilities gets smaller and smaller." That same year, however, he must have found some issue, for a radio play written in English, *All That Fall,* was performed on the BBC's Third Programme in January, 1957, and in April Beckett's second long play, *Fin de partie (Endgame),* opened in London, produced in French by Roger Blin, the same daring artist who had introduced *Godot* to the Parisian public. On the same bill was a one-act pantomime entitled *Acte sans paroles (Act Without Words).* The two plays were later transported to Paris where they had a much shorter run than *Godot*.

Endgame was coupled with a new one-act play, *Krapp's Last Tape* (written in English and later translated as *La Dernière Bande*) when it began its English-language run in London. A second pantomime, *Acte sans paroles II*, and another radio play in English, *Embers*, both dating from 1959, complete Beckett's dramatic catalogue.

When Roger Blin was looking for a theater in which to present *Endgame* in Paris, he was unable to find a producer willing to take the financial risks involved. "Performed or not," wrote the French dramatist Georges Neveux in *Arts*, "Beckett's second play will soon be as famous as the first." *Endgame* achieved fame, but it certainly did not enjoy the success which was accorded the earlier work. For the general public today Beckett is above all the author of *Waiting for Godot*, and it is largely this play that prompted the claim made by the French weekly *Arts* that Beckett may be considered "one of the great creators of the modern theater."

Waiting for Godot

More than one critic has pointed out that the story of *Waiting for Godot* may be expressed in the words of Estragon, one of the two bums who are the protagonists of the piece: "Nothing happens, nobody comes, nobody goes, it's awful!" It is a fact that the action of *Godot* is reduced to a minimum, this is part of its originality. Vladimir and Estragon, on a deserted country road distinguished only by a pitiful tree, wait for a mysterious person named Godot who at some indefinite time in the past, under somewhat uncertain circumstances, made a rather imprecise appointment to meet them in some ill-defined place at an indeterminate hour. While they wait Didi and Gogo (for these are the nicknames invariably used in the play) encounter a pitiable pair passing down the road, Pozzo the

25

master and Lucky his slave. Finally a boy arrives to announce that Godot will not come tonight, but the following night. The second act only repeats, in a slightly different way, the happenings of the first.

Although it may be true that "nothing happens," that there is virtually no action in this play, it is not true that "nobody comes, nobody goes," for *Godot* contains a great deal of external movement. Not only do Pozzo and Lucky enter and exit one or more times in each act, but Gogo and Didi move about the stage, and even leave for brief moments, and at the end of each act the young boy makes his entrance and exit. This movement gives variety to the groupings on the stage and helps to sustain audience interest. But it is only a superficial kind of action, for one of the basic assumptions of the play is that life is meaningless and monotonous, and leads us from nothing to nowhere. If action is, as Aristotle states, the principle and soul of tragedy, then *Waiting for Godot* is not a play without a principle and a soul but one in which, paradoxically, the conviction that nothing ever really happens, that there is no such thing as action, forms the fundamental action of the play. And this is represented in the very structure of the work, for it is a precisely structured play.

It seems superfluous to point out that *Godot's* structure is not like that of the conventional play. The categories of exposition, inciting moment, rising action, turning point, falling action, climax, and conclusion are not observed in any strict sense. There is, of course, a certain amount of exposition as the play opens. In fact, the setting, the beginning action, and the first few speeches suggest much of what is to follow, and are indicative of Beckett's power of synthesis. The stage is bare, suggesting a stark and empty universe. The only hint of nature is a skeletic tree, which at once recalls a gallows, a cross (both instrument of torture and religious symbol), and the various trees of mythical literature. We are at the center of the world, so to speak, at the point where enlightenment should come, if enlightenment is possible. The symbol of the tree of life, the Boh-tree, Yggdrasill, prepares the perceptive viewer to accept Gogo and Didi as representative of all suffering humanity. And it is precisely humanity's suffering which is stressed as the drama begins and we see Gogo struggling with his shoe. We are in a world where men are not at home, where they are tortured by objects which should rightfully add to their comfort. Man's hopelessness and anguish is betrayed in Gogo's first words: "Nothing to be done." His efforts have no results, just as his waiting will have no results, and his temporary reaction is to give up.

Vladimir's entrance introduces the theme of sickness and decay, for he advances "with short, stiff strides, legs wide apart." Didi, like most of the characters in Beckett's world, is ailing. His hernia prevents him from laughing —"Dreadful privation," comments Gogo ironically—and he makes frequent exits to answer nature's call. This is a universe without any spiritual values; man is caught within the physical, unable to rise above the numerous bodily functions and needs which, in the last analysis, are the only sure things we know.

Vladimir has overheard Estragon's exclamation of despair, and comments upon it: "I'm beginning to come round to that opinion. All my life I've tried to put it from me, saying, Vladimir, be reasonable, you haven't yet tried everything. And I resumed the struggle." Substantially the two men are saying the same thing, but whereas Gogo's comment was primarily directed at his present effort, Didi is speaking in much more general terms. He has actually misunderstood what his friend was talking about, for real understanding is impossible. Time and again the two tramps think they are communicating, but are in fact speaking at cross purposes.

Within a few moments three or four important themes are introduced: the need for affection and the presence

27

of others; the difficulty of knowing anything with certainty; the presence of death, which causes both fear and a sense of relief; and the Christian themes of salvation and atonement.

The skillful exposition, one might almost say, continues throughout the play, for there is no inciting moment, nothing which occurs to disturb the tedium of Vladimir and Estragon, unless it be the arrival of Pozzo and Lucky. But the wretched pair only bring about a momentary interruption of the endless boredom, and when they leave, the bums are at the same point we found them before; the action does not rise to any turning point because of their brief passage. We might, if compelled to do so, consider the arrival of the young boy as the turning point, but it is followed neither by falling action, climax, nor conclusion. The action—or lack of it—simply goes on. The second act is constructed like the first, and by the end of the play we are back where we began if, indeed, we have moved from there at all. *Godot's* structure might be described as circular with the stress on similitude, monotony, and endless repetition. Each act could be considered complete in itself, but the first without the second would not be so conclusively despairing, for we might still hope that on another day Godot would indeed arrive. Act II, however, shows us that this monotonous rhythm is a recurrent one, and will probably go on forever. If there were a third act, it could but repeat the patterns and rhythms of the first two. Beckett was surely right in his answer to those critics who had claimed that *Godot's* structure and "message" left him free to lay down his pen at any moment: "One act would have been too little and three acts would have been too much."

The eternal recurrence without meaning or direction is pointed up on various levels in the play. At the beginning of Act II Vladimir sings a song about a dog who came into the kitchen and stole a crust of bread, but was beaten to death by the cook, whereupon all the other dogs dug him a grave and wrote upon the tombstone that a dog came into the kitchen and stole, etc., etc. In her very discerning article on *Godot* (*Yale French Studies*, No. 14), Edith Kern identifies this as a "doleful little ballad of German origin," and points out the inescapability and perpetuation which it suggests.

The actions of the characters also help to stress such a feeling. Gogo returns frequently to fiddling with his shoes, Didi time and again takes off his hat and feels around inside it in an attempt to discover just what it is that is scratching him. Of course he never finds out. In the second act the two tramps discover the hat Lucky had dropped there the day before. They now have three hats, and in a magnificent piece of stage business, they pass back and forth the three hats, from head to hand, to hand to head, and back again. Lucky, the slave, suggests the idea of endless and meaningless activity in his constant putting down and picking up of all the objects he is forced to carry: whip, folding stool, picnic basket, suitcase, overcoat. Each time that Pozzo gives him an order, he must put down all the objects, except the one involved in the order, comply with his master's command, then return to the objects and pick them up again. The suitcase, we discover, is filled with sand.

But the most significant and constant level on which this major theme is represented is that of speech. The dialogue, particularly between the two tramps, stresses the monotony and motionlessness of their situation. Vladimir observes, "Time has stopped." The pointless waiting which will go on forever is suggested by a little exchange which takes place toward the end of the play:

Estragon. But night doesn't fall.
Vladimir. It'll fall all of a sudden, like yesterday.
Estragon. Then it'll be night.
Vladimir. And we can go.
Estragon. Then it'll be day again.

And so, on and on. "What'll we do, what'll we do!" cries

Estragon despairingly. Of course the only answer can be, "Wait for Godot." And it is given so frequently, that it becomes a kind of refrain. Six times the following dialogue takes place:

Estragon. Let's go.
Vladimir. We can't.
Estragon. Why not?
Vladimir. We're waiting for Godot.

Beckett's genius has been to present this so-called static play, where "nothing happens" in such a way that it sustains our interest from one end to the other. When destructive critics claim that absolutely nothing happens in this play, we might answer, says the brilliant young Spanish playwright Alfonso Sastre, "Does this seem no small achievement to you? This is precisely the fascinating thing about *Waiting for Godot:* nothing happens. It is, in this sense, a lucid testimony of nothingness. And it cannot be denied that, while many dramas of intrigue in which a great deal happens leave us cold, this 'nothing happening' of *Godot* keeps us in suspense."[2]

There are many elements in *Godot* which contribute to such a feeling. The action of waiting is, of course, based upon suspense. During the first act we continue to wonder whether Godot may not indeed show up. We even ask ourselves for some time whether Pozzo is not in reality Godot. In fact, some critics have claimed that this is the case. As the second act opens we have almost given up hope, but we, like Gogo and Didi, tell ourselves that perhaps, after all, he might come today. It requires two acts to establish the fact that this waiting must go on forever. A third act would lose all suspense, therefore, and undoubtedly be unbearable. Beckett has skillfully varied the events just enough in the second act to avoid exact imitation of the first, and yet has preserved enough of the similarity to remind us that things are never very different from what they always were, and tomorrow and tomorrow will undoubtedly creep on its petty pace.

The characters hold our interest constantly despite

their lack of psychological development. In fact, it is partly because they are stripped of traditional character development that we are prepared to accept them as representative of humanity. Although Estragon and Vladimir resemble each other in many ways, however, they are distinctly alive and memorable characterizations. The former is instinctual, eager for food, money, and sleep; the latter, analytical, possesses more dignity, and is given to philosophizing. It is he who must remind the forgetful Gogo that they cannot leave because they are waiting for Godot. Estragon has a peculiar kind of memory: either he forgets immediately or he will remember forever. Significantly, the things he remembers are connected with his appetites and his sufferings. He forgets Pozzo and Lucky from day to day, but he remembers that someone threw him a chicken bone, and that he was kicked.

The behavior of Didi and Gogo is clownish, and reminds us, in its dependence upon slapstick, of the circus and the music hall. Their rapid exchanges of questions and answers, or brief commentaries on what is (or is not) happening, their misunderstandings and *non sequiturs,* all go back to the comic techniques of vaudeville, farce, and circus. But whereas vaudeville and farce were almost exclusively comical, *Godot* identifies its clowns particularly with those of the circus by infusing their behavior with pathos. Gogo and Didi are in the sad yet amusing tradition of Charlie Chaplin, and Henri Michaux's hapless Plume. "At last," sighs Alfonso Sastre, "a real tragicomedy!" In Beckett's play, he declares, we find the "pure tragicomic situation: that mysterious situation before which, although horrified we laugh. We laugh, but are paralyzed with horror. We laugh, but our eyes are wet."

The element of cruel humor, what the French call *humour* as opposed to *esprit* or simply *le comique,* dominates a large part of Beckett's work, both novelistic and dramatic. In *Godot* its function is double: it affords

31

relief from the depressing atmosphere and at the same time heightens the tragic effect, for it stresses the role of man as sufferer who does not belong, and who cannot ultimately be taken seriously, because there is no one to witness his suffering. "Do you think God sees me?" Estragon wonders naively. And as he watches Gogo sleeping, Didi says to himself: "At me too someone is looking, of me too someone is saying, He is sleeping, he knows nothing, let him sleep on. (*Pause*) I can't go on! (*Pause*) What have I said?"

Vladimir the "thinker" is not at all convinced by his "thinking"; it is a pitiful effort to reassure himself, rather than a statement of conviction. And even if he succeeds in believing, is not his hypothetical "Watcher" persuaded that Vladimir is sleeping and knows nothing, and therefore certainly cannot be considered a sufferer?

The characters' insecurity is reflected in their obsession with play-acting. So hopeless is their situation that they must keep up a running conversation in order not to remember their wretchedness, even if what they say is a lie. "Say you are [happy], even if it's not true," says Vladimir to Estragon.

Estragon. I am happy.
Vladimir. So am I.
Estragon. So am I.
Vladimir. We are happy.
Estragon. We are happy. (*Silence.*) What do we do now, now that we are happy?

A few moments later, having run out of anything to say, Gogo suggests, "In the meantime let us try and converse calmly, since we are incapable of keeping silent."

Vladimir. You're right, we're inexhaustible.
Estragon. It's so we won't think.

There follows a highly poetic and evocative dialogue in which they describe the dead voices of the past which rustle like leaves, like feathers and ashes. Even the voices of the past must talk about their lives:

32

Vladimir. To have lived is not enough for them.
Estragon. They have to talk about it.

The same is, of course, true of Gogo and Didi. The silences during which forlorn man becomes aware of his solitude and nothingness, lost between the infinities, is unbearable, and Vladimir constantly beseeches his friend, "Say something!" It is not surprising that Jean Anouilh, most aptly, called *Waiting for Godot* a "music hall sketch of Pascal's *Pensées* performed by the Fratellini clowns." Almost with a feeling of terror, Vladimir and Estragon invent their lives as they go along, playing scene after scene of their eternal waiting for meaning. "We don't manage too badly, eh Didi, between the two of us?" asks Estragon. "We always find something, eh Didi, to give us the impression we exist?" Without words, without the little actions they perform, the two bums of this "metaphysical farce" (the term is Rosette Lamont's) would feel themselves inexistent, annihilated. Their "scenes," like the monologue of *The Unnamable,* gives them an illusion of living. Their few moments of real lucidity usually result in exclamations such as "I can't go on like this!" or "This is becoming really insignificant."

The tragedy of these sufferers-out-of-context is heightened by the fact that they are performing for no one —their solitude is complete. When Gogo, believing himself surrounded by enemies, attempts to escape through the backdrop, Vladimir informs him that there is no way out there, and taking him by the arm he drags him to the front of the stage where, gesturing toward the audience, he cries: "There! Not a soul in sight!" They are playing to an empty house.

Beckett's cheerless but entertaining first play has been understood in various ways. A number of critics seemed to take pleasure in pretending they were completely mystified, and termed the work puzzling, baffling, enigmatic. *Waiting for Godot* is, of course, enigmatic in the sense that anything new or different is a mystery to the casual or untutored observer. But the confusion of critics and audiences is probably due to the fact that Godot contains no clearly indicated message, no single meaning or lesson. We have been accustomed by the naturalist theater to a serious play that states something in more or less specific terms. *Waiting for Godot* says a great deal, but its method is so indirect that it can speak in different ways to different people. It has even been suggested—apparently by a nonpartisan, for the portrait is not flattering—that Godot represents De Gaulle!

It is probably wise not to be too literal in our interpretation of Godot. The play reveals man's anguish as he waits for the arrival of something that will give life meaning and bring an end to his suffering. Ultimately there is no arrival and no meaning. In a striking image, Vladimir describes the course from birth to death: "Astride of a grave and a difficult birth. Down in the hole, lingeringly, the grave-digger puts on the forceps. We have time to grow old. The air is full of our cries. . . . But habit is a great deadener." Man is born through suffering into a world in which he continues to suffer, until soon, numbed by habit, he is overtaken by death. Bogged down in the crassly physical, preoccupied by his bodily needs and functions, he is hard put to find any spiritual values. Only the arrival of Godot can set things right.

A Christian interpretation of *Waiting for Godot* seems justified—or rather an interpretation that considers Didi and Gogo as reflections of a writer nurtured on Christian tradition. Two tramps—mankind—lost in a world of suffering, have managed to find something that will give them a bit of comfort: the hope that some day someone will come along to feed and clothe them, and give them a warm place to sleep. "That's worth waiting for, isn't it?" asks Vladimir (in the French text, p. 30; not found in the English text). Beckett does not, of course, assert in so many words that their hope is right

34

or wrong. But everything about it is disturbingly vague, for they are not sure when, or where, or under what circumstances their appointment with Godot was made. Perhaps they have imagined it all. All that is certain is that they are waiting for someone or something. It is typical of Beckett's universe that the comforts they expect are physical in nature, and reflect no spiritual preoccupations.

If Vladimir and Estragon represent humanity waiting for a savior, it is possible (and even extremely probable, considering the large amount of Christian mythology distributed throughout the play) that they represent also western man who has received as part of his inheritance a belief, however vague, in some supernatural power. The Judeo-Christian tradition has pictured this power variously as a loving father and as a fearful God. Godot (whose name, Edith Kern has pointed out, combines the word "God" with the French suffix "-ot," interpreted by Rosette Lamont as a diminutive, for she calls Godot "the Little God") is both loving father and unjust dictator. He will bring comfort when he arrives, but in the meantime we discover that he punishes without reason (the messenger boy is treated well by Godot, he tells us, whereas his brother the goatherd is not), is capricious in his refusal to show up for the appointment he makes from day to day, and perhaps even expects his creatures to come in "on our hands and knees."

The portrait of Godot is woven of two kinds of material: that which we assume to be mostly true, since it is reported by his messenger, the shepherd boy; and that which may be only fantasies of the imagination of the tramps. But the matter is further complicated by the fact that Beckett may be writing with tongue in cheek. Is he making fun of the conventional anthropomorphic concept of God when he makes his shepherd boy tell Vladimir that he thinks Godot's beard is white? Is Beckett simply confusing us when he claims that he named his ever-awaited savior after a bicycle racer?

Whether we wish to think of Godot as God or as a vague power that gives some direction or meaning to life, it is clear by the end of the play that he will never come. Professor Charles McCoy has, however, written an interesting "Biblical Appraisal" of *Godot,* in which he claims that perhaps Godot did indeed come, but Vladimir and Estragon do not realize it. He bases his argument largely upon Vladimir's line, "Hope deferred maketh the something sick," which is clearly enough a reference to Proverbs 13:12, "Hope deferred maketh the heart sick; but when the desire cometh, it is a tree of life." And indeed, in the second act we see that the lonely tree has sprouted leaves; but there are only four or five: it is an exceedingly scrubby tree of life.

'That for which Gogo and Didi wait does arrive," concludes Professor McCoy. "It is they who miss the appointment. The tree, the Cross, becomes a tree of life. But those who wait in self-satisfied blindness remain dead."[3]

In the original French version of the play, Vladimir makes no reference to "hope deferred," but simply says, speaking of death, "It's long, but it'll be good." This, of course, does not vitiate the "biblication interpretation," since Beckett obviously found the quotation from Proverbs relevant, otherwise he would not have translated Didi's line so freely. It would seem, however, that if Godot has indeed come, and the bums remain disconsolate, this constitutes a condemnation of Godot: mankind, helpless, and God, all-powerful if not all-loving, operate on such different levels that there is no chance of their meeting. Only a Kierkegaardian *credo quia absurdum* could furnish an answer to the dilemma.

If Godot is largely depicted as a negative value in this universe, we are justified in asking, are there then no positive values? What answers does Beckett offer? He offers no answers in the sense that Shaw or Brieux offer them. There are only implications; from the rather dismal total picture offered by the play we may infer certain convictions.

A man who, like Beckett, may wish to believe in some transcendant power, but obviously does not, is inevitably thrown back into the closed universe of humans. Significantly, his characters are either traveling, vaguely searching, like Molloy, Watt, and McMann, or they are closed within four walls like Murphy in his rocking chair, Malone in bed, or the two characters of *Endgame*. In the final analysis, man is reduced to complete solitude like the armless character of the *Unnamable*, sitting motionless on the sawdust in his jar. But before this last agonizing state is reached (and it is reached dramatically in *Endgame*), man is often cast into situations where he must be with other men. *Waiting for Godot* dramatizes effectively two basic human relationships: that of friend to friend, and that of master to slave. The latter is shown to be immoral in the sense that it leads to decadence in both master and slave. Lucky, we are told in Act I, used to dance the farandole, the brawl, the jig, and a dozen other dances. Now all he can do is writhe in an agonized step which his master tells us he calls "The Net,"—a reflection of his entanglement in life and in a degrading relationship. Formerly he spoke beautifully, and even taught his master, but when we hear him "speak" in his performance for Vladimir and Estragon, his speech is the sad remains of a once reasonable being. In Act II Pozzo has become blind and has lost his memory, and Lucky now cannot even speak. The long rope, visibly representing the servitude of Lucky, has been shortened, and Pozzo constantly bumps into him causing both to fall in a heap on the ground. The degenerative relation of master and slave reduces both to animality and helplessness. Pozzo, lying among his scattered baggage with Lucky, calls out for help.

Vladimir responds joyfully, for now time will pass: "We are no longer alone, waiting for the night, waiting

37

for Godot, waiting for . . . waiting." Man has found a mission, something to occupy him, to amuse him, to help him forget his own pitiable condition. As they listen to Pozzo's cries for help, Vladimir reminds us that he and Estragon are all humanity:

> Let us do something, while we have the chance! It is not every day that we are needed. Not indeed that we personally are needed. Others would meet the case equally well, if not better. To all mankind they were addressed, those cries for help still ringing in our ears! But at this place, at this moment of time, all mankind is us, whether we like it or not.

The implication is not only that man needs other men, but that he must feel that he is somehow necessary. After posing the intellectual's problem of action versus thought, Vladimir chooses action, since nothing in the realm of thought is certain, except that they are waiting for Godot. Vladimir, attempting to help Pozzo, tumbles to the ground, and Estragon, helping Vladimir, soon follows. Four wretched creatures lying on the ground: "We've arrived," exclaims Vladimir. "Who are you?" asks Pozzo. "We are men."

Pozzo is a monster of egoism, but he is not independent of other men. "Yes, gentlemen," he admits, "I cannot go for long without the society of my likes . . . even when the likeness is an imperfect one." His pathetic insecurity, in spite of a blustering manner, is obvious as he prepares to depart. The clownish scene in which he reluctantly leaves is a parody of real-life situations, and a rather sad commentary on the absolute solitude of the egotist:

> *Estragon.* Then adieu.
> *Pozzo.* Adieu.
> *Vladimir.* Adieu.
> *Pozzo.* Adieu.
> (*Silence. No one moves.*)
> *Vladimir.* Adieu.
> *Pozzo.* Adieu.
> *Estragon.* Adieu.

38

(*Silence.*)
Pozzo. And thank you.
Vladimir. Thank *you.*
Pozzo. Not at all.
Estragon. Yes yes.
Pozzo. No no.
Vladimir. Yes yes.
Estragon. No no.
    (*Silence.*)
Pozzo. I don't seem to be able . . . to depart.
Estragon. Such is life.

The only rewarding relationship in life, Beckett intimates, is that of friend to friend. Man cannot bear life alone, but when he shares his suffering with others it becomes tolerable. Unfortunately, those moments when we need affection rarely coincide with those of our friends: when Vladimir wishes to embrace him, Estragon is not in the mood; and when he does feel like it, Vladimir no longer wishes to. When they finally embrace, the result is not pleasant, for while one has stinking breath, the other has stinking feet. Several times they suggest that it might be better to go their separate ways, but they inevitably return to each other's company. Their relationship at times is moving because of the comfort their mutual tenderness affords. "Don't touch me! Don't question me! Don't speak to me! Stay with me!" cries Estragon, expressing his need for a human presence with whom to share his suffering silently, after a particularly miserable night spent, as usual, in a ditch.

In this bleak world of waiting, the only solace given wretched humanity is the knowledge that we are in the company of others, and they are suffering with us.

Endgame

If in Beckett's first play we are waiting for a significant arrival, in *Endgame* we might be said to be waiting for an insignificant departure. But Clov does not leave any more surely than Godot arrives. In a bare, gray-lighted

39

room with two small windows looking out on empty land and empty sea, two men struggle, bound together by hate and a vague necessity. Hamm, the master, and perhaps the father of Clov, is confined to a chair, his legs paralyzed, his eyes blind ("it seems they've gone all white"). Clov can get around rather stiffly, and obeys the orders of Hamm, giving him his toy dog, moving his chair to the window where Hamm may think he feels the nonexistent sun upon his face, examining from time to time the two garbage cans down stage which shelter the legless bodies of Hamm's parents, Nagg and Nell. And when there is nothing else to do, Clov goes into his kitchen to "lean on the table, and look at the wall."

There is much less surface movement in *Endgame* than in *Godot*. Once again nothing happens, and at the end of the play we have described a circle, if we have moved at all. Professor Lamont points out that the final tableau of the play is the same as the opening one: Hamm is at center stage, his face covered by his bloody handkerchief, while Clov stands by the door watching him motionlessly.

Clov's opening speech, recalling, Ruby Cohn notes, Jesus' last words from the Cross, sets the tone of the play, and describes the point we have reached: "Finished, it's finishing, nearly finished, it must be nearly finished." Near the end of the work, Hamm, believing that Clov has left him, sits in his chair center stage and says wearily, "Old endgame lost of old, play and lose and have done with losing," expressing at the end what Clov had expressed at the beginning. In between nothing has happened. No one has come, no one has gone. No Pozzo has entered, no Lucky has danced, no messenger from the outside has arrived, for in the world of *Endgame* there appear to be no other living beings on our tired planet. The only movement in the play is given by Nagg and Nell who occasionally pop out of their garbage cans to hold a brief conversation, or to call for their porridge. Needless to say, there is no more porridge.

Endgame is the truly static play which many playgoers had seen in *Godot*. Beside it the first play is abounding in action and incident. Here there is no hope, there is nothing to look forward to, the end has come before the play begins, and we do not honestly care whether Clov leaves or not, for it can make no difference. "The end is in the beginning, and yet you go on," says Hamm.

Beckett admits that his second play is "rather difficult and eliptic, mostly depending on the power of the text to claw, more inhuman than *Godot*."[4] Whether we enjoy it is, of course, a matter of personal taste. Georges Belmont, writing from London after the opening of Roger Blin's production there, claimed that "With *Endgame* Beckett has attained classical perfection." Most reviewers, however, agreed that the play failed to hold their attention, and one even found time during the performance to compose a bit of doggerel reflecting his attitudes:

> Clov and Hamm and Nagg and Nell
> Lead us steadily to hell.

or:

> Life is fleeting; none can check it:
> Hear at once the worst with Beckett.[5]

Suspense of some kind is essential to any drama, whether it be basically emotional or intellectual in nature. In *Endgame* the element of suspense is minimized; we are waiting for nothing to happen, since we realize from the start that everything has already happened, and this is the end. We can feel little involvement with the unsavory characters. But this does not preclude our being interested in them as symbols. Despite the equivocal meaning of the play, assiduous homework cannot be more rewarding than a viewing in the theater, because the drama is more than a literary or philosophical text. In an intelligent article Thomas Barbour concludes:

> *Endgame* is not so much a short play as a very long metaphysical poem; and the staging of it, though

it may add color and interest for the initiated, does not, seen only once at any rate, disclose essential significances that could not better be discovered by assiduous homework. Its value as a theatre piece, unlike that of *Godot,* is but secondary to its values as a literary, and, if you will, philosophical document; and as such it must eventually be assessed.[6]

Endgame may be a metaphysical poem, but it is a dramatic metaphysical poem. Barbour's attitude, it seems to me, overlooks the visual drama which Beckett has put into his play, the dull colors, the painful movement, the extended pantomime with which the work opens and closes, stressing the ritual aspects of the play and adding thus to the religious overtones gained by the frequent use of quasi-Biblical phrases; all of which forms a part of the works "essential significances." It is this visual wound inflicted upon us, as well as the "clawing" text of which Beckett speaks, which constitutes the theatrical effectiveness of this play. Its suspense lies in our reading of what Artaud would have called the "hieroglyphs" that are presented before us.

I think we must admit, however, that it requires a special sensibility to appreciate the drama in *Endgame.* The average playgoer is not ready to forget the usual pleasures afforded by the theater in order to discover new ones, theatrical and nontheatrical, in this play. We must confess, with Beckett, that the "inhumanity" of the play makes it more difficult of access. As a matter of fact, *Endgame* shows a step away from the moving, humane, and more dramatic universe of *Godot* with the tossing of the ball back and forth between two dialoguers, toward the more static world of the novels which are essentially monologues. Structurally, *Endgame* resembles *Malone Dies* and *The Unnamable,* for example, more than it does *Godot.* The first novel is a monologue written by Malone as he lies paralyzed in his bed. From his window he can scarcely see a corner of sky, and part of the house across the street. For a time he is left soup by a shriveled arm that appears through the door. As he lies waiting for the end, Malone draws his various possessions to him by means of a stick with a hook on the end. He soon drops the stick, however, and cannot take inventory of his "things." He amuses himself by telling stories, and commenting on his condition until finally death overtakes him, and his voice simply dwindles away.

The Unnamable is the monologue of a person, uncertain of his identity, armless, resting upon sawdust in a vase outside a restaurant. Because of the vase's rim, he cannot turn his head. Condemned to this motionless state, he mercilessly analyzes his meaningless existence and his own thought processes. "The hermetically self-sealed solipsist," Jerome Stone calls the protagonist of Beckett's novels, "whose mind, in mad lucidity, gnaws away like a galvanized mouse at the trivial underpinnings of man's logical existence, until the whole superstructure of the world of human dignity is reduced to a tissue of nihilistic absurdity."[7]

Because of the more objective manner of presentation of drama, we are not so aware of the monologue in *Endgame*. And yet Hamm, almost glued to center stage, dominates the play from one end to the other, like some malevolent deity, torturing Clov, reviling his parents, commenting almost detachedly on the disintegration that takes place as life grinds to a stop. Like Malone, he tells a story, and interrupts to comment upon it: "Nicely put, that. . . . A bit feeble, that. . . . That should do it, etc." All Beckett's characters seem cruelly aware of what is happening to them. This is why they must talk, find a sounding board in someone, or at least monologue endlessly, "to prevent the discourse from coming to an end, this futile discourse" (*The Unnamable*, p. 26).

Even *Malone Dies*, emptied of plot and character, has some movement, for Malone does die. In *Endgame*, Hamm does not die, and Clov does not leave. Perhaps the better analogy is with *The Unnamable*, for as it ends, the maimed body, which does not know its name, is just where it was at the beginning: "You must go on, I can't go on, I'll go on."

Beckett is a linguist, and many of his critics have enjoyed toying with the possible meanings of his characters' names. A vast majority of his novelistic creatures have names beginning with "M": Murphy, Molloy, Moran, Malone, and so on. *Endgame* has afforded a field day. Hamm has been associated with Hamlet, a ham actor, and the Home owner, Ham the son of Noah, and a hammer insofar as he is the central personage who drives the other three "into the nothingness of life and death."[8] Clov may be a corruption of the French word for nail, *clou*, whereas Nagg and Nell are simply variant forms of the word "nail." Nagg, furthermore, is a nagger, and Nell has a sweet bell-like, knell-like voice, while Clov is a combination of love plus "C" for Christ.

These interpretations seem to add nothing essential to the meaning of *Endgame*, although they may help to corroborate the belief (which scarcely needs corroboration) that Hamm is the central and dominant character of the play.

Who are these characters? Are they simply the remains of humanity after some dreadful catastrophe which has left the world deserted? Or are they symbols of God and man? Hamm and Clov look very much like Pozzo and Lucky. We have fallen into a world where friendship and tenderness no longer exist (unless we count the senile sharing of memories and biscuits by Nagg and Nell as an indication of tenderness—but how terrible a commentary on human tenderness after the more meaningful sharing of suffering we could see in *Godot*), where the only relationship left is that of master and servant.

We must ultimately admit that Hamm and Clov are representative of man, however tempting it may be to see in the former a God-image. It is true that he plays the father-role to Clov, and that his position is central at almost all times. He very fussily insists that Clov place his chair in the very middle of the room after their brief tour to the wall and window. It is also true that he enjoys knowing that the toy dog is standing before him in an imploring attitude, and takes a sadistic pleasure in making his subordinates suffer. But the Hamm-God interpretation is invalidated by the fact that it is Hamm who invites the others to pray to God, and joins in prayer himself. There is no response, and the angry conclusion of Hamm is, "The bastard! He doesn't exist!" Godot has died, and the world-in-waiting has become a world with nothing to wait for.

Professor Lamont makes the very pregnant suggestion that Hamm is the wounded Fisher King, with Clov as Parsifal and the Holy Grail a jar of dry cookies. Now, the Fisher King is a kind of scapegoat who suffers for all humanity, but in Beckett's play he refuses to suffer alone, and drags Clov, Nagg, and Nell along with him. The ultimate irony is that there is no humanity left for these sufferers to redeem: they are suffering for themselves alone, their suffering has no transcendence, no meaning. "Outside of here it's death," warns Hamm twice, but within is death also. Outside is only the "other hell" which corresponds to the hell these people are suffering in their prisonlike room.

Even the pitiable tree of *Godot* has disappeared. There is no more nature, we are told. The world has run down and Clov, looking out the window with his telescope, describes it aptly as "corpsed."

> What in God's name do you imagine? [cries Hamm
> violently to one of the characters in the story he
> is telling]. That the earth will awake in spring?
> That the rivers and seas will run with fish again?
> That there's manna in heaven still for imbeciles
> like you?

There are no more sugarplums, no more seeds that sprout, no more rugs to keep us warm, no more coffins, and of course no more painkiller. The only two things from our familiar world which still seem to exist are rats and lice: Clov has trapped a rat in his kitchen, and a louse in his pants. Both must be exterminated immediately: "Humanity might start from there all over again!" cries Hamm, perturbed. "Catch him, for the love of God!"

A grim humor lightens some few moments of the play, and the clownish antics of Gogo and Didi survive weakly in the business of Clov and Hamm. But the dominant note is one of tedium. Time and weather never vary. Yesterday is only "that bloody awful day, long ago, before this bloody awful day." "All life long the same inanities." One only has a vague feeling that something is transpiring, but what? "Something is taking its course," asserts Clov. "Have you not had enough . . . of this . . . this . . . thing?" asks Hamm. The audience never learns precisely what it is that is taking its course, because Beckett's characters, and perhaps Beckett himself, cannot understand it, much less define it. Hence the play seems to stand still, and the fetid odor of human suffering is the strongest impression that reaches us. The stench of sickness, rotting limbs, blood, and wet diapers. Or the smell of death, for are not all Beckett's characters ultimately dead spiritually? Didi says as much (*Godot*, p. 59), and Hamm describes part of his decrepitude:

Hamm. Last night I saw inside my breast. There was a big sore.

Clov. Pah! You saw your heart.

Hamm. No, it was living.

Readers, spectators, and critics are not alone in hoping to find some meaning in *Endgame*. Hamm himself asks rather incredulously:

Hamm. We're not beginning to . . . to . . . mean something?

Clov. Mean something! You and I, mean something! (*Brief laugh.*) Ah that's a good one!

Hamm. I wonder. (*A pause.*) Imagine if a rational being came back to earth, wouldn't he be liable to

46

get ideas into his head if he observed us long enough.

Certainly the intelligent and "rational being" observing *Endgame* is "liable to get ideas into his head," but he may have difficulty in finding coherence in the total pattern. He might even be justified in complaining that, although the ideas have been presented in a way that piques the intellect and stimulates the imagination, they lack the necessary theatrical qualities to hold the interest of the average theater-goer during the hour and a half that the single act lasts. At the same time, it cannot be denied that this play constitutes a profound experience for the person who is willing to overcome his prejudices and inertia and will participate intellectually in the presentation. It remains a terrifying picture of the disintegration of a human universe, and a vivid document of an era which has lost its faith in an absolute.

The Short Plays

Thematically the short plays add nothing new, for they exploit the same feelings of tedium, meaninglessness, and frustration we have seen in *Godot* and *Endgame*. Technically, however, they explore two new media: mime and radio.

Pantomime has apparently always interested Beckett, for it plays an important part in his work. Both long plays contain intricate descriptions of stage business, such as the passing of the hats in *Godot* and the ultimately useless movements of Clov with ladder and telescope in *Endgame*. The novels too make use of such a technique. In *Watt*, for example, there is a masterly description of an academic committee whose members begin to look at one another, but it is no simple matter and requires three or four pages of accurate description:

> For example, Mr. Fitzwein looked at Mr. Magershon, on his right. But Mr. Magershon is not looking at Mr. Fitzwein, on his left, but at Mr. O'Meldon, on his right. But Mr. O'Meldon is not looking at Mr.

Magershon, on his left, but craning forward, at Mr. MacStern, on his left but three at the far end of the table. But Mr. MacStern is not craning forward looking at Mr. O'Meldon, on his right . . . etc., etc.

Such pantomime, usually amusing in itself, inevitably underlines the major themes of the plays and novels, adding to the feeling of absurdity, meaningless repetition, and futility. And these are precisely the emotions evoked in *Act Without Words I* in which the man, victim of a hostile universe, is cast into a desert where various objects are offered for his comfort: a palm tree with its shade, a bottle of water suspended from the flies. He is even offered the means to obtain the water, which is always kept just beyond his reach: various blocks, rope, and scissors. When he cannot get the water, and attempts to hang himself with the rope, the palm tree disappears into the flies. When he decides to cut his throat with the scissors, they too disappear skyward, leaving the man alone, lying on his side staring toward the audience. He looks at his hands, and the curtain falls. Has he resigned himself and crawled into a shell recalling the foetal position, or has he learned that he must count only upon himself?

Act Without Words II is a tightly compressed little piece which suggests a great deal through its three short scenes. Two sacks, each containing a man, are in turn pricked by a goad. The first man rises, prays, dresses, eats, and performs sluggishly all the activities symbolic of a human day, then returns to his sack. The second man does much the same thing in a gay, brisk manner. As the pantomime ends the goad pricks the first man again and he climbs out of his sack to begin the same routine. Aside from the usual commentary about the monotony and repetition of human life, *Act Without Words II* seems to say that no matter how you go about it, the end result is the same: back into the sack. The meaningless rhythm is not only that of the life of a single

48

day, it is also the rhythm of a lifetime, for the sack sym-
bolizes womb and tomb as much as it does sleep. The
goad, which first enters from the wings without sup-
ports and subsequently enters on one and then on two
wheels, further suggests that the play is a representation
of the whole history of humanity. Ironically, the goad
which pricks us may be improved, but human tedium
remains forever the same.

All That Fall, a radio play, contains a great deal of
movement, and Thomas Barbour has suggested that it
is better adapted to the needs of experimental cinema
than to the radio. Beckett has, however, laid great stress
on the sounds in his script: rural sounds such as those
of various animals; the dragging feet of Mrs. Rooney
as she plods along the country road; cars, trains, bicycle
horns, and so on.

Unlike Beckett's other work, *All That Fall* is not
allegorical. The characters reveal the human predicament, but they are more clearly individuals than are
Didi and Gogo or Hamm and Clov, and to that extent
are less symbolic. Their antecedents are found in the
Irish drama of Synge and Lady Gregory, and Beckett
has conserved the subtly beautiful music of Irish speech
in his dialogue. We meet an entire gamut of Irish rural
character types: the lonely and pain-ridden ancient Mrs.
Rooney, the prim and bigoted (and significantly named)
Miss Fitt, the crusty station master, the thoughtful young
race course clerk, the crotchety blind husband of Maddy
Rooney. Each is characterized simply by a few lines of
dialogue. Mrs. Rooney, the central personage, goes to
the train station to meet her husband returning from
work on the 12:30 train. Unlike Godot, the train does
arrive, but somewhat late, and Mrs. Rooney is upset.
Her husband offers no explanation for the tardiness, and
it is only at the end that we discover that a child had
fallen out of one of the cars and under the wheels of the
moving train, perhaps murdered, it is suggested, by old
Dan Rooney.

Once again suffering, anguish, solitude, physical decrepitude, and decay are stressed. Mrs. Rooney walks in pain, can scarcely climb the steps at the railroad station, Mr. Rooney cannot walk and talk at the same time, he is blind and his heart is ailing. When someone inquires after another's health, the latter is invariably worse off, or only getting along, or has just had all her insides removed. This universe is as uncomfortable as that of Gogo and Didi, bicycle tires will not stay inflated, cars are so high off the ground that it is only with great physical effort and a push from behind that Mrs. Rooney can get in. When she and the blind Mr. Rooney prepare to undertake the descent of the station stairs, poor Dan is perplexed and frightened by the number of steps. Like the character in the first story of *Tales and Texts for Nothing*, he has never been able to ascertain the exact number of steps, for does one count the ground at the bottom as the first step, and the level at the top as the last? Or only the steps between? Or perhaps only the intervening steps along with the top level, or only the steps along with the ground at the bottom? Mr. Rooney, like all of Beckett's characters, is lost. He can find no absolute to hang onto, and must simply get along as best he can, with a tapping cane and the aid of the trembling Mrs. Rooney. "We shall fall into the ditch," he prophesies. "Oh, Dan!" cries his wife, ecstatically, "It will be like old times!"

The title of this little picture of unhappy humanity comes from a Biblical quotation. Maddy tells her husband that the preacher for next Sunday has announced the following text: "The Lord upholdeth all that fall and raiseth up all those that he bowed down." There is a brief silence, and then "they join in wild laughter." It is only too apparent to these miserable characters that, although they have fallen and are indeed bowed down, no Lord has upheld them. The consoling lie is too good a joke for them to refrain from laughter even in the midst of their privations.

The almost grisly dialogue of *Krapp's Last Tape* takes place between man-become-animal and a machine. There are no more living presences. Even the hopeless world of *Endgame* is outstripped, as the nearsighted Krapp, sitting alone in a circle of light surrounded by what he considers a comforting darkness, listens to a tape made thirty years ago, when he was a young thirty-nine. The pathos of the act does not arise so much from a comparison of the corroded old man with the creature evoked by the tape of many years before, for there is no great difference. At thirty-nine, Krapp was already laughing at his youthful idealism. Our horror comes rather from the realization that his life has been a downward plunge all the way. The addiction to drink and large bananas, which he denounced in his old tape, is still a part of him. And his pleas for a less engrossing sexual life have apparently not been realized either. Together the tape and the old ruin laugh at the youthful idealism as the tape recalls the young man he once was. The tragedy of Krapp, and of all men in Beckett's view, is not that we become what we were not, but that we are now and evermore the same. The basic animal does not change: Krapp at sixty-nine is still swilling alcohol, still eating bananas (whose peels he discards into the orchestra pit), and still sleeping with whores. What has disappeared is hope and intellect, the non-physical appetites. He must now search in the dictionary for words he used thirty years ago. What has increased is physical disintegration: nearsightedness, deafness, cracked voice, laborious walk, a cough; these characterize Krapp. The only happiness that remains is the joy of pronouncing the word "spool." "Revelled in the word spool," Krapp reports on his last tape; and adds with relish, "Spooool! Happiest moment of the past half million." As the play ends Krapp sits motionless staring before him while the tape runs on in silence. For there is nothing left to say.

Embers, Beckett's second radio play, reminds us

once again of the novels, for although there are several voices, one has the impression that everything is going on inside Henry's head. Henry, sitting by the sea, recalls "the good old days when we wished we were dead." Telling himself unending stories, talking to his dead father, reliving moments with his wife and child, Henry evokes the bitter chill atmosphere of a world whose fire has gone out. Desperately he clutches at words, at sounds—for "every syllable is a second gained" —in an effort to drown out the noise of the sea which captivates him, draws him to its side with the fascination of death and nothingness.

Like Krapp, Henry is in an empty world. Even a machine is denied him, and all that remain are his memories slowly burning out. All the voices we hear are called forth by Henry, and the sounds are those which he imagines, except for the sound of his own footsteps and the sea. Ada may sit beside him, but she makes no noise, for she is nonexistent. And soon, she tells him, "You will be alone with your voice, there will be no other voice in the world but yours."

Beckett's view of life and man's tragic place in the universe is illuminated by a passage from his study of Proust:

> Tragedy is not concerned with human justice. Tragedy is the statement of an expiation, but not the miserable expiation of a codified breach of a local arrangement, organized by the knaves for the fools. The tragic figure represents the expiation of original sin, of the original and eternal sin of him and all his "soci malorum," the sin of having been born.

The picture presented is an elemental one, in which social relationships are but one aspect of man's metaphysical anguish. He is a creature paying for a sin he did not commit, or was unaware of committing. God, the villain, either does not show up for his promised appointment, or what is worse, he does not exist, and man is left alone in a meaningless universe, attempting to find the reason for it all. His moments of lucidity bring no revelation, only suffering, and he tends to sink into habits that, although boring, are at least a "great deadener." But unfortunately man is a thinking animal, in spite of Herbert Gould's clever assertion that one of Beckett's characters is "a perverse Descartes, proclaiming: 'I stink, therefore I am.' "[9] He cannot avoid moments of lucidity in which he asks certain embarrassing and unanswerable questions: Who am I? Where am I going?

Many critics have pointed out that Beckett's works constitute a search for the self, that they exploit the mystery of self-identification. The answer to the mystery seems to be, as Richard Eastman states, "that the true self is so much of a myth that people, like certain actors, can exist only by devising their roles." We have already noted how Gogo and Didi improvise scenes as they go along, how Hamm, like many characters in the novels, is obsessed with telling a story. Beckett's creatures must build a screen of words between themselves and nothingness—or rather, between a fancied image of themselves and their ultimate unreality. And yet they are frequently aware of what they are doing, and comment, "We're getting on," or "How boring!"

"The sin of having been born," recalls the doctrine of original sin. The sense of guilt is strong in Beckett's work, rich in religious connotations. Vladimir and Estragon, like Malone, remember the thieves crucified with Christ, and realize that their role must be that of suppliants. They even contemplate repentance. Throughout the novels God and Jesus are mentioned, the characters often comparing themselves to the latter. God is perhaps awaited in *Godot* and Watt actually spends some time in the mansion of the enigmatic Mr. Knott. Biblical passages are quoted or evoked. The Cross, the Crucifixion, and the two thieves seem almost an obsession, for they recur with greater frequency than other Biblical allusions. They would stress, of course, the suffering of man who is daily crucified, giving some vague hope of salvation, and imparting, as Horace Gregory remarks, a strong "emotional charge" to the writing.[10]

Beckett's view of life is basically a religious one: it is the view of a man who seeks some meaning beyond the trivial happenings of everyday life, a purpose beyond the physical needs of a specific time and place. The painful recognition of the absurd, and the ensuing struggle for meaning, reflect a more profoundly religious attitude than any facile acceptance of inherited beliefs. Beckett appears to be struggling within the framework of the Christian religion, but has apparently not found a valid attitude aside from that lucid awareness of man's miserable condition and the ever-present threat of annihilation.

One would expect a rather sober reaction to such a pessimistic outlook, but Beckett is a comic writer of great skill and originality. "Nothing is funnier than unhappiness," says Nell in *Endgame*, and she adds, "Yes, yes, it's the most comical thing in the world." Beckett almost succeeds in convincing us that Nell is right, for his humor is invariably based upon man's wretchedness. Ruby Cohn assigns Beckett to that "cruel comic tradition" in which "laughter arises from a malicious feeling of superiority over a victim."[11] And yet we do not remain completely immune, for, as Cohn suggests, "doubt gnaws through our triumph. . . . Before very long we are laughing on the other side of our mouths." At first we may find Gogo pathetically amusing as he fiddles with his shoe, and Didi comical as he feels the inside of his hat in a vain effort to locate the source of discomfort. But when Gogo returns time and again to his shoe, and Didi repeatedly examines his hat, although it may become more laughable than before because of the mechanical repetition, our laughter begins to be tinged with uncertainty. When at the beginning of *Endgame* Hamm says "There's no one else" and Clov claims "There's nowhere else," it is depressing enough. But when we discover a few moments later that there are no more bicycle wheels, no more pap, and no more nature, the situation becomes at once both more amusing and more horrifying. Beckett's humor is largely based upon such repetition of human misery until it becomes terrifying because of its enormity, and at the same time grotesque because of its triviality. Bicycle wheels, pap, and nature are included with sugarplums, coffins, and painkiller in the same mounting crescendo toward nothingness.

Many of the stock methods for inducing laughter are used, such as repetition of words and even entire sentences, misunderstandings, surprising contrasts and contradictions, and of course the slapstick humor of the circus. The laughter they elicit is not usually the loud guffaw, but the wry chuckle. In most of the situations we are laughing *at* the characters of the drama. But there is another kind of laughter in which we join the characters as they themselves laugh grimly at their own dismal situation. It is based upon irony and disillusionment, a laugh of awareness. We see it, for example, in *Krapp's Last Tape* when Krapp joins his tape in deriding the idealism of his youth; and as *Endgame* opens and Clov verifies once more the state of affairs, each new proof that nothing has changed, that the situation remains as grim as ever—emptiness out the right window, emptiness out the left window, corroding Nagg and Nell in their garbage cans, and Hamm at center covered by his bloodstained handkerchief—brings forth a brief chuckle. Again, Hamm promises Nagg a sugarplum if he will listen to his story.

Nagg. You swear?
Hamm. Yes.
Nagg. On what?
Hamm. My honor.
　　(*Pause. They laugh heartily.*)

It seems a measure of *Waiting for Godot*'s greater humanity that it is distinctly lacking in such disabused and bitter laughter. The characters are still mercifully blind to the complete hopelessness of their situation; and this undoubtedly accounts, at least in part, for the greater success of *Godot*.

"My work is a matter of fundamental sounds made as fully as possible," Beckett says in his letters on *Endgame*,[12] "and I accept responsibility for nothing else. If people want to have headaches among the overtones, let them." We have spoken of the "fundamental sounds" in the sense of the major themes, and perhaps dallied among the "headaches" of the overtones in Beckett's plays. We cannot leave them, however, without saying a word about the "fundamental sounds" in a more literal sense, for, as Horace Gregory reminds us, "the first thing to be said about Samuel Beckett . . . is that he is essentially a poet." Gregory goes on to say that Beckett writes in the "economical, sometimes ambiguous language of poetic imagination."

Poetry, since Symbolism, has aspired to the condition of that most abstract of the arts, music, and attempts to speak a language that suggests, or reveals indirectly, rather than stating outright. The direct appeal is made to the emotions by means of images, rhythm, tone color, and connotation. The poet's meaning, while immediately apprehended by the affective faculties, is not always obvious to the intellect. This is probably one of the major problems of poetic drama today: the dramatist must succeed in finding that point where the mystery of poetry is retained but at the same time due importance is given to the wakeful mind that—for better or worse—is apparently an indestructable part of the theater spectator, at least as he has been conditioned by the twentieth-century Occidental world.

Beckett has usually succeeded in finding that mysterious point where suggestivity meets intelligibility. Only the most crassly insensitive person could fail to *feel* intensely the essential meaning of Beckett's work. And if he is wakeful he will easily *comprehend* the basic dramatic situation, and the issues involved. Beyond this may lie "headaches" for the overzealous analyst. And yet, the pleasure of interpretation and discovery is certainly one of the greatest afforded by contemporary art, and only the blind, the lazy, or the hidebound traditionalist—but has not obscurity been a tradition in modern literature for at least three quarters of a century?—will refuse to risk at least a few migraines.

Beckett's favorite stylistic devices—brevity of line, stychomythia, repetition, and frequent use of silence—contribute on another level to the feeling of isolation and absurdity which dominates his work. Simplicity of sentence structure and brevity of line point to the same nudity and forlornness stressed by the bareness of the décor. Stychomythia in Beckett, unlike that dynamic interchange found in Corneille, suggests a lack of communication as each man follows his own train of thought almost oblivious to what the other is saying. The frequent pauses isolate the words and brief phrases, just as the characters are isolated, and intimate that the final and inevitable answer will be silence. The repetitions and refrains (one almost hesitates to reiterate) underline the tedium of this world, its interminable futility.

It is *Waiting for Godot* that best embodies these characteristics, and uses them to fullest advantage. And from the dramatic point of view, I believe it is *Godot* that must be considered Beckett's masterpiece, for it is most successful in presenting characters who are sympathetic and clearly defined in an action that, although reduced to the minimum, contains the requisite amount of movement. The vague element of hope, the humanity of the author's attitude which we can feel in his treatment of Didi and Gogo, the tempting ambiguity, and the terse poetry of the dialogue make of this drama what Anouilh has called "one of the key plays of the contemporary theater."[13] *Godot* was the first of the so-called avant-garde plays to gain world-wide recognition, and it remains one of the most accessible. An appreciation of Beckett's meaning and methods as they are embodied here can help us to approach his more difficult, or more "dehumanized" plays, just as it can give us a perspective on the other dramatists of the avant-garde.

3

Eugène Ionesco

EUGÈNE IONESCO was born in Slatina, Rumania, in 1912, was brought to France the following year, and remained there until he was thirteen. His mother was of French background and Ionesco's upbringing and education were completely French. He returned to Rumania in 1925 to attend the University of Bucharest, study symbolist poetry, teach French, and write literary criticism. It was at this time that he composed an essay entitled *No*, which attempted to demonstrate the identity of opposites.

In 1938 Ionesco obtained a government grant to study contemporary poetry in Paris, where he was to prepare a thesis on the subject of death in modern poetry. Anyone familiar with Ionesco's work will recognize one of his major preoccupations, and it is interesting to note as early as 1938 the scholarly interest he apparently planned to devote to the subject. The thesis, however, was never written.

Ionesco began to write for the theater about the same time as Beckett, and although several of his plays were produced before *Godot* achieved its world-wide renown, they did not at first enjoy its enthusiastic reception. *The Bald Soprano*, written in 1949 and produced the following year, lasted barely six weeks, often playing to empty houses. Productions of *The Lesson* in 1951 and *The Chairs* in 1952 were scarcely more successful. It was only in 1954 with *Amédée or How to Get Rid of It,* presented by Jean-Marie Serreau at the Théâtre Babylone, that Ionesco finally found a larger audience. Since then his plays have been frequently revived in France and abroad, and each new play is anticipated eagerly by those devoted to the noncommercial and experimental theater. The more conservative elements have not accepted Ionesco, and it is unlikely that they ever will. In France, where bitter word battles are still waged through the newspapers and magazines, Ionesco's two staunchest enemies have been the critics of the country's most widely distributed dailies, Jean-Jacques Gautier of *Le Figaro* and the late Robert Kemp of *Le Monde.* Ionesco has not hesitated to dub them "the personification of universal stupidity." They in turn have described Ionesco thus:

> Monsieur Eugène Ionesco is a fellow of the same kind as Alfred Jarry. Monsieur Ionesco represents, in the eyes of a small, a very small, group, a "libertador," a sort of Bolivar of the theatre. . . . Let him keep his flattering illusion. He is an insignificant "curiosity" of today's theatre. [R. Kemp, *Le Monde*]

> I do not believe that Mr. Ionesco is a genius or a poet; I do not believe that M. Ionesco is an important author; I do not believe that M. Ionesco is a man of the theatre; I do not believe that M. Ionesco is a thinker or a madman; I do not believe that M. Ionesco has anything to say.
> I believe that M. Ionesco is a hoaxer (I don't want to believe the contrary, it would be too sad), a mystifier, hence a practical joker. [J.-J. Gautier, *Le Figaro*]

For his admirers, Eugène Ionesco is a "theater man par excellence,"[1] and his plays form an "implacably human theater."[2]

There is some justification in considering Ionesco the

unofficial spokesman for the avant-garde theater since he has published more explanatory writing than any other dramatist we are considering. "If only M. Ionesco would put into his plays a bit of the clarity and wisdom which he puts into his polemical writings, he could become a great dramatist," declared a reader of the London *Observer*.

Ionesco has stated his position firmly and clearly: "I can only affirm and repeat that the theatre is the theatre." With these words he rejects the conventional theater of ideas, psychology, or philosophy and attempts to return to a primitive theater that seeks only to be itself. The essence of theater, he claims, is enlargement. To go beyond that twilight land that is neither life nor theater, we must exaggerate, push our characters, our stories, and even our settings beyond the bounds of the true or the likely in order to arrive at something that is truer than life itself; the amplified and theatrical image of life which strikes deep below the surface of reality.

The world created by Ionesco is strange and nightmarish, but at the same time familiar, for it is our own little world, and the grotesque figures moving upon the stage remind us of ourselves. We have become gigantic puppets, often moving senselessly back and forth, with little apparent meaning in our words or actions. This theater recalls the Punch and Judy show, as is natural, for Ionesco had his first lessons in dramatic art at the guignol.

> The spectacle of the guignol [he tells us] held me there, stupefied by the sight of these puppets who spoke, who moved and bludgeoned each other. It was the spectacle of life itself which, strange, improbable, but truer than truth, was being presented to me in an infinitely simplified and caricatured form, as though to underline the grotesque and brutal truth.

Such a description is almost a methodology: in Ionesco's plays we see just such caricatures as they reveal to us our uselessness, our vanity, and our own stupidity. At the same time, these figures possess a metaphysical dimension, for men are not only social animals, they are also victims of the antispiritual universe that crushes them beneath the weight of an overwhelming mass of dead matter. In several essays, Ionesco has described this terrifying feeling that is at the base of many of his plays. In "The Point of Departure" he explains that there are two fundamental states of consciousness from which his works take their being. One is that of lightness, evanescence, and it gives rise to an attitude of wonder, surprise, and even of liberty. Things seem unimportant, and man can laugh. But this state is very rare, and the author most often feels himself dominated by a heaviness, a thickness, an opacity, a universe which crushes man. The self is separated from the world, and also from its real self, spirit dies and matter is victorious. After brief moments of euphoria man is inevitably thrown back into this opaque world of things.

I have no other images of the world, [Ionesco claims] aside from those which express evanescence and hardness, vanity and anger, nothingness or hideous and useless hate. Existence has continued to appear to me in this way. Everything has only confirmed what I had seen, what I had understood in my childhood: vain and sordid furors, cries suddenly stifled by silence, shadows swallowed up forever in the night.

Such a point of view, like that of Beckett, would seem to indicate a somber and lugubrious theater. On the contrary, most of Ionesco's plays are surprisingly gay, for the author wishes to underline through these tragic farces and comic dramas, not only the inseparability of the comic and the tragic, but the fundamental absurdity of the human predicament. Tragedy reveals the dignity of man crushed by an incomprehensible destiny. But comedy is even sadder, for it suggests that there is no such thing as human dignity, that there is nothing to understand behind the cruel jokes that life plays upon us. Ionesco mingles the comic and the tragic, and his audience is pulled from one to the other until it no longer knows what to think. An Ionesco audience is rarely indifferent: its members are either vehemently opposed to what they are witnessing, or are just as vehemently in favor of it.

Starting with ordinary events which are taken most frequently from our daily existence, then modifying and distorting them to nightmarish intensity, Ionesco arrives at the unusual. This vision, he believes, forms a realistic appraisal of life, for reality is deeply rooted in what seems unreal, just as life is rooted in death. It is a vision, he reminds us, that is attested by Buddha, Shakespeare, John of the Cross, and Job.

Ultimately, as with all the dramatists of today's avant-garde, Ionesco is dealing with the human condition, and taking a stand, however nondogmatically, on the fundamental issue of man's existence and its meaning. A work of art, he claims, cannot avoid expressing some fundamental attitude:

> It is nothing if it does not go beyond the temporary truths and obsessions of history, if, stopping at such and such a symbolist, naturalist, surrealist or socialist-realist style, it fails to find a definitive and profound universality.

Ionesco is therefore violently opposed to a theater that deals with current problems as such. Of course an author who deals in universals will have something to say for men of his day, unless he speaks in too abstract a manner. But the author who espouses a political system, or attempts to preach a particular ideology from the stage is branded as an imposter—a thinker attempting to look like a dramatist, or a dramatist parading as thinker. The theater is autonomous, gratuitous. This is not to say, however, that Ionesco is a partisan of the art for art's sake school. He refuses to belong to any school, and stands for the absolute liberty of the dramatist. His theater is, he tells us, a confession, an avowal, a projection of his inner drama upon the stage, and "it is by being entirely oneself that one has the best chance of being others at the same time."

The dramatist's refusal to bind himself by any rules is amusingly set forth in the one act play, *The Alma Impromptu or The Shepherd's Chameleon*, written in 1955. Like Molière's *Versailles Impromptu* and Giraudoux's *Paris Impromptu*, this work is interesting chiefly as a revelation of the author's ideas. The Place de l'Alma gives its name to the play, for it is just around the corner from the tiny theater of the Studio des Champs-Elysées where the first performance took place.

As the *Impromptu* (which in translation bears the title *Improvisation*) begins we find Ionesco dozing among his books and manuscripts. His slumber is soon interrupted by a visitor, Bartholomeus I, a producer and critic who has come to pick up a play commissioned for a new theater that boasts a scientific director, a troup of scientific young actors, a small house with twenty-five seats, and standing room for four—and best of all, an elite popular audience. The author is embarrassed, for he obviously has scarcely begun the play, and has difficulty in describing it to Bartholomeus I. What he does say, however, offers a rather faithful description of his plays and their genesis:

> Er . . . you know I never know how to talk about my plays. . . . It's all in the dialogue, in the acting, in the stage effects, it's very visual, as usual. . . . With me there's always first some image, some line or other which sets off the creative mechanism. And then I just let my own characters carry me along, I never know exactly where I'm going. . . . For me every play is an adventure, a quest, the discovery of a universe that's suddenly revealed, and there's no one more surprised than I am to find that it exists. . . .

64

As Ionesco finally starts to read the play, which begins precisely as the *Impromptu* we are witnessing, he is interrupted once again, this time by two more critics, Bartholomeus II and Bartholomeus III. The three critics are depicted as narrow, dogmatic, and unintelligent clowns, much in the same tradition as the doctors of Molière. They are, in fact, doctors of theatrology, for they believe that everything related to the theater can be reduced to rules and precepts. They take it upon themselves to teach their benighted author the rules of theatrology, costumology, decorology, and spectato-sociopsychology, for Ionesco, they claim, is a dramatist and therefore necessarily stupid. Only the critic is intelligent or allowed to think, and it is his duty and his mission to take exception to everything.

In his three doctors Ionesco has parodied two attitudes toward the theater: that of the conservative critic who believes the theater has no purpose beyond amusement, and that of the socially-oriented critic who, taking Brecht as his god, believes the theater must be didactic. It must be organized like a night school course, they decree, with rewards and punishment. Much fun is made of the Brechtian principle of alienation, and Ionesco is told that he must no longer identify himself with himself: "You've always made the mistake of being yourself. . . . Be Ionesco not being Ionesco! . . . Look at yourself with one eye, listen to yourself with the other!"

Bartholomeus III, a partisan of Bernstein and the old-fashioned boulevard theater he represents, is soon quarreling with his colleagues who proclaim Brecht the only god, and themselves his prophets. Soon, however, they decide to present a unified front to their common enemy: the author. They reject everything which does not conform to their ideas, and which does not represent their own social context. Poetry is gibberish, and Shakespeare a foreigner to be suspected:

Ionesco. I was made to read the works of Aeschylus, Sophocles, and Euripides . . .

Bartholomeus I. Outdated, outdated, all that! It's dead . . . of no value at all . . .

Ionesco. And then . . . and then . . . Shakespeare!

Bartholomeus III. He's not a *French* writer. The others may be, but *he's* a Russian.

Even Molière is not safe, for if his work is still valuable today it means that he did not express the society of his own time.

Finally, the author, almost hypnotized by the senseless speech of his three critics, teaching him the various -ologies, begins to bray like the ass they would make of him. At this point the voice of reason is heard: Marie, the cleaning woman who has been knocking at the door for some time now, cries out, "Ah, zut alors!—Curses!" and brings us back to reality. She breaks down the door, drives out the doctors, and gives a drink of water to Ionesco who, taking a paper from his pocket, puts on his spectacles and addresses the audience. Much of what we have heard, he tells us, is taken directly from the writings of the honored doctors. He accuses them, the representatives of dogmatic criticism (and the name Bartholomeus recalls rather clearly the name Barthes, one of Ionesco's arch-critics, whom he has called "the mystified demystifier"), of having obfuscated the truth by covering it with complicated terminology. There is, moreover, no such thing as absolute truth, and even elementary truth becomes dangerous when it is pronounced infallible. Therefore the critic should be aware of attitudes other than his own, and his criticism should be descriptive rather than normative.

Our learned doctors, as Marie has just told you, have everything to learn and nothing to teach, for the creative artist himself is the only reliable witness of his times, he discovers them in himself, it is he alone, mysteriously and in perfect freedom,

66

who can express his day and age. Constraint and control . . . falsify this evidence and distort it by pushing it in one direction or the other.

The theater, he proclaims, is for him the scenic projection of an inner world. As he goes on to construct a system based upon this belief, beginning to sound strangely doctoral and dogmatic, the voice of reason once again calls him to order: Marie takes a doctoral robe and places it upon his shoulders as the curtain falls.

The dramatist who enjoys real liberty and is allowed to express his deepest preoccupations, will resemble himself even in diversity, much more than the playwright who follows the dictates of changing fashions. Ionesco's plays, covering a wide range of types, show a homogeneity of vision and of the techniques employed to present that vision. At the same time one can note a definite development when one compares the first plays with the later ones. Interestingly enough, Ionesco seems to be growing in a direction diametrically opposed to that taken by Beckett. We noted that *Godot* is the most human and sympathetic of Beckett's dramatic works, while the later plays tend to become dehumanized. In Ionesco's theater we can see a process of humanization. The first plays picture machines in a world without real feeling. The author remains detached from his creatures. Beginning with *The Chairs*, however, an element of pathos can be perceived. And with *Rhinoceros* Ionesco appears to have achieved a humanity that has found him a wider understanding and appreciation than heretofore.

From The Bald Soprano *to* The Chairs

For most people Ionesco is the author of *The Bald Soprano, The Lesson,* and *The Chairs.* Both abroad and in France he is known primarily for his early works in which unreal characters, speaking a disarticulated and fantastic language that somehow resembles our own, behave in an incredible and outlandish fashion. This is an accurate, if somewhat superficial, description of *The Bald Soprano* (1949), *The Lesson* (1950), *Jack or the Submission* (1950), and its sequel, *The Future is in the Eggs* (1951). *The Chairs* (1951) has much in common with these plays, but it is more credible in some ways, more human, and reveals a new dimension of Ionesco's theater.

The author has called *The Bald Soprano* an anti-play, and has given it the subtitle "The Tragedy of Language." These suggest two levels of meaning in this play which at first glance appear to be trivial and meaningless. There are other and deeper levels to be explored also, for *The Bald Soprano* constitutes a commentary on society, and on man's predicament as well.

Ionesco tells us that he first came to the theater because he hated it. It seemed to him false: the actors were not really themselves and yet they were not the characters they were trying to impersonate either. Somehow they were lost in an intermediate zone which was too exaggerated to be life, and not exaggerated enough to be theater. When he wrote *The Bald Soprano*, Ionesco had decided to poke fun at such a theater, and in this anti-play we see caricatured many of the clichés of conventional drama: polite drawing-room conversation, melodramatic situations, mysterious asides.

The people we meet behave in a way which at first seems natural, but their mannerisms are exaggerated to such a degree that we cannot accept them as real. But at the same time as we realize that they have become mechanical and foolish, repeating their meaningless clichés, we realize somewhat painfully, that they are behaving as we behave. They are members of what Ionesco has called a perfect society, that is to say, a society in which everything is so well regulated that there are no problems. Neither are there any real pleasures, and life is emptied of meaning. So tedious have their lives become that the Smiths and the Martins are fascinated by the trivial tales with which they amuse each other. Or are they merely being polite? For these puppets most often observe the rules of a society which is hollow within, but we feel no real conviction behind their polite inanities.

As the curtain rises, Mr. and Mrs. Smith are "enjoying" what is apparently a typical evening at home. It is made up of trivial chitchat, misunderstandings, and arguments. Mr. Smith makes no reply to his wife's observations; he merely clacks his tongue. It is clear from the start that there is little understanding and no real communication between the two. The remainder of the play justifies our suspicions, for Mr. and Mrs. Smith rarely agree upon anything and most often are talking at cross purposes.

Bobby Watson is perhaps the most famous character in the play, and yet he—or rather *they*—never appear. For Bobby Watson is an entire family, nay, a whole clan. Every member bears the same name, and as Mr. and Mrs. Smith discuss the mother, the father, the children, the aunts, and uncles, we realize with growing hilarity that it is impossible to distinguish one from the other. Mr. and Mrs. Smith cannot speak about them with any lucidity or accuracy, and their very friends frequently cannot recognize them. For we are in the frenzied world of Ionesco where men have lost their true identity. All have become anonymous, and even the language we use to distinguish our friends one from the other has begun to break down.

Mr. and Mrs. Martin arrive, and while they wait for their host and hostess to dress, a pathetic scene takes place in which Mr. Martin shyly asks Mrs. Martin if he has not seen her somewhere before. As it turns out, they both live in the same house and sleep in the same bed. Indeed, they are man and wife, but living together for many years by no means assures that man and woman will know each other.

The embarrassed silences, the coughs, the platitudes and polite phrases, the disagreements that make up the scene between the two couples are realistic enough to remind us of certain painful evenings we have spent with people to whom we had nothing to say. The arrival of the fireman saves the evening, and the time passes with the telling of stories, each one more meaningless than the last, until the fireman achieves the ultimate in confusion and meaninglessness with his tale, "The Cold."

A society based upon hypocrisy must ultimately disintegrate, and this is precisely what happens at the end of the play as the characters, totally isolated from one another and no longer able to communicate, shout meaningless phrases back and forth, and finally nonsense syllables. Throughout the play we have witnessed the destruction of language. Entire sentences are bereft of their meaning by the context in which they are placed. Words which in another situation might be significant now become absurd. Meaningless arguments about unimportant matters, plays on words suggested not by logic but by unconscious association, nonsense syllables, all contribute to the atmosphere of uselessness, as well as to the humor of the play. The original title of *The Bald Soprano* was to have been *English Without Toil* (*L'Anglais sans peine*), for many of the sentences are taken directly from the Assimil conversational method for learning English. But they are thrown pell-mell into the conversation and have no connection with what precedes or follows.

The extravagant exaggerations and the monstrous humor of the play suggest the solitude of man's condition in a world where husband and wife can no longer speak meaningfully with each other; where indeed they cannot even recognize each other. All men have become anonymities in this world where one word may be substituted for another and where one name will do as well as the next. This is demonstrated impressively by the ending of the play as it is now performed: the lights go out, and when they come up Mr. and Mrs. Martin are sitting where the Smiths were at the beginning, and the play starts over again with exactly the same dialogue. Spectators are perplexed to find no soprano, bald or otherwise, in this play. The title, as a matter of fact, has no real connection with the play but was discovered purely by accident when the actor rehearsing the role of the fireman mistakenly said "une cantatrice chauve" (a bald soprano) instead of "une institutrice blonde" (a blonde schoolteacher). Such a disparity between title and content is justified in Ionesco's theater, for it emphasizes two aspects of his dramaturgy: a nondidactic approach to a theater which is only an exteriorization of the contradictions and anguish of the author's inner life; and the saving grace of humor which not only makes palatable what would otherwise be lugubrious and distasteful, but also suggests at one and the same time the fleeting presence of an unattainable happier world and the meaningless absurdity of the world in which we find ourselves.

If *The Bald Soprano* has nothing to do with a bald soprano, *The Lesson* is a lesson in every sense of the word. In this "comic drama" a professor receives a new pupil who wishes to study for her "total doctorate." He coaches her in mathematics and languages, but is finally driven to distraction by her lack of attention, for she develops a toothache and can think of nothing else. In desperation and anger he kills her with an invisible knife. The maid had warned him that "mathematics lead to philology and philology leads to the worst!" She now chides him for his childish behavior, for this is the fortieth student he has killed today. As the curtain falls, she goes off to answer the door and admit the next new pupil.

The Lesson has the same circular structure as the first play, and suggests again the perpetual but senseless activity. "A vicious circle has its virtue," one of Ionesco's characters says. But whereas *The Bald Soprano* may be dismissed with a snicker, *The Lesson* is terrifying, for it

71

reveals the dangers of totalitarianism. In this little tale we witness the gradual demoralization and destruction of one being by another, as the professor dominates his student, forces her to learn, to become more like him. According to the stage directions the student is lively, gay, and smiling at the beginning and becomes progressively sad, morose, and tired. At the same time the professor, who at the start is very gentle and apologetic, becomes more domineering, until he shouts and strikes the now passive student in the most savage manner. From a more or less human relationship, in which they were communicating with each other (even if only superficially), they degenerate into a useless relationship of animal and object. We see a kind of cannibalism practiced before our eyes. And when the professor takes his invisible knife to stab the girl, he has no need of a real blade, for she is spiritually dead already, and his melodramatic gesture only finishes the job.

The "lesson" given by the professor recalls (or rather foreshadows) the logic of the three Bartholomeuses, and as he delivers his tirades of pedantic gibberish, things become more complicated, logic goes out the window, and language once again breaks down. There is a significant commentary on language in the professor's lecture on philology. In absurd terms he discusses the so-called neo-Spanish tongues. The differences between these related languages, we learn, are imperceptible, since all the words of all the languages are the same. As an example he employs the sentence: "The roses of my grandmother are as yellow as my grandfather who was Asiatic." In all languages it is identical, and yet when the student repeats the sentence, it is never correct according to the professor. The only really safe words, it is suggested, are nonsense syllables, for words that are very heavy with meaning always end up succumbing, crumbling, or bursting like balloons.

A similar degeneration is seen in the "naturalist drama" *Jack or the Submission* and its sequel *The Future*

is in the Eggs or It Takes Everything to Make a World.
Jack, a nonconformist, sits silently in the middle of the
room while his parents make every possible attempt to
get him to speak. He must admit that he likes hash
brown potatoes (in the French version, it is potatoes
with bacon), a phrase that simply represents his acceptance of society, its norms, and its hypocritical little
games. This Jack refuses to do for some time. Finally
his sister prevails upon him, and he admits, with little
enthusiasm, that he likes hash brown potatoes. There
is great rejoicing, and his bride Roberta is brought forth.
She has only two noses, and Jack refuses her, claiming
he will marry only a woman with at least three noses.
A three-nosed Roberta is brought in, and left alone with
the recalcitrant young man. First she gains his sympathy,
and then proceeds to seduce him. Jack, in a weakened
state after the violent sex-play suggested rather than
described through their dialogue, finally gives in, accepts Roberta II as his bride and even consents to take
off his hat—last symbol of rebellious individualism. As
Jack and Roberta II crouch upon the floor, the parents
joyfully cavort about, mewing, whining, and croaking.
The animal has won out again, and man the individual
is dominated by those antispiritual forces which Ionesco
feels are so oppressively omnipresent.

The Future is in the Eggs takes up where *Jack* left
off: Jack and his wife are wrapped in a close embrace
which has apparently lasted for three years. They are
oblivious to all others and purr happily to each other.
The acceptance of marriage, which in *Jack* had been
at the same time an acceptance of society, has now become exclusive and antisocial. It is unproductive, we
are told, and therefore the families must take a hand to
set things right. In the name of tradition, of materialism, and of duty, Jack is told he must produce! His sister
Jacqueline once again brings him round, and the couple
both partake, before our astonished eyes, of a plate of
hash brown potatoes. Jack, it must be said to his credit,

has some small misgivings, remembering his now distant rebellion. He learns to accept the hypocrisy of society and weeps copious tears over the death of his grandfather (who is now standing in a frame and making friendly faces at his grandchild), although he is obviously not moved at all. Finally Jack settles down to the serious business of production. As he makes violent efforts to push, we hear Roberta II off-stage clucking madly, and the members of the family bear in large baskets full of the eggs she has laid. They are placed on a hatching machine, and Jack is forced to sit upon them. More and more eggs are brought in, piled on and around him, until he is scarcely visible. Again the happy family dance and rejoice as the stage takes on the look of a factory: Jack is chugging away like a machine while the clucks of his animal-wife are heard off-stage; the rest of the family is running around passing baskets of eggs as they shout, "Production, production, production!"

The future of humanity is evoked: from the eggs they will make sausages, omelettes, athletes, generals, leeks and onions, idealists, relativists, existentialists, but above all omelettes! There will even be, Jack suggests to the consternation of the others, some pessimists, anarchists, and nihilists. For Jack has not quite forgotten his past, and as he is slowly swallowed up by animalism and materialism he expresses a last vain hope: "I want a fountain of light, incandescent water, fire of ice, snows of fire." The evanescent state of lightness and transparency has disappeared forever, and the curtain falls upon the ghastly cries of "Production, production!" and the repulsive cackling of Roberta II.

As with Bobby Watson, the anonymity of humanity is pointed up by the names of the characters. All of Jack's family bear the name Jack or some derivative, while Roberta's parents are Robert Father and Robert Mother. The hypocrisy and shallowness of these characters can be stressed, Ionesco points out, by having them wear masks, whereas Jack's real face is visible. All of them are exaggerated, weeping at the least provocation and dancing wildly to express their happiness. Jack Grandfather and Jack Grandmother are senile Punch and Judy dolls. Grandfather can scarcely speak, and spends most of his time singing snatches of a song, while his wife constantly tries to give advice to which no one will listen, and she is reduced to cursing, and vents her wrath by hitting her husband over the head.

The family picture presented is not a particularly happy one, and the relations between in-laws are even more strained, as the Roberts accuse Jack of the unproductiveness of the marriage, and the Jacks lay the blame on Roberta II. The crass materialism of society is condemned by Ionesco through these people who leave no room for individuality, and insist that to be meaningful everything must give material results. Even Jack at the end of the first play has succumbed to middle-class values, and as he takes Roberta II's nine-fingered hand, he exclaims, "Oh! You've got nine fingers on your left hand? You're rich, I'll marry you . . ."

The domination of the individual by a system imposed from the outside is simply another form of totalitarianism, and one that is present in every play of Ionesco's in some way or another. The theme is emphasized and tied in with political totalitarianism in *The Future is in the Eggs* by the assertion of Jack Father that their race must be continued: "Long live the white race!" he cries. And the cry is later repeated by the other Jacks and Roberts.

Language again runs riot, words are no longer used as counters, but, emptied of meaning, are simply there for themselves, because they have been suggested by another word or sound. There is a feeling of exuberance in the linguistic invention, illogical, nonsensical, they smack of surrealist trickery and remind us of the fertile imagination of a Jarry. Jack is overwhelmed with invective by his family, for whom he is a *mononstre,* a

75

vilenain, and an *actographe.* Jacqueline cries to her brother, "Je te déteste, de t'exertre," while his mother reminds him how she taught him to "progresser, transgresser, grasseyer," for she had been all things to him, "une amie, un mari, un marin." Trite phrases underline once more the mechanical quality of these people. The triumph of linguistic absurdity takes place in a scene at the end of *Jack* when the young fiancée asks her husband-to-be what he is wearing on his head. It is a kind of "chat" (cat), he answers her, for it is, of course, a chat-peau (chapeau—a hat). There follows a kind of litany during which Roberta II attempts to guess just what it is, using words beginning (in French) with the syllable cha—: a plough, a chagrin, a bullhead fish, a launch, a chalet. And at last, having guessed, she confides that in the basement of her *châ*teau everything is "chat"—cat. Cats are called cat; insects, cat; chairs, cat; one, cat; two, cat; and so on. So whether one wishes to say "I'm terribly sleepy, let's go to sleep" or "Bring me some cold noodles, some warm lemonade and no coffee," one says, "Cat, cat, cat, cat, etc." "Oh," concludes Jack, "It's easy to talk now . . . In fact it's scarcely worth the bother . . ."

The Bald Soprano, The Lesson, Jack, and *The Future is in the Eggs* belong to a period when Ionesco was very much preoccupied with language. In these plays it has become the symbol of that antispiritual, antihuman presence that inevitably wins out. Words no longer have any profound meaning, or stand for any real idea. Rather they have become objects, things, that by their very presence crowd out the meaning that might otherwise have existed.

This oppressive presence is further represented in these early plays by the mechanical quality of the characters. None of them are living beings who feel deeply what they do or say. They are all hollow puppets who live only on the surface, doing what society expects of them, like the Smiths and the Martins or the Jacks and the Roberts. Or else they fall into some mechanical pattern from which they cannot free themselves, like the professor in *The Lesson*. They all feel the need to conform to a group pattern, and thus they deny man's innate uniqueness, his sacred individuality which makes him something living and changing rather than a dead object incapable of independent thought. The Jacks and Roberts must belong to society and behave as society decrees—it is the duty of their children to produce off-spring, and perpetuate the white race. The professor, who strikes us as so antisocial in his behavior, is as dependent as the others. After having killed his student, he is frightened, and to calm him the maid places around his arm a band with a swastika (or some such symbol) on it, saying, "Wait, if you're afraid, wear this, then you won't have anything more to be afraid of." At last he too belongs. And of course the swastika is a very fitting insignia for a man who has murdered a living spirit.

The machinelike characters are of course very amusing. Bergson long ago suggested that comedy arises when a human being behaves like a machine, losing the elasticity we expect men to exhibit. Ionesco's humor is largely based upon this belief. But paradoxically the very element that gives rise to laughter also suggests the heaviness and opacity of man's universe, and we laugh both at the characters and at our own terrible predicament which they embody.

The visual element does not yet play an excessively important part in these first plays. Ionesco, however, like Beckett, from the beginning depends to some extent upon the visible to reveal his deeper meaning. The plays are usually set in a rather shabby décor with characters in threadbare costumes, but the author does not specify this for the first two plays. Only *Jack* and its sequel are described as taking place in a somber, grayish set. The people's clothing, we are told, is wrinkled and worn out. The physical attributes of Roberta II

77

seem significant, since she has three noses and nine fingers on one hand. But she is puzzling: does this super-fluity of appendages mean that Jack will not accept an ordinary woman, and will only compromise partly with society? Or are we to infer that once he has compro-mised, he will go all the way, and materialistically re-quire a woman who has more to offer than the usual one?

The most interesting visual device—and one that pre-figures those used in the plays to follow—is that of the eggs piled about Jack at the end of *The Future is in the Eggs*. Here Ionesco has materialized the antispiritual presence, and caused it almost to drown poor Jack as he hatches out his progeny. The multiplication of dead matter will occur as a central device in three of the next four plays, while the mechanical comportment of the characters and the anarchy of language will no longer be stressed.

The Chairs is a transitional play in the sense that it shares characteristics of the earlier works, and at the same time looks forward to the later plays of Ionesco. It is characterized by the author as a "tragic farce," and, indeed, the exaggerations of farce are once again grafted upon the terribly real situation: the fundamental re-lationship of man to wife, and of both to a nonexistent, but at the same time all too-present, society. The earlier plays form, each in its own way, an amusing if pessimis-tic exposition of the absolute incompatability of hus-band and wife on any level other than the superficial and purely physical, and suggest that no matter how closely associated men may be, they will never, or only rarely, understand each other. But we may be tempted to dismiss them, for the Smiths and Martins, the Jacks and Roberts remind us curiously of excited animals. They do not have the immediacy for us which a more warmly human creature might. They do not speak to us with the urgency of a Didi and a Gogo, and we cannot feel any profound sympathy for their situation. For they are themselves unaware of it. Where Beckett's characters constantly analyze themselves and their predicament, Ionesco's automatically accept without questioning. The Old Man and Woman of *The Chairs*, however, are pathetically aware of their failures, even if they are unwilling to admit it to themselves.

Semiramis, aged 94, and her husband, 95, living in a dilapidated apartment on a lonely island, await the arrival of their guests to whom the Man will reveal his "Message" before the two leap to their deaths. The guests arrive and a chair is brought for each. The guests are, however, invisible, and soon the stage is cluttered with chairs. The last guest to arrive is the Emperor, and in spite of strenuous efforts to reach him, neither of the characters is able to get through the mass of chairs. Finally the Orator who is to deliver the Old Man's message makes his entrance—the only other visible character in the play. After the old people have jumped from the windows at either side of the stage, the Orator opens his mouth to speak, but he is a deaf-mute and of course cannot utter a word. He leaves, and after a pause during which we hear a murmur of conversation, then only the lapping of the sea, the curtain slowly falls upon silence, and the large central door opens upon darkness.

The central device of the play is, of course, the use of the accumulation of chairs to represent a society that is more physical than it is spiritual, more dead than alive, and is an obstacle to man's happiness and understanding. This presence is at the same time an absence, for the overwhelming mass of chairs only stresses more poignantly the emptiness of any human presence on the stage, the inevitable solitude of the old couple. As they prepare to leap to their deaths, they are separated from each other by the many chairs, and are consoled vaguely by the thought that they will be united in eternity, for the "eternal Emperor" will remember them. But, alas, the Emperor is as absent as the other guests, and his arrival is accompanied, the author tells us, by a "cold, empty light." The God-image, with his "divine forehead," his "celestial glance," his "halo," who is the "savior" and "last recourse" of the old people, is unattainable, for the chairs, society, and dead physical matter prevent any approach to him. In the last analysis each of the characters is entirely alone. And the final grim joke is that the great message, which was to have saved humanity, is nonexistent. Or if it exists, there is no possibility of communicating it, for when it comes to exchanging real meanings, we are all deaf-mutes.

In *The Chairs,* the décor assumes a greater importance than heretofore. The author describes it in great detail and even includes a sketch. There are no less than ten doors in this room, nine of which are used interchangeably by the Old Man and Old Woman as they answer the bell, or go off to fetch more chairs. They may leave by one door and return by another on the opposite side of the stage, for all these doors are meaningless and lead ultimately nowhere, just as does the large double door upstage through which the invisible Emperor makes his "entrance."

The Old Man and Woman present a pitiful picture of the married couple; their union is based upon lies, hypocrisy, and a resolute refusal to face the truth. The Old Man is satirized as a mediocre nonentity who has convinced himself that he is different from other men, for *he* has an ideal in life. He takes himself very seriously, devotes two hours a day to his message, is self-satisfied, and foolishly optimistic. Because he is superior, he believes that he has been misunderstood, that life has not offered him the opportunities he deserved. He thus excuses his lack of accomplishments, when he is clear-sighted enough to admit his failures. More often, however, he blindly asserts that he has lived a full life, and as the two plunge to death they cry out optimistically, "We will have a street named after us."

The Old Woman seconds him in his false beliefs, for her role is that of the perfect wife, and she is all things to him, even taking him upon her knees and playing the mother when he feels himself a deserted child. When he falters, she bolsters his male ego, assuring him, "You're very gifted, my darling. You could have been head president, head king, etc." She repeats this refrain so often it soon appears automatic and therefore devoid of meaning.

A truer picture of this "rich" life is revealed through the dialogue of the couple as they describe their activities to their first guest, and we perceive the real emptiness of their existence:

Old Man. We live a retired life.

Old Woman. My husband's not really misanthropic, he just loves solitude.

Old Man. We have the radio, I get in some fishing, and then there's fairly regular boat service.

Old Woman. On Sundays there are two boats in the morning, one in the evening, not to mention privately chartered trips.

Old Man. When the weather's clear, there is a moon.

Old Woman. He's always concerned with his duties as general factotum . . . they keep him busy . . . On the other hand, at his age, he might very well take it easy. . . .

Old Man. In the winter, a good book, beside the radiator, and the memories of a lifetime.

Old Woman. A modest life but a full one . . .

They come dangerously close to an admission of their uselessness, and yet continue the pretense. Together they present a unified false front to the world, for their marriage is, in the words of Rosette Lamont, "an association of two helpless, self-indulgent, egocentric individuals who try to find in each other their own image and the comfort they have lost in growing out of childhood."[3] Like Didi and Gogo, together they may face what alone might be intolerable. And like the two tramps of Beckett's play, they still preserve the dim memory of some happy Eden from which they were excluded many years ago. Of all that, there remains today only a song, an allegory, they claim, with the ironic title, "Paris Will Always be Paris." In one of her rare moments of lucidity, the Old Woman whines that all of this has gone, "Down the big black hole."

In spite of their apparent unity, we begin to wonder just how well man and wife know each other. In a curious scene the Old Woman speaks with one of their guests and makes indecent suggestions to him, raising her skirt and revealing coquettishly her outlandish red petticoat. "Do you really believe that one can have children at *any* age?" she demands coyly. At the same time her husband is reliving the past with his first love, a wrinkled old woman with a long nose. A few minutes later, while the Old Woman tells her friends that her husband was a model son and that they too had a good-hearted son who left home, the Old Man is, on his side, telling a friend that he left his mother to die alone in a ditch, and he and Semiramis have never had any children. Which is true? Have they both lost their memories or their minds in an advanced stage of senility? Or are they merely inventing?

In spite of the "deep humanity of Ionesco" (Lamont), and the relatively complex characters he has given to his old couple, they remain machinelike in many ways. Anyone who has forced his life into a pattern and is willing to accept certain beliefs without examining them is bound to exhibit mechanical traits. Ionesco has exaggerated these in his senile pair. We have already seen that Semiramis repeats her comforting words until they become a senseless refrain. Her husband has his own peculiar refrain: "Drink your tea, Semiramis," he tells his wife many times. There is no tea. The absurd phrase seems to mean, "Be quiet!" Throughout the play the comforting little clichés of life crop up. "What's yours is mine," says the Old Woman to her husband, and when he weeps for his dead mother she assures him that she is "in heavenly paradise . . . she hears you, she sees you, among the flowers." Platitudes of uninspired conversation also run through the play, as they speak of what the French call "the rain and good weather," and reply politely and vapidly to the discourse of their guests in scenes which remind us of *The Bald Soprano*.

As the play progresses, the old pair become more mechanical. When the guests begin to arrive at a vertiginous rate the Old Man hurries back and forth answering the door, and the Old Woman hastens at a hysterical pace to find more chairs; without a word, from one door to the other they run—"as though rolling on wheels," Ionesco tells us. When the room is overflowing with chairs and invisible guests they gently slow down, like machines that have run out of steam, and the Old Woman, falling into the role natural to someone who has admitted people to seats, begins to sell programs and candy. The Old Man, following the protocol of such situations, must thank everyone who has had a hand in the success of their gathering, from the august Emperor down through the technicians and "electrocutions" to the manufacturers of the paper for the programs.

Linguistic techniques similar to those used in earlier plays are again in evidence. One word suggests another because of sound, regardless of meaning, and we become aware of the absurd physical presence of the word rather than of the reality which it represents. "Were you sure to invite everyone," asks the Old Woman, "Le Pape, les papillons, et les papiers?" (The Pope, the butterflies, and the papers). Several times words are repeated so frequently that they become only a sound, totally emptied of meaning, as when one repeats one's own name so long that it becomes simply an object in itself. Will the Orator come to reveal the Old Man's message? "Il viendra [he will come]," says the Old Man confidently. And the word is repeated ten times, then changed to the present tense, and repeated five more times.

The ultimate irony is that life itself, even a rich and successful life that contributes something to society (certainly not the case with the two old ruins on the stage before us), is finally reduced to nothing but a word, to a street name. "Let's die in order to become a legend," says the Old Woman. "At least, they'll name a street after us . . ." And the old couple plunge to death repeating ecstatically, "Nous aurons notre rue!"

It seems to me that *The Chairs* is one of the summits of Ionesco's theater, for it uses effectively the devices so typical of his art, but at the same time it strikes deeper than the earlier plays because the characters are considerably more complex and human despite the grotesque features they share with their predecessors. The author appears to be less detached than is usually the case, and we sense some slight "engagement of the heart." The phrase is Thomas Barbour's, but Barbour does not feel that *The Chairs* exhibits this involvement. Indeed, he claims that "no play of Brecht's better illustrates than Ionesco's the Brechtian principle of alienation."[4] In my opinion Mr. Barbour's observation may certainly be applied to the first group of Ionesco's plays, where we are almost assured of remaining distant and objective as we view the extravagant conduct of these Punch and Judy characters. We may realize that they are like ourselves in many ways, but they are too exaggerated to allow us to identify with them. It is in *The Chairs* that we first feel this identification, slight though it may be, for the old couple are not only amusing, but touching, and they draw us to them through bonds of sympathy if not through those of direct self-identification. This bond of sympathy can be detected in the plays of the following period, and becomes definitely established in the last plays, *The Killer* and *Rhinoceros*.

Victims of Duty, The New Occupant
and Amédée

Any grouping is ultimately arbitrary, and we must be careful to avoid forcing plays into an interpretation that will fit our groups, rather than seeing them with an unjaundiced eye. The plays of what I have called the second group recall in some ways the first plays of Ionesco. Occasionally the characters become mechanical and the language totters on the edge of meaninglessness. But most often such tendencies are absent, and we see more complex, and consequently more realistic, characters placed in situations that are frequently treated in an expressionistic manner. They continue the process used so effectively in *The Chairs,* and objects take on a new and terrifying meaning.

Victims of Duty (1952), a "pseudo drama," begins very much like *The Bald Soprano,* with a quiet evening at the home of Choubert and Madeleine. We see quickly that husband and wife are indeed very different from each other. Madeleine is a real conformist and even enjoys obeying the laws, pointing out that "it really is very nice indeed to be a good, law-abiding citizen and do one's duty and have a clear conscience." Choubert, on the other hand, is an ineffectual rebel, and is concerned that "a recommendation has a way of turning into an order," for "we know how suggestions suddenly come to look like rules, like strict laws."

Quickly Choubert's fears are realized, and the totalitarian regime asserts itself in the person of a detective who arrives looking for a certain M. Mallot. Like the professor in *The Lesson,* he is at first timid and polite, but soon becomes brutal and domineering, as he conducts his pseudopsychoanalytic investigation to discover the whereabouts and the identity of Mallot. Choubert is forced to go back in time in search of Mallot, and in a scene reminiscent of the expressionistic drama of the 'twenties, he wanders about the room, crouching

85

under tables and climbing upon chairs in his efforts to locate the lost personage—perhaps some facet of himself with which he has now lost contact. In order to stuff the holes of his memory, the Detective feeds Choubert bread, which he forces him to chew and swallow until the poor man is almost ill.

Choubert is saved by the arrival of a friend and poet, Nicolas d'Eu (a pun on Nicolas Deux—the Second—of Russia) who kills the Detective. As the latter dies, he proclaims that he has been a victim of duty, and gives the terrifying but familiar cry, "Long live the white race!" Nicolas, repentant, and moved by the exhortations of Madeleine, takes it upon himself to find Mallot, and begins stuffing Choubert with bread, as Madeleine claims, "We are all victims of duty." "Chew, swallow, chew, swallow!" they shout at each other, and as the curtain falls the enigmatic woman, who for some time has been sitting at one side of the stage, joins them in their exhortations.

In this play, as so often elsewhere, Ionesco is preoccupied with totalitarianism. Choubert, the dramatist, attempts to be a liberal, and he is finally freed from the yoke of his search for Mallot by a poet. But they are too weak to resist the pull of "duty," and along with the foolish Madeleine and the Lady who appears at the end, and who may represent destiny or the presence of duty itself, they succumb. *Victims of Duty* begins calmly, but soon takes on a serious and anguished tone. The inane conversation between Madeleine and Choubert is followed by the painful investigation by the Detective and climaxed by the savage scene in which Choubert is fed the bread, a materialization of his loss of liberty. Such a loss is further represented by another accumulation of matter: while Choubert is being tortured, his wife begins to serve coffee for the Detective. Back and forth between kitchen and living room she goes, placing cup after cup of coffee upon the sideboard, until finally it is completely covered. Madeleine

86

has, in the process, become another automaton, as might be expected, since she is willing to accept automatically the dictates of society. All of Ionesco's peripheral characters, and many of the major ones, sooner or later take on the appearance of a machine, even when they are realistic at other moments.

Victims of Duty is Ionesco's first play to contain any direct statements about the theater. Choubert, believing himself a dramatist, discusses with his wife the possibility of writing something really new for the theater. She assures him that there is "nothing new under the sun. Even when there is no sun." Choubert acquiesces, and decides that every play that has ever been written has been a thriller, in the realistic vein, with a detective in it somewhere.

> Every play's an investigation brought to a successful conclusion. There's a riddle, and it's solved in the final scene. Sometimes earlier. You seek, and then you find. Might as well give the game away at the start.

Ionesco's play belies Choubert's statement, for the enigma of Mallot's identity is never solved, and the author suggests it is possible to write drama that is new and different. Nicolas d'Eu describes at length the theater of which he dreams: a non-Aristotelean, irrationalist theater based upon what he calls a psychology of antagonisms. There would be no unity of personality, rather one would become aware of the contradictions and changes which are constantly appearing in people. As for plot, it will be ignored, at least in its old forms, which were "too clumsy, too obvious," and the genres will lose their identity as the tragic becomes comic, and the comic tragic. Nicolas does not write dramas, he tells us, for there is Ionesco, and Ionesco is enough.

Needless to say, the Detective does not understand these nontraditional notions, for he is enslaved to a way of thinking which does not allow change: "As for me I remain Aristotelically logical, true to myself, faithful to my duty and full of respect for my bosses." He, and Madeleine who resembles him, during Choubert's long search into his past, seat themselves at one side like spectators at the theater. But this drama, which is an exploration of a man's inner life, does not impress them. "My dear," says Madeleine to the Detective, "we'd far better spend the rest of the evening at a cabaret." And she adds, "All he does is contradict himself. . . . So dull and ordinary. It could have been so much more amusing . . . or at least instructive, couldn't it . . ." Like the usual spectator, Madeleine wants to be amused or instructed and is unable to accept the theater on terms other than those to which she is accustomed.

For Ionesco, however, the theater has affinities with poetry, for its true function is revelation: stripping us before our very eyes of those comforting illusions to which we cling so tenaciously, he reveals us as lonely, useless, enslaved. There is no *useful* conclusion in the play, and Mallot is, of course, never located, for Ionesco is showing us that here at last is one play in which the common pattern is not followed. With that strength which only the blind possess, the Detective can press on to his goal, becoming savagely inhuman in order to secure his ends as he forces the humiliating bread into Choubert's mouth. Firm in his belief in a coherent universe, unaware of the absurd, he can require conformity to the only pattern he is capable of understanding. It is natural that Nicolas d'Eu, the would-be poet and liberator, should free his friend from this dogmatic domination. But men are weak, and even Nicolas who espouses the author's ideas, may become dogmatic (just as we saw Ionesco doing in *The Alma Impromptu*), or even shift allegiance.

Such an interpretation of the enigmatic ending of *Victims of Duty* is the proper one—or one among several, for others are also possible—for it stresses the author's attitudes toward theater, and that is what interests us first of all in this play, which Ionesco has called a "pseudo drama." Pseudo, indeed, for it is first of all a defense and illustration (but far from the best) of a dramatic method, and only secondarily is it drama. There are the usual amusing satire of the self-satisfied bourgeois, the commentary on marriage, the criticism of intolerance and dogmatism, and a few dramatically effective scenes, particularly those in which Choubert's joy or anguish is exposed, and we are overwhelmed by masses of bread and teacups. The long central scenes, however, during which we witness Choubert's search for Mallot, become too diffuse, too protracted, and our interest flags. This is theater that is "surrealizing" as Nicolas admits to the Detective, "insofar as surrealism is oneirical." To reveal our hidden beings to ourselves through patterns that, however chaotic, can take on meaning, is one thing; but simply to present extended dreamlike sequences that have no distinct correlation to our own experiences, seems to be quite another.

When the Old Woman and Man in *The Chairs* evoke their past, or when they receive their invisible guests, we can all recall similar moments in our own lives, we can establish some bond with the characters or actions we see before us. But when Choubert begins to wander about the room like a man swimming in deep water, it may interest us for a few moments as a curiosity or an adventure, but as the adventure drags on, we find it difficult to follow, particularly since the clues are few and far between. His conversation as a child with his father effectively suggests the lack of comprehension between two people who desired nothing so much as to communicate. But it is confusing to hear the Detective assume the role of the father, and then become once more the Detective, just when the audience has finally become accustomed to him in the other role. Because of such obscurity in the dramatic action, and perhaps too explicit a statement of dramatic theory,

Victims of Duty, I believe, fails to come off as real drama. Ionesco was wise to add his subtitle, for it allows us to accept the play on one level, while making certain reservations on another.

The New Occupant (1953) and *Amédée or How to Get Rid of It,* (1954), like *The Chairs,* depend largely for their effectiveness upon the author's (as well as the director's and the actors') skill in handling the central device of an overpowering mass which is used to represent the oppressive domination of matter over spirit. In the first of these plays, a gentleman comes to occupy a new apartment. The movers arrive with the furniture, and carry it into the room, until every inch of space is covered, the windows blocked, the doors obstructed. The stairway, we learn, is still full of furniture, the streets are crowded, traffic has stopped, the subway system is paralyzed, and even the Seine, dammed up, has stopped flowing. The entire universe has been overcome by matter, and there is apparently nothing to do but follow the example of the New Occupant who, invisible, behind tall screens and cupboards, asks the movers to turn out the lights as they leave.

The realism of the play with its fussy old concierge, the sounds from the courtyard below, the commonplace pieces of furniture in a bare old room, makes what happens all the more terrifying, for it is more than a dream sequence, it seems to lie within the realm of possibility. *The New Occupant* has an immediacy which is lacking in *Victims of Duty.* The author stresses this realistic style in the description of the set which was omitted in the English translation:

> The acting should at first be very realistic, like the setting and furniture which will be brought on stage later. Then the rhythm, almost imperceptibly, gives to the actions the character of a ceremony. Realism will dominate once again in the last scene.

90

As the movers scuttle back and forth with the cupboards, tables, chairs, and vases, they begin to behave
automatically almost, and the moving becomes a kind
of religious ceremony in which the placing of a vase
one or two inches to the left or the right of a door
appears to be very important. What we are actually
witnessing is the burial of a man, complete with flowers:
before he leaves, the First Moving Man climbs a step-
ladder to peer within the enclosure of furniture, assuring himself that the New Occupant is comfortable,
and throws him some flowers.

This is a willful burial, a picture of conformist man
—for what else is the Occupant in his tidy black suit,
gloves, and shiny shoes, with his polite, quiet, almost
sinister manner?—who accepts, or rather invites, the
living death that the universe seems to force upon us;
he has come prepared for his own funeral, and the title
has a double significance.

If the Occupant is frightening in his inhuman and silent acceptance, the amusing Concierge almost matches
him, but in a somewhat different way. She is a caricature of a type well known to devotees of French films.
Crotchety, grumpy, suspicious, self-pitying, possessive,
she is the ruler of her building and domain, and it is
only with great bitterness that she relinquishes any
part of her power. The Occupant's refusal to hire her
to tidy up his apartment is a keen insult, and she mut-
ters about it to herself, to the movers, to the Occupant,
and to the wall. Her speech is speckled with platitudes
and clichés, and humorously sets forth her lack of originality or independent thought, while her frequent contradictions, reminding us of Nicolas d'Eu's psychology
of antagonisms, emphasize the meaninglessness of her
idle chatter. She becomes frightening when we realize
how true to life this narrow little lady is, and what
power she may wield in her own little universe. Although no one pays the slightest attention to her threats

and curses, she is there, twisting and perverting the words of the Occupant, reviling him, sounding for all the world like the voice of an incomprehending yet ever-damning society. She too is inhuman, inelastic, following the pattern of her suspicions, rather than looking and listening with a wakeful intelligence.

If we except *The Future Is in the Eggs,* which is after all a sequel to the "naturalist comedy" of *Jack, The New Occupant* is the first play to bear no descriptive subtitle. The plays that follow it will simply be called "pièce," or "comédie," generic names in French which merely mean "play," without specifying its nature. Perhaps Ionesco felt by this time that he had stressed sufficiently his belief in the mixture of genres, and his conviction that comedy and tragedy were inseparable, that a dramatic work could not be conveniently pigeonholed once and for all. It also seems likely that the author could count upon a more perceptive audience for these plays. Not because he was well known, for *Amédée* was written before Ionesco's name had become synonymous with avant-garde theater. Rather, the dramatist's development had gradually, almost imperceptibly, led him from a kind of play in which mechanism and fantasy have the upper hand —and which might very easily be dismissed by the audience as an amusing oddity—to a kind of drama where the major characters are more human, more complex, and perhaps command a bit more sympathy than the Smiths or the Jacks, and therefore may be taken more seriously by the public. *The Chairs* had already pointed to such a development, while *The New Occupant,* although a later play, appears in some ways to belong to the earlier period. As I have observed, there is no clear-cut break between an old technique and a new one; they are mingled from one end of Ionesco's production to the other, but there are tendencies that serve to distinguish most of the later plays from most of the earlier ones.

Amédée is a sad commentary on love and marriage. Its main theme resembles the secondary themes of such plays as *The Bald Soprano, The Chairs,* and *Victims of Duty:* the failure of an aging couple to keep their love alive. The love of Amédée and Madeleine, in fact, died fifteen years ago, and since then a mysterious cadaver has been slowly growing in their old bedroom. It has become so large that they have moved it into another room. Toadstools have sprouted all over the floor of the body's room, and as the play opens Amédée discovers one growing in the living room. Before the first act has ended we are given a rather complete picture of the monotonous and loveless relationship between the tired, irresolute husband who has never been able to get beyond the first two lines of the play he intends to write, and his cross, bitter, disappointed wife, who must earn a meager living for the two of them. And the body has begun to grow at such a rate that his feet push through the door. By the end of the second act the immense legs of the corpse stretch across the living room and threaten to break down the front door. It is clear that something must be done.

While they wait for dark to fall so that Amédée may drag the body out the balcony window and down to the river, the couple sit in the twilight dreaming, and we see the phantoms of their past play out the fundamental misunderstanding which has always existed between the hopefully idealistic young Amédée, blinded by poetic fancies, and the unimaginative, too-sensible, and materialistic Madeleine. Their opposed natures are depicted in the dream scene by Amédée's ecstatic cry, "We are happy. In a house of glass, a house of light," which Madeleine changes to "A house of brass, a house of night!" Finally, beaten, Amédée also begins to use Madeleine's words, for she has won, her critical and unloving attitude has brought them to the sad predicament in which they find themselves: prisoners of the corpse they have created, they no longer dare leave the house, and live in utter fear lest someone come in and discover what has happened. For they are unaware that this body is their dead love, and Madeleine accuses her husband of having killed her lover of many years ago in a fit of jealousy, little realizing that this lover was perhaps none other than the young Amédée.

At midnight Amédée pulls the body through the window, and drags it through the streets. But he is discovered before he can reach the river, and as the police pursue him he simply rises into the air, borne up by the body which has become a kind of parachute. "He's going to vanish into the Milky Way!" cries a prostitute to her American soldier. And, indeed, it appears that Amédée, free at last of his nagging wife, has found again that feeling of lightness and buoyancy recalled for us through the dream scene of Act II when he had cried out:

> If only you wished. . . . Nature would be so bountiful. . . . Wings on our feet, our limbs like wings . . . our shoulders wings . . . gravity abolished . . . no more weariness. . . . An insubstantial universe . . . Freedom . . . Ethereal power . . . Balance . . . airy abundance . . . world without weight . . .

For once the feeling of lightness seems to have won out. But the ending is, after all, a fantastic one, and does not possess the finality that a more realistic denouement would have had. A magical evasion has sidestepped the problem rather than facing it: and who among us, with our own oppressive corpses, can simply fly into the Milky Way? Although Ionesco has prepared us for a bit of magic in his play by using such fantastic elements as the sprouting mushrooms, the growing body, the dream sequence, and a clock whose hands are seen to move, the human relation depicted is extremely lifelike, and a more realistic solution (or even lack of solution) would have been more satisfying.

As in *The New Occupant*, the central device is that

94

of a huge physical mass which gradually forces the living characters almost off the stage. As a matter of fact, the body in *Amédée* has already dispossessed the couple of their room, and as the play continues it pushes them into one corner of the living room. The furniture from the bedroom, along with that of the living room, has been shoved to one side to make place for the body, and Amédée and Madeleine are scarcely visible among the cupboards and chairs. The body has been stricken with "geometrical progression . . . the incurable disease of the dead," observes Amédée, and for a moment he sees through his foolish optimism, admitting that "There's nothing to be done." It occurs to him, however, that their love might save the situation—if only they could love each other again. Madeleine dismisses this as rubbish, for her spirit is dried up, and she cannot imagine love dominating an obstacle. Here Ionesco identifies the embittered shrew with his own critics: "Love can't help people get rid of their troubles!" she cries. "You know nothing about real people! When are you going to write an ordinary play?"

The truth is that their dead love is so much a part of their life that it is only with the greatest difficulty that Amédée and Madeleine can get rid of it. "Our home will seem quite empty when he's gone . . . He's been the silent witness of our entire past," says Amédée. As he finally drags the body to the window, plaster falls from the ceiling and the set trembles. "This should give the impression," the author indicates, "that as the body is steadily pulled nearer the window, it is dragging the whole house with it and tugging at the entrails of the two principal characters." For the body represents the habit of a lifetime.

Amédée, it should be noted, is quite attached to the cadaver, and rather hesitant about getting rid of it, for it is all that remains of what was once his love. For Madeleine, on the other hand, it has no meaning; she has apparently never really loved her husband. That is why she must imagine the body as a dead lover. As Amédée pulls it from the room, she constantly gets in the way, unintentionally impeding the progress of the operation. But once he is free of her, Amédée may ride his love, now idealized and perhaps revitalized, into the beautiful night sky he had described earlier in such glowing terms to his unappreciative spouse.

Amédée is Ionesco's first long play, but in many ways it is similar to the shorter plays that preceded it. It is essentially a one-set play, and as produced at the Théâtre Babylone the last act was played in the living room whose back wall had disappeared. It is, like the plays written before it, and like the dramas of Beckett, a mono-situational play in which there is little or no development. In each of his works up to this point Ionesco had shown us a simple, sometimes amusing, often frightening, situation that suggests to us something about our own predicament as social animals and as human beings in a hostile universe. "His characters remain strangers," Thomas Barbour claims, "and he is wise to realize one act is long enough to spend with them." This may be true of the earlier personages who are inaccessible because they are basically inhuman, but *The Chairs, Victims of Duty,* and *Amédée* show us characters who are, despite some exaggeration, more complex individuals and hence more recognizably human. And by the time he wrote *The Killer* (1957), and *Rhinoceros* (1958), three years had elapsed since *Amédée's* creation, and Ionesco had found a central character with whom he clearly identified himself, and who, because of his human warmth, speaks to us in more compelling terms than the earlier characters.

The Killer *and* Rhinoceros

The Killer (1957), Ionesco's finest play according to Pierre Marcabru of *Arts,* effectively contrasts the two opposed feelings of evanescence and opacity. As the play opens we are in a radiant city, whose entire décor, according to the author's directions, is made up of lights. Bérenger, a kind and conscientious, almost absurdly naïve, gentleman, is being shown about the city by its Architect. He is overcome with joy, and cannot help comparing this radiant city of light with the gloomy quarters outside its confines where most of humanity must pass their lives in the wet and cold of a meaningless world. He is so blinded by his feeling of euphoria that he fails to note the ominous hints given him almost from the beginning. The Architect seems to have some reservations about the perfection of his city, and we soon discover that all is not well. There is a strange calm about the place—a calm of death; the Architect's secretary, Dany, claims that she absolutely *needs* a vacation; stones are thrown at the visitor by invisible hands. And we quickly learn that the city is almost deserted because a mysterious killer has been murdering two or three people every day. In the face of death's inevitability, existence seems useless to Bérenger, and his happy dream collapses. Before the act ends we are back in the gray outside world where everything is more real and palpable. In the gray city we can actually see the décors, whereas the buildings of the happy city which Bérenger claimed were "concrete, palpable, solid" are no more existent than the visitors in *The Chairs*. When the Architect's secretary is announced as the Killer's latest victim, Bérenger decides that something must be done, for he had become very fond of her in the few moments he spent with her. The Architect seems peculiarly insensitive to these killings, as he is to all human suffering—after all, it permits newspapermen to earn their living. Besides he, as a member of the Administration, is immune, and Dany was murdered because she wanted her "liberty," and so left her job.

Who is this strangely inhuman Architect who calmly eats his sandwich and coolly drinks his Beaujolais while people suffer and die about him? He would strike us as a sadistic god-image if Ionesco had not had him say, "All of us are mortal." I rather think he represents the impersonal institutionalization of life, someone who has become Architect and Administrator and forgotten that he is above all a human being. Even within the so-called radiant city everything is organized into iron-clad hierarchies, a scientifically perfect society that is sterile and lifeless. Bérenger, describing his impressions, says to the Architect, "I'm not expressing myself clearly, am I?" The Administrator responds, "I'm not capable of judging. It's not one of my duties. The logic department sees to that."

The second act takes place in Bérenger's apartment, and we are back in the familiar dilapidated old room dominated by worn furniture, but empty of human presence. "The décor of Act II," the author tells us, "is very much constructed, heavy, realistic and ugly; it contrasts strongly with the lack of décor and the simple lighting effects of Act I." The weather outside is, of course, dismal: a fine mixture of snow and rain is falling. The first half of Act II is a tour de force: for fifteen pages no one enters the set. We only hear the voices from the outside, and see a few people passing by the window, yet the impression of the feverish life of a city is created. The emptiness of the stage suggests the vacuity of the people portrayed, while the sound background of machines and the yelping of the students in a nearby schoolroom stress the mechanism of the human circus. The effect should be one of "a half-disagreeable, half-comical ugliness." The portraits sketched include those of the grumbling, self-pitying, suspicious concierge who engages one of her occupants in pseudo-philosophical chitchat similar to that of earlier Ionesco plays; two little old men for whom nothing is good any more; the voice of the confused teacher next door crosses with a voice from the streets, producing the bizarre impression that the hungry people before the gates of Versailles cried out, "We have fifty-eight delivery boys!" Snatches of conversation reveal nonsense tales and imaginative linguistic inventions reminiscent of *Jack* or *The Lesson*, or parody hilariously the overorganization of modern life to which Ionesco is so strongly opposed.

Finally Bérenger enters, and is surprised to find his friend Edward waiting for him in the apartment. Edward is racked with a cough. Diseased and decaying, his arm shriveled, he reminds us of the disintegration that living entails. Bérenger describes his horrible discovery to his friend, but Edward is not surprised, for the Killer's activities are evidently common knowledge, and the whole city has already accepted the fact that they must live with death, and that life cannot be as beautiful as they might have wished. "There comes a time," says Bérenger, "when you can no longer accept the horrible things that happen." And he rebels against what is apparently the human condition. Unlike all the other inhabitants of the gray city, who have lost the vision of what should rightfully be theirs, Bérenger becomes even firmer in his conviction that something must be done.

As the two are about to leave the room, Edward's briefcase falls open, and some photographs spill upon the table. Bérenger recognizes them as the "photographs of the Colonel" which the Killer is known to carry in his briefcase, and which he shows to his victims in order to distract them. Upon investigation, Bérenger discovers that his friend's briefcase contains the baubles said to be sold by the Killer, and even the Killer's calling card. For a terrible minute we suspect that Edward is none other than the Killer, but this suspicion apparently never crosses Bérenger's mind, although Edward cannot explain how he came by all the strange objects that come pouring out of his briefcase like the dozens of clowns out of a tiny circus auto. Since they at last have some definite clues, Bérenger drags the apathetic Edward off to the police station to denounce the criminal.

Act III opens with a parody of political demagoguery

and abstract idealism as Mother Pipe, inciting the people to support her and her geese, cries, ". . . tyranny restored will be called discipline and liberty. The misfortune of one is the happiness of all." This is followed by a guignolesque struggle between Mother Pipe and a free-thinking drunkard. In the meantime Bérenger arrives with Edward, but the latter has misplaced his briefcase, so they seize the briefcases of the drunkard, of a lost old man, and of Mother Pipe, but none of them contains the necessary proofs. As Edward goes off to look for his own briefcase, two gigantic traffic police enter. They are the personification, once again, of dehumanized organization. Their sole function is to direct traffic, and Bérenger's efforts to find the Killer do not concern them. As Bérenger sets out for the police station, the back walls fall away, the policemen disappear, and the little man finds himself alone on a dark road headed toward the setting sun.

The last fifteen or twenty minutes of the play form a monologue spoken by Bérenger as he walks to the prefecture. He is alone in the empty street as he goes to face his death. At first he is strong in his convictions, but quickly a vague fear overtakes him, and grows slowly into an inexplicable anguish. He is frustrated by a feeling that in spite of walking, he is not advancing. Even objects conspire against him: his watch stops. He becomes hesitant, willing to wait till another day, even to place the responsibility on others, and he turns around to retrace his steps, when the Killer is suddenly before him, small, badly shaven, with a torn hat upon his head, his single eye gleaming like hard steel. He never speaks, but only accentuates Bérenger's words with an ironic chuckle or a sneer.

Bérenger is almost a giant beside the tiny Killer, and his vigor contrasts with the latter's indifference. Unfortunately, he wishes to understand his enemy, but comprehension is untenable in the face of an inhuman adversary. In a series of naïve commonplaces he attempts to convince the Killer that he must reform. His efforts are of course useless, and he realizes that with such opponents dialogue is impossible. Nervously wiping his forehead, Bérenger brings out his battery of old accepted truths, but religion and brotherhood of man have no power to convince. Nor does ridicule frighten the Killer, or the suggestion that after all "Crime doesn't pay!" For this is a Killer without wages (and such is the original French title of the play). Bérenger's defeat is more and more visible, and he who at first seemed to dominate, now falls upon his knees and implores. He cannot even pull the triggers of the two antique pistols he had brought along: "How weak my strength is against your cold determination, your ruthlessness!" And as the Killer advances with raised knife, Bérenger mumbles in despair, "My God, there's nothing we can do! . . . What can we do . . ."

"The Sphinx has given no answer," says Pierre Marcabru, and "the silent Killer, whom nothing can touch, the very image of a universe conquered by the laws of devastation and madness," is grimly victorious.

Who is the Killer? Obviously it is not Edward. But then why does he carry a briefcase exactly like that of the Killer? And why does the Architect carry a briefcase? And the drunkard, the lost old man, and Mother Pipe? Because we are all killers. The Architect because he has become inhuman, coldly regulated, lost in his official functions; Mother Pipe because her ideology blinds her to men as individuals; Edward and the others, because of their resignation, their indifference and apathy.

In an article published in *Arts,* when *The Killer* was first performed in Paris, Ionesco asks:

> Don't we have the vague feeling that beyond all ideologies we cannot help being at the same time murderer and murdered, . . . instrument and victim of death triumphant?
>
> And yet [he adds, leaving us some small hope

in spite of the desperate ending of his play] we are here. It just may be that there is some reason, beyond our comprehension, for living. Everything is so absurd, that this too is possible.

Bérenger, I think, is Ionesco's most appealing character. Despite his pathetic naïveté, his almost ridiculous desire to match strength with incomprehensible evil, or rather precisely because of these qualities, we find Bérenger loveable and profoundly human. In him Ionesco has, except for one insignificant moment, forgotten his robots of the early works. Bérenger feels the emotions he expresses, and his good will, however blind, is an indication of his commitment to man. Although he falls back upon the platitudes of our common heritage in his attempts to convince the Killer, he is no unthinking receptacle. In fact, his pain arises, like that of Beckett's characters, from an awareness of his situation. The men outside the radiant city, he tells the Architect, are drab and ugly, for they are neither happy nor unhappy, neither ugly nor beautiful, they feel no real nostalgia, and they suffer from life unaware that they are suffering. "But I was aware of the discomfort of living. Perhaps because I'm more intelligent, or on the contrary less intelligent, less wise, less resigned, less patient." Bérenger has had a glimpse of the happy city that man through strength of will might perhaps make his own. It reminds him of the paradise he once had, and lost. Unlike Vladimir and Estragon, he does not sit and wait for the arrival of an uncertain Godot to set things right. He decides to act for himself, but he encounters the same absurdity that lies behind the despair of Didi and Gogo, and like theirs, his quest turns out to be fruitless.

We meet Bérenger again in *Rhinoceros* (1958), but it is a more indolent, easygoing Bérenger who cannot settle down to the dull routine of his office job, and takes frequently to the bottle, much to consternation of his very proper, conservative, and condescending friend Jean. The action of the play begins when Jean's well-intentioned preaching to his friend is interrupted by a rhinoceros thundering offstage past the café terrace where they are seated. The appearance of a second rhinoceros leads to some entertaining hypotheses regarding its identity, its origin, and its classification, and gives Ionesco the opportunity to satirize the mechanical behavior implicit in mass reaction, at the same time he caricatures various town types. The human world does not begin to disintegrate until Act II when one of Bérenger's colleagues fails to show up for work. His wife arrives, breathless and upset, having been chased by a rhinoceros, to announce that M. Boeuf is ill and in the country. Before long we discover that the truth of the matter is that he has become a rhino, and it is he that has been chasing his wife down the street. Rhinos, it seems, are turning up everywhere, and the fire department is hard put to rescue all the people whose stairs have been destroyed by the heavy hooves. Things take a terrifying turn when Bérenger goes to visit his humorless friend Jean, with whom he had quarreled the other day, and finds him in bed, a sickly green color. Jean, it soon becomes apparent to the audience, is slowly turning into a rhino, and before our very eyes the metamorphosis takes place: at first his voice is hoarse and he cannot hear well, his memory is failing, he has headaches, and slowly a bump is forming on his forehead. When Bérenger wants to call a doctor, he expresses more confidence in a veterinary. Gradually his breathing becomes heavier, his skin thicker, his voice progressively more hoarse, and his words more difficult to understand. Each time he runs to the bathroom to cool himself off with water, he emerges a deeper shade of green, his bump having grown a bit more. Finally he throws off his clothes, bellows out his yearning for freedom, the law of nature and the swamps, and bears down upon Bérenger, who succeeds in locking him in the bathroom and runs to the concierge for help. A rhino-headed woman answers the door!

In the third act, things have become worse. Swarms of beasts are heard roaming the streets, bellowing, looking in the windows, and even crossing the orchestra pit of the theater. Bérenger is awakened from a nightmare by the arrival of his office colleague Dudard. Little by little Dudard begins to see the rhino's point of view, and when he refuses Bérenger's invitation to dinner, saying he feels like eating on the grass, we know that he is lost. Finally Bérenger's girl friend, Daisy, arrives, and the two of them decide they will remain together, the only human beings in a rhinoceros world, for the animals have, like conquerors, taken over the telephone service and the radio stations. Daisy, with a telltale headache, suggests they should attempt to understand the rhinoceroses, and even learn their language; and she wonders whether in a world where everyone else is a rhinoceros, she and Bérenger are not the misfits, the only unhappy and uncomfortable animals in existence. Daisy, of course, is lost also, and slips off to join the throngs in the streets, leaving poor Bérenger dazed. As in the ending of *The Killer*, the pathetic hero is left to face the inhuman forces alone. In complete solitude, out of any human context, he asks himself whether his language can mean anything, since there is no one with whom he can communicate. And how now can he recognize one man from another, if he is the only man left? To surround himself with a human presence, he takes from a closet two or three large portraits which he decides are of himself, but when he hangs them we see that they represent two hideous old men and a huge woman, and contrast grotesquely with the rhino heads that are nodding in at all corners, doors, and windows and from the orchestra pit, for in this animal world, the rhinoceroses have become more and more beautiful, and their bellowing now sounds like a musical background.

Ready to give in, Bérenger discovers he is too human to become a rhinoceros, it is too late. Instead, he will retain his ugly originality in this world of beautifully conformist animality. "I'll put up a fight against the lot of them, the whole lot of them! I'm the last man left, and I'm staying that way until the end. I'm not capitulating!" he cries as the curtain falls.

The meaning of *Rhinoceros* is clear enough. Ionesco laments the lack of independence, of free thought, and individuality that inevitably result in totalitarianism of one kind or another. We have already met this theme in other plays where a professor dominates a pupil, a detective his interlocutor, an entire society the nonconformist, and where cries of "Long live the white race!" are occasionally heard. In *Rhinoceros* most of the characters are presented from the start as creatures of habit, caught within a pattern to which they have adhered for years. The inhabitants of the little provincial town, whose acquaintance we make in the first act, are mechanical in their reactions to situations. As excitement rises and ebbs, heads pop, puppetlike, from doors and windows. Upon the appearance of the first rhinoceros everyone but Bérenger is shocked and cries out "Ça alors!—Well, of all things!" "What do you think of that?" asks Jean four or five times. And when a second rhino is seen the characters shriek, one after another, "Oh, a rhinoceros!" followed, of course, by the inevitable, "Ça alors!" Bérenger's colleagues in the publishing world are no better: M. Papillon, the head of the department, thinks only of his work and is less dismayed by M. Boeuf's metamorphosis than by the realization that he must be replaced; while the retired schoolteacher, Botard, refuses to believe that there are any rhinoceroses at all, and when he is brought face to face with M. Boeuf bellowing on all fours, he claims it is an illusion. He too, however, finally relents, and we are told later that he has joined the throng, declaring in his last human words, "We must move with the times!"

Only Bérenger resists to the end. Here, at last, is a character in Ionesco's theater who develops. At first his attitude is one of complete indifference, and like the others he feels that the phenomenon is a temporary and unimportant one. But as the metamorphoses become more frequent, and the town is overrun with bellowing animal matter, Bérenger wakes to the dangers involved, and takes a surprisingly firm stand for the man who had been denounced by friends and fellow workers as a spineless drunkard, not to be taken seriously.

When *Rhinoceros* had its world *première*, November 1, 1959, in Düsseldorf, it had a very special meaning for the German audience, and they applauded every reference that could be applied to the evils of Nazism. The Paris production, which opened several months later, at Jean-Louis Barrault's Théâtre de France, apparently played up these references to Nazism, and Pierre Marcabru in his review in *Arts* (Jan. 27, 1960), rightly complained of the too narrow interpretation of the play's meaning forced upon it by using the goose step, and "Lily Marlene" in the Barrault production. All of Ionesco's theater, it seems to me, presents us with symbols of an antispiritual victory which may be interpreted in a variety of ways, and applied to a number of situations. It seems a mistake to narrow their scope by too specific an application. *Rhinoceros* may be a commentary on political dictatorship and its unthinking followers. But it is just as valid a commentary on educational and religious "truth," for the method is indirect, as nondidactic theater must always be. It is an error to state, as the *New York Times* news story does, that this is Ionesco's first play "on a purely political theme" (Nov. 3, 1959). There are political implications in the play, but there is nothing *purely* political about it. It so happens that the political implications strike us more forcefully today, whereas in another era the savage and thoughtless animals might stand for something else. Indeed, preceding plays of Ionesco suggest that this preponderance of unthinking, if not dead, matter is but another materialization of that oppressive universe which is constantly crushing in upon us and preventing us from realizing the spiritual possibilities which lie inherent in human nature.

The terror implicit in the situations is alleviated, as is usually the case in Ionesco's theater, by the grotesque symbol that has been chosen. The idea of a man actually becoming a rhinoceros is, of course, fantastic. Yet within the framework of the play the characters accept it so naturally that they become laughable. It is only when we suddenly realize how naturally we accept the monsters we encounter in our own lives that the laughter freezes on our lips. How frequently we might make the inadvertent slip of Bérenger speaking of his still-human colleague: "He's a good fellow with his four feet planted firmly on the ground."

"For ten years," declares Ionesco, "I have been fighting against the bourgeois spirit and political tyrannies." And since "the petty bourgeoisie [is] the personification of accepted ideas and slogans, the ubiquitous conformist[,] his automatic use of language is, of course, what gives him away." From the Smiths and Martins of *The Bald Soprano* to the townspeople and office workers of *Rhinoceros,* we hear the tired clichés, the empty talk of people who are "speaking because there is nothing personal to say," and who reveal "the absence of inner life, the mechanical aspect of daily existence, man bathing in his social environment, becoming an indistinguishable part of it."[5] These words, which Ionesco wrote about his first play, apply equally well to the last, and show how faithful he has been to his fundamental beliefs and techniques at the same time he has evolved as a dramatist. Despite a slight turning toward realism, which Ionesco himself fears may be a compromise with his ideals, the later plays are still abundantly supplied with trite language, repetitions, cut and dried expressions, and vehement discussions over nonessentials, all of which help to suggest the deadness of the characters. In *Rhinoceros* one of the favorite targets is the Logician, who represents the drying up of feeling, the reduction of living thought to a formula that can no longer cope with reality:

> *Logician.* Here is an example of a syllogism. The cat has four paws. Isidore and Fricot both have four paws. Therefore Isidore and Fricot are cats.
> *Old Gentleman.* My dog has got four paws.
> *Logician.* Then it's a cat.

In one of the most brilliant scenes of the play, Bérenger is seated in the café telling his friend Jean of his feeling of solitude and estrangement. At a nearby table the Logician is discussing logic with his old friend. As the two conversations progress, they begin to resemble each other, until Jean and the Logician, Bérenger and the Old Man, are using almost the same words apropos of entirely different discussions. This tour de force implies the breakdown of a language which can be used interchangeably, and suggests the stupidity and uselessness of the two conversations, if not of all conversations and efforts at communication.

The empty characters of this drama can easily play follow-the-leader and turn into indistinguishable rhinos, for they have been indistinguishable from the start, unable to think or express themselves as individuals. Again we may apply the author's words describing *The Bald Soprano* to this later work: "They can 'become' anybody, anything, for, having lost their identity, they assume the identity of others, become part of the world of the impersonal; they are interchangeable." And he adds, looking forward to a character he would develop eight or ten years later: "The tragic character does not change,

he is crushed; he is himself, he is *real*. Comic characters, fools, are people who do not exist."

I think no one would seriously contend, Ionesco least
of all, that the two Bérenger's are tragic characters of
great stature. But because of their awareness, because
of their unwillingness to accept the automatic life that
has overcome their fellows, they have a dignity and a
reality that is unique in Ionesco's theater. From the
vantage point of Ionesco's tenth year in the theater, and
through the development of more than twelve plays,
we can look back upon a production that has grown
from the simple and exaggerated puppet play of *The
Bald Soprano* to the more complex *Killer* and *Rhinoceros*, where a heroic character attempts consciously to
resist the leveling forces of life. Into the framework of
gross caricature a human element is introduced.

With his usual perspicacity, Thomas Barbour remarked in 1958 that if Ionesco progressed no further,
he would be reduced to parodying himself, and pointed
out that "one direction in which M. Ionesco might move
would be toward a greater engagement of his heart." I
think this is precisely the direction Ionesco has taken
in his latest plays. At the same time, he has not left behind those characteristics so peculiarly his: the grotesque characters, "dead" language, and a visible representation of what J. S. Doubrovsky calls "the inevitable triumph of the object over the subject."[6]

In *The Killer* and *Rhinoceros* we see a skillful blending of subject-symbols (Bérenger—the conscious human being) and object-symbols (the machines-become-
rhinos) which permits us to remain the detached and
amused observer of humanity that we had been while
witnessing the earlier plays, and at the same time
to identify sympathetically with the pathetic hero. In
The Bald Soprano or *Jack*, no matter how clear a revelation of our own weaknesses we perceived in the
empty people before us, we remained the cool observer,

109

standing *outside* a world that represented our own. Through Bérenger we are allowed now to penetrate somewhat into that world and to experience the horror of man alone in the presence of his death, alone surrounded by an inhuman universe.

The later plays with their greater complexity, show that Ionesco is capable of developing an action beyond its initial stages. Whereas the earlier plays are simple situations, often circular in structure, *The Killer* and *Rhinoceros* are dramas that have a beginning, a middle, and an end, take a character in a given situation, and trace his growth or development through decisions and acts, to an ultimate defeat. When Barbour, however, sees Ionesco only as a "very clever and audacious contriver of theatrical effects," he is stressing the importance and originality of the form (which admittedly is of great importance in this experimental drama —it might also be pointed out that Barbour's article was written before he had read either of the last two plays) at the expense of the author's ideas, which are equally important, and, as a matter of fact, actually *determine* the form. Beckett, we noted, sees life as pointless tedium without purpose or direction, and this, of course, is reflected in the structure of his plays which have a minimum of movement or development. Ionesco's view is similar to Beckett's, for he too is aware of an underlying absurdity in life, but he is not so preoccupied with our awareness of boredom and suffering as he is with the breakdown, the complete disintegration of the meaningful forms with which we mask futility and chaos. Consequently his form stresses that disintegration by a structure that is circular, or by a straight downhill plunge ending in silence; by characters who for the most part have no personal identity; and by language that becomes solidified and actually disintegrates before our eyes.

Similarly Ionesco's humor is not a humor of human suffering, like Beckett's, for his characters lost in mechanism are usually unable to appreciate the pain of their predicament, J. S. Doubrovsky, in his fine article on "Ionesco and the Comic of Absurdity," finds three types of comedy: the comedy of circularity ("destinies, like personalities, are interchangeable"), the comedy of proliferation (the domination of objects), and the comedy of language ("which, in its essence, never was anything but systematic delirium"). All three types derive from their automatism, which focuses our attention upon the surface rather than the deeper *human* element we would expect to see in them. This reduction of the living to the mechanical on the three levels of plot, character, and language, exposes us to ourselves in all our absurdity. Instead of the anguished reaction one might expect, we laugh, for Ionesco has pushed beyond that area where man can continue to take himself seriously: "Man becomes suddenly so unimportant," says Doubrovsky, "that tragedy turns into a farce, and an absurd laughter bursts forth. . . . The 'useless passion' which existentialists thought man to be now becomes eminently laughable." Laughable because of that very uselessness, precisely because lucidity allows no other reaction.

4

Theater and Anti-Theater

THE DAY AFTER the opening of *Waiting for Godot*, the newspaper *Aurore* carried a review entitled "The Anti-Play of Samuel Beckett." Three days later Luc Estang, in *La Croix*, pointed out that such theater might well be called "anti-theater when compared with the ordinary conceptions of dramatic art." Four years earlier Ionesco had called his *Bald Soprano* an anti-play, and in 1955 he published an essay entitled "Theater and Anti-Theater," in which he declared that he created anti-theater "only to the extent that the theater that one usually witnesses is taken for real theater." Today the term is common currency, and is applied not only to the works of Beckett and Ionesco, but to those of many of the avantgarde writers who in one way or another disregard traditional ideas of drama. The term stresses the unconventionality of the plays, as well as suggesting the difficulty with which they have been accepted by a public accustomed to something quite different.

The term "anti-theater" is a coin with two faces and both are faces of revolt. On the one hand, it suggests that the new drama is fundamentally different from other theater that we know, and for that reason is either a hopeless nondramatic perversion, or an exciting exploration of unknown territory. On the other hand, anti-theater suggests an attempt to return to the roots of drama, to free the theater from what the proponents

112

of this kind of drama consider to be superfluous and un-
authentic elements that, over the years, have encrusted
it:

> Artistic creation [Ionesco tells us] finds again the
> fundamental laws, rises up against dessicated the-
> atrical conventions, prudence, and what through
> an incredible misunderstanding has been called
> realism.[1]

No longer earthbound by enslavement to exterior realism, freed from such extraneous preoccupations as philosophy, theology, or other kinds of discursive reason-
ing, the dramatist will attempt to create a poetic or
dramatic universe that, like the primitive theater of
ceremony, speaks to some deeper level of man. I should
like to investigate briefly these two veins of anti-theater
as they are embodied in the works of the two most important dramatists of the avant-garde.

The Mythical Mode

Serious theater at its beginnings, whether we consider
that of Greece, European drama in the Middle Ages, or
the drama of the Orient which has remained so close to
its origins, is always religious. Although it may become
profane and lose all conscious connection with its sacred
beginnings, beneath the surface there always remains
the mystery of man on the stage becoming what he is
not, the god made man, or man made the hero: the
mystery of transsubstantiation.

The young French critic Morvan Lebesque has suggested that the history of the theater might be divided
into three periods. In the first, man attempts to entice
his unknown gods to earth, or else he puts himself in
their place, imitating them and hoping thus for recognition of his existence. "This is the period of religious
invocation which begins with the simple sacred dance,
and then becomes profane through the Egyptian then
the Greek, *representation*." It is the age of tragedy. In
a second period, man, tired of calling upon the un-

responsive gods, turns to himself and places man in the center of the stage. This is the age of comedy. Finally, having made himself godlike in his ability to explore the universe, and to destroy whole worlds, man becomes his own god. But now he contemplates himself not in society, but from above: "from the dizzying heights where his intelligence has preceded his body."[2] This presumably is where we stand now. It seems to me that our age must then be one in which tragedy and comedy mingle, for man has continued to center his attention upon himself as in the second period, but has added to this contemplation the vertical dimension that was present only in tragedy and religious ceremony. Himself become god, modern man may now set about to create myths about himself, or find once again through his art the old myths which arose perhaps in a less self-conscious way in a less self-conscious age when man was searching for god and meaning in a universe that allowed him to find both in something exterior to himself.

As in any clear-cut division, there are weaknesses in this one. But I think it offers us a very fruitful point of view from which to look at today's theater. It is a frame which might very well have been accepted by that most important of twentieth century metaphysicians of the theater, Antonin Artaud. For Artaud, we have noted, the theater must be a mystical and magical experience that reveals rather than analyzes. He inveighs against Shakespeare and his presumed preoccupation with psychology and plot.

> Shakespeare himself is responsible for this aberration and decline, this disinterested idea of the theater which wishes a theatrical performance to leave the public intact, without setting off one image that will shake the organism to its foundations and leave an ineffaceable scar.

Just as the religious ceremony cannot perform its function of renewal until it has destroyed the old self, so

114

the theater that is to be a revelation must first "hypnotize the sensibility of the spectator seized by the theater
as by a whirlwind of higher forces." Only by running
this risk of physical shock, claims Artaud, can we hope
to revitalize our world. Rejecting, then, the man-cen-
tered, psychological theater that belongs to Lebesque's
second period, he redefines the theater's purpose as that
of creating myths: "to express life in its immense, universal aspect." And these myths will be those of Creation, Becoming, and Chaos, myths of a cosmic order
which will "furnish a primary notion of a domain from
which the theater is now entirely alien. They are able to
create a kind of passionate equation between Man, Society, Nature, and Objects." Needless to say, such metaphysical ideas are introduced only indirectly, creating
what Artaud calls "indraughts of air" around the ideas.
In other words, the method of suggestion through images, symbols, humor, and other means will be employed.

The theaters of Beckett and Ionesco go a long way
toward creating these myths of which Artaud speaks.
We are dealing here with the conscious (or at least
partly so) creation of myth as a modern device for
reaching levels of consciousness, and degrees of universality, which may not be approached by any other
methods. Such a method is only indirectly related to
what we may assume was a spontaneous creation of
myth in the so-called "mythical age," but it shares with
those significant tales certain characteristics that, I believe, account for its profound suggestiveness: myth attempts to recognize truth; it employs a metaphorical
presentation; it is related in some way to religious ritual;
its hero is something more than any individual.

> Myth, [says Susanne K. Langer] at its best, is a
> recognition of natural conflicts, of human desire
> frustrated by non-human powers, hostile oppres-
> sion, or contrary desires; it is a story of the birth,
> passion, and defeat by death which is man's com-

mon fate. Its ultimate end is not wishful distortion of the world (as is fairytale), but serious envisagement of its fundamental truths; moral orientation, not escape.[3]

The worlds of Beckett and Ionesco are based upon a lucid awareness of life's emptiness and lack of meaning. The almost unbearable picture they sometimes give us is often presented in a comic way, for the comic is "the intuition of the absurd," but that comedy in no way blinds us to the horror of our situation. On the contrary, it may point it up by stressing the hopeless mechanism in which we are caught. Both dramatists, apparently convinced that there is no system to give a direction to life, show us a universe that is hostile to man. In Beckett it is a hostility of absence, a lack of response to man's needs, a vacuum where man would have hoped for some significant entity. Ionesco's hostile universe is more menacing, for it is not an absence, but a presence, and where Beckett's bums could worry and wait, Ionesco's harried couples are attacked, surrounded, and buried by victorious matter. The struggle, the solitude are intolerable, but there is no solution, for we are faced with an honest picture of man's condition as Ionesco and Beckett envisage it. We may argue with the truth of their vision, but I think that no one will challenge its sincerity or accuse them of attempting to flee from reality into a world of magic and illusion.

Mythos is Greek for tale, fable, story, hence the concept implies some plot line. It is interesting—and significant—to note that the plot has been reduced to the minimum in many of these plays that, nonetheless, retain their mythical richness. In an earlier age, man was an adventurer heading toward a known goal. It is a commonplace of literary criticism to point out that while the *Odyssey* and the *Divine Comedy* trace journeys to fixed points (home and paradise), Baudelaire's disillusioned masterpiece, *The Voyage,* reveals modern man as wandering almost aimlessly in his search for meaning, and ultimately returning to his starting point having found nothing but ennui. Beckett's and Ionesco's sad creatures are the heirs of Baudelaire's man without a goal, and the lack of narrative element is a corollary of the cruelly lucid view that man is going absolutely nowhere.

Myth does not speak the language of reason, or only does so superficially. Beneath the surface, through images, through symbolic language, the myth suggests more than is immediately apparent.[4] That is why, Philip Wheelright states, we may characterize both the Eden story and the Krishna-Arjuna tale as myth:

> because, although accepted as true by large respective circles of believers, they convey also, to the more religiously sensitive and the more intellectually acute of those believers, something more than appears at first glance. Each embodies an archetypal idea—a set of depth-meanings of perduring significance within a widely shared perspective, and transcending the limits of what can be said via ordinary literal speech.[5]

The laziest approach to myth is simply to accept it as a story, without making an attempt to grasp deeper levels. This explains, at least in part, why so many spectators have rejected the drama of the avant-garde. The surface realism, or the superficiality of the greater part of today's theater, has accustomed us to accepting what we see on the stage as a picture of life, or a pleasant diversion from everyday cares. We are not often prepared to become involved on a level which would respond to the mythic mode, either by making an effort to comprehend the deeper meaning of what we are witnessing, or simply by allowing the magic of the nonrational to do its work by relaxing our hold upon the rational. If we are to experience the full dramatic impact implicit in the terrible struggle between human yearning and universal denial, we must prepare ourselves, not by rejecting the rational completely, but by accepting the truth of other modes of perception. We must suffer within ourselves the pain of Didi and Gogo before the gallows tree where they wait for life and meaning; and become aware of the reality of the all too present chairs in Ionesco's tragic farce. We must be willing to admit that the Bobby Watson tale is not just an absurd linguistic invention of the dramatist, but stands for something more general; that Hamm crying out for his painkiller is something more than a sadistic invalid. In short, we must be prepared to admit that the metaphorical method is as valid a means of reflecting reality as is the so-called realistic manner.

The reality of life (which is also that of myth) cannot be expressed in so many words, for life goes far beyond the logic of language and vocabulary. The ideas of Creation, Becoming, and Chaos, of which Artaud speaks, cannot be limited or even formally depicted. They must be suggested. That is why myth never speaks directly, and it is also, I suspect, one reason that Ionesco has so frequently pronounced himself against the theater of philosophy, theology, or thesis. Facts may be known, but Truth can only be experienced.

The "moment of truth" may perhaps best be reached by appropriating the devices of religious ritual, for it is through religions that man has most often attempted to perceive truth, and particularly through the mystical experience of ceremony in which time is transformed into eternity. Lord Raglan has even suggested (but this theory is largely discredited today) that myth is only the form of words associated with a rite. However this may be, the dramatists we are concerned with, particularly Beckett, and Genêt to whom we shall turn presently, lean rather heavily upon ritual method.

Horace Gregory declares that one reason Beckett's later works "strike below the surface of entertainment is, of course, the emotional charge of their religious associations." Beckett is quite frequently considered to be more "profound" than Ionesco, and I think we may

118

ascribe such an evaluation at least in part to the religious echoes which abound in the works of the Irish Protestant, and which are almost totally lacking in those of Ionesco. It may also arise from the fact that Beckett's universe seems more anguished, even in his humor that is based upon suffering, whereas Ionesco's world is exaggeratedly gay, with a comicalness that sometimes seems gratuitous. But the laughter of Ionesco, although thick and deep, reveals by its very exaggeration a view so pessimistic and so lucid that no other reaction is possible. At the same time, as Artaud has suggested, the comic view is more anarchic than the tragic, for it separates us from what we are viewing, and separates the various objects viewed from one another. It serves therefore as another reminder of universal solitude and chaos.

Virtually the only ritual technique employed by Ionesco is his circular plot structure. Mythical time, like ritual time, is felt to be cyclical, therefore recurrent. The rhythm of sacred ceremonies, repeated according to traditional patterns, recalls the rhythm of nature, the seasonal changes, and the rhythm of life itself. But the recurrence of religious ritual suggests something vital and meaningful: the re-enactment in time of what is true also in eternity, and hence an assimilation of this mystical act of the human to the divine, the temporal to the eternal. In such plays as *The Bald Soprano* and *The Lesson,* as well as in Beckett's two major dramas, cyclical time has a different implication. It is no longer vital and has lost touch with a meaningful eternity. In Ionesco it signifies a world of senseless anonymity and mechanism. In Beckett it suggests the monotony of a universe abandoned by God, and consequently by meaning. But although the ties with any eternal ground have been cut, one feels that the wound is still fresh, even bleeding; it is this wound perhaps which gives *Godot* the dimension that seems lacking in Ionesco's theater. Day after day, in scene after scene, Vladimir and Es-

tragon re-enact before the stunted tree, the ritual crucifixion of man by life.

In addition to the many direct references to God,
Jesus, the Crucifixion, the Last Judgment, and so on,
which have been mentioned in chapter 2, there are in
Beckett's theater numerous words, phrases, and situations which point to religious preoccupations, and make
us realize that this dramatist is a profoundly religious,
if completely unorthodox, man: the name Godot, the
settings of the two plays, the relationships between the
characters, the theme of atonement and of the scapegoat, the kind of lost paradise evoked by Hamm and
Clov as well as by Vladimir and Estragon.

The characters of myth, I suggested above, are something more than individuals. In the old world myths
they usually are bigger than life. When we witness the
great Greek tragedies, no matter how profoundly human the characters may be, we are always aware of the
distance that separates us from them. Obviously the
characters that we find in Beckett and Ionesco do not
exist on the same exalted plane with Oedipus and Elec-
tra. But they do live in a world which is at one remove
from our own, because they are either too exaggerated
to be accepted as "realistic" representations, or what
happens to them is so impressively grim that we can
imagine ourselves in such circumstances only with difficulty. Because we cannot accept them as individuals,
in the sense that we might consider Willy Loman or
Blanche Dubois as a possible neighbor, we feel they
must stand for something beyond their own identity.
To a certain extent both Ionesco and Beckett have
availed themselves of characters already belonging to
a restricted and somewhat civilized mythology: that of
the circus, the vaudeville team, and the guignol.

Whether consciously or not, Beckett and Ionesco have
found through their plays some of the fundamental
dramatic schemata that are at the same time inherent in
myth and ritual. Through characters who are somehow

different from us, presented in patterns vaguely reminiscent of ritual and ceremony, they suggest obliquely rather than directly, truths about the human condition and man's role in an oppressive universe. I do not mean that these dramatists have created myths possessing the same degree of universality, the same richness and profundity as the great world myths. Nor do I wish to suggest that they are the first to employ the techniques of myth. But I do believe they have taken a step away from the play that is based upon more superficial theatrical values, such as suspense, involved intrigue, themes of current interest, and so on, and in the direction of the profound dramatic encounter suggested today, for example, by the Mass, and in an earlier age by the tragedy of Aeschylus; and that it is a step sufficiently great to justify the epithets "cosmological comedy,"[6] "ontological theatre,"[7] and "metaphysical farce."[8]

Tradition and Anti-Theater

Throughout the ages dramatists have been more or less faithful to the traditional dramatic elements of plot, character, dialogue, spectacle, and theme or idea. They have sometimes minimized one and exaggerated another, but rarely if ever have they done away with any of the major categories. Artaud, we have seen, wished to reject both plot and character, and even dialogue, in favor of spectacle. For him the scenic space to be filled became the major preoccupation of the dramatist-director. Anti-theater implies a similar rejection of conventional dramatic elements. Let us attempt to ascertain to what degree Beckett and Ionesco have repudiated these elements.

The plot is, in Aristotle's words, "the arrangement of the incidents," or as Edward Wright puts it, "the statement of the play in specific terms."[9] A play's success or failure frequently depends upon the structuring of the plot, the degree of skill with which the author has put together the elements from exposition to conclusion. In the traditional theater the spectators are accustomed to a certain amount of "story," which will grip their interest and lead them from inciting moment to climax, and at the end of which they will feel the situation "has run its course or been resolved." Beckett affords little satisfaction here. As we have already seen, he pays scant attention to the plot, and his two major plays scarcely get off the ground in this respect. One is hard put to find any inciting moment, climax, or denouement. In *Godot* the waiting and hoping give the play a certain movement, or at least a forward look, but neither it nor *Endgame* satisfies Wright's dicta that "there must be a conflict or at least some element of crisis in the action," and "a play must possess dramatic movement which means something is happening to the characters through reaction." There is, to be sure, a conflict of wills between Hamm and Clov, if Clov can be said to have a will, but it is a conflict that is never resolved, or only temporarily so, for Clov never leaves his "master." Some critics considered *Endgame* a completely classical play because of its unity, its purity of line, and its lack of any extraneous elements. But even that most static of classical French tragedies, Racine's *Bérénice*, is brimful of action, reaction, crisis, and decision when set beside Beckett's rundown world.

Ionesco, speaking of his own work, has also evoked the classics: "This theatre progresses not through a predetermined subject and plot, but through an increasingly intense and revealing series of emotional states. Thus I have tried to give the play a classical form."[10] Classical in their simplicity, perhaps, but nonclassical insofar as they ignore the crisis and decision which lie at the heart of classical drama. In place of plot and peripety, Ionesco tells us, he works with intensity and emotional states. This is particularly true, as I pointed out, of his early short plays in which there is little incident. But even here Ionesco's drama possesses more plot in the traditional sense than does Beckett's. We can actually recount the story of what happens in any of his plays, and it adds up to just about as much as we could tell about the plots of *Riders to the Sea* or *The Three Sisters*. In *The Killer* and *Rhinoceros*, however, plot is largely handled in the traditional manner. There is an inciting moment which "disturbs the picture of their world": the discovery of a killer in the happy city, and the arrival of the rhinoceros in the provincial town. Rising action, turning point, falling action, climax, may all be found in these two plays in which the hero must react to a given situation and make a decision. Where Ionesco differs from traditional plot-builders, it seems to me, is in his handling of the denouement: the conclusion, rather than giving the feeling that the situation has "run its course or been resolved," is simply an intensification of the climax, and leaves the hero in a state near paroxysm, his dilemma unsolved because it is insoluble.

Where Ionesco shocks the orthodox theatergoer is in his treatment of characters. For many years the exploration of character has appropriated the terrain that formerly belonged to plot. In Morvan Lebesque's tripartite division of theater history, he shows the interest shifting from the depiction of the gods and their imitators or representatives on earth, to man. In what he calls the second period, man holds up a mirror and studies himself—the result is an age of comedy. Although we are now, Lebesque claims, in a third period, the spectators, accustomed to the psychological comedy of the preceding era, still look for sentiments, passions, and characters, and when they do not find them, feel lost and cheated.

"The contemporary theatre . . . never got beyond the psychology of a Paul Bourget," declares Nicolas d'Eu in *Victims of Duty*, and Ionesco, in an attempt to correct the situation, introduces his "psychology of antagonisms." We might expect the result to be an extremely dynamic creation of characters in the manner

123

of Stendhal or Dostoyevsky. On the contrary, the personages we encounter in Ionesco's theater are, as I have indicated, overgrown puppets, monstrous machines, caricatures of ourselves, blown up to grotesque proportions. Bypassing the psychological realism of the late nineteenth century, they join hands with the comic creations of Labiche, Jonson, and Molière. They seem inhuman not because they behave differently than we do, but because they behave precisely as we do, only with an intensity so increased that they become improbable. This inhumanity gives us a certain objectivity in regard to them, and although we may recognize the caricatures of ourselves, and even be made uncomfortable by it, we still remain emotionally uninvolved. It is only with *The Chairs*, when the author himself begins to become more humane in depicting his pathetic characters, that we are able to feel some warmth in them. And although Bérenger in the last two plays is not the object of a concentrated psychological study, his portrait is reasonably realistic and reminds us of characters we have already encountered in the theater. It is the mechanical peripheral characters who remain monstrous and unreal.

Beckett's miserable characters, although types we are less likely to meet in real life, are treated in such a way that we can accept them as living individuals. They are not so exaggerated that they become impossible caricatures, and yet they are sufficiently enlarged to be characters of the theater which come across the footlights. It is their human attitudes which strike us, their suffering, questioning, hoping, waiting, despairing. In Ionesco, particularly in the early works, it is the inhuman attitudes which strike us: the empty repetition, unresponsiveness, blindness, and narrowness.

Symptomatic of this difference is the language. Ionesco's disarticulated language bespeaks a personality that no longer exists, a person who has disintegrated. This is of course why the diction becomes less exaggerated as the characters become more human, and in the last plays it is only the social caricatures who speak this once-dominant disarticulated language, while Bérenger and his more realistic friends utter sentences similar to those we are accustomed to hear in the theater.

Beckett's people, on the other hand, speak a language that, surprisingly enough, is not disintegrated. His universe is one of physical disintegration and moral torment, but language has not yet decayed so far that it falls apart; it continues to present a coherent surface, even if the characters can no longer really communicate with this worn out instrument. There are no gratuitous inventions or combinations of words. The characters usually speak in complete, if extremely brief and dried up, sentences. The only exception is Lucky's pseudo-philosophical spiel in *Waiting for Godot,* which is an indication of his fallen state, rather than any comment on language in general. There are phrases repeated from time to time in Beckett's plays, but they are repeated within a pattern, like the "Let's go–We can't–Why?–We're waiting for Godot" exchange. Or they are used to stress a given idea or theme, for example, the numerous repetitions of "we're getting on" and "there are no more . . ." in *Endgame.* Ionesco's more irrational repetitions or nonsense syllables betray the mechanical quality or shallowness of his characters, as well as suggesting a surrealist source of inspiration.

But neither Ionesco nor Beckett uses language simply to further understanding of character or to develop plot. The latter uses it not as an object in itself, as Ionesco does, but in the manner of poetry since Baudelaire, for its suggestivity. A great deal of what Beckett has to say remains unsaid, and must be discovered by the spectator for himself, for he speaks what Horace Gregory has called "the economical, sometimes ambiguous language of poetic imagination." A poetic process of condensation has taken place, giving a few words the power to suggest much more than is immediately apparent. With

Ionesco one has the impression that instead of a few words covering an extensive meaning, the opposite is true: innumerable words simply mask emptiness. It is true that Ionesco uses language to suggest, but in an entirely different way from Beckett. While the latter depends upon connotations, silence, the power of rhythm and speech patterns, and the bareness of his rhetoric, the former takes language as something with a physical existence all its own, and tears it down in order to reveal the vacuum beneath. "The rationality to which we desperately cling," says J. S. Doubrovsky, "only exists in and by our words." But "Ionesco's reasoners . . . demonstrate that language, in its essence, never was anything but systematic delirium." And as it crumbles, language pulls down the entire superstructure of our reasonable world with it.

"It is the duty of the playwright," states Edward Wright, "as an artist, to make clear to his audience what he thinks and feels and what he is trying to do." The avant-garde dramatists have often been taken to task for obscurity. It is a criticism leveled at almost every artist who brings something new before the public. It is immediately apparent that these dramatists do not speak directly of their preoccupations, in the way that a Shaw or a Curel might. Plot, character, and dialogue contribute only indirectly to the meaning of the plays, and frequently they seem only to confuse the issue because of their grotesqueness, their absurdity, or apparent meaninglessness. The meaning, or theme, of these plays must be found in the entire texture of the production, not in any one part. It is the way in which plot, character, language, and spectacle are used together which indicates what the author is attempting to tell us. Spectacle plays a large role in helping us to understand —a much larger role than it has heretofore, and this is one of the most original contributions of the avant-garde theater. Not only symbols, like the tree in *Godot*, but the actual gestures or movements made by the characters on the stage (in which respect it is related to the theater of the dance, and moves at least slightly in the direction envisaged by Artaud), the kinds of décors that surround the characters, and the objects with which they come in contact during the play: shoes, hats, clocks, pipes, empty suitcases, whips, toy dogs, water carafes, noses, chairs, eggs, teacups, photographs, corpses, and rhinoceroses.

Such everyday objects (except of course corpses and rhinoceroses) remind us that these dramas, which may at times appear fanciful, have their point of departure in a solid realism. Ionesco has taken the trouble to tell us several times that he is depicting an inner realism which he believes to be more real and more universal than any exterior form. And yet he clearly takes as his starting point those tedious quotidian situations with which we are all familiar. But in his theater they usually get out of hand, and with a growing feeling of anguish we perceive that man has lost control, and we end up in a world dominated by some monster, animal, vegetable, or mineral. Beckett's anguish remains closely tied to the humdrum situation that never becomes animated enough to get out of hand.

Beckett and Ionesco, we may conclude, are anti-the-atrical writers when compared to traditional dramatists insofar as they tend to neglect certain categories usually considered essential; at the same time they compensate to some degree by giving added importance to the spec-tacle, but in a way that is the very opposite of the usual superficial display so frequently made in an effort to hide lack of substance. Moreover, they use language in refreshingly original ways, suggesting much more than they actually say.

It is immediately apparent that they are attempting to do considerably more than tell a story by means of actors on a stage before an audience. They are making a comment upon the human condition. But they are not doing so in the same way that Sartre, for example, has done, employing the frame of a more or less well-made play, in which realistic characters comment in an intelligible fashion upon their predicament. Ibsen had already done this in a masterly way a century ago. The avant-garde dramatists are renewing the theater today by taking it in a direction followed by poetry almost a hundred years ago when Rimbaud wrote, "This language will be of the soul for the soul, summing up everything, odors, sounds, colors, thought grabbing hold of thought and pulling it" (*Lettre du Voyant*). It is only natural that the art form which is dependent upon a large public for its very life should be the most conservative of all the arts. Music, poetry, painting, and even the novel, long ago explored realms which until recently had only been touched upon by the theater. Today for the first time a movement of considerable breadth is investigating methods and forms which had been ignored by all but a few eccentrics in the field of drama. The result is a theater which approaches the richness, the ambiguity, and at times the obscurity, of modern poetry. Beckett's and Ionesco's language (both visual and oral), like Rimbaud's, is of the soul and for the soul. It speaks to a deeper level than the waking consciousness, and hence is capable of expressing something more universal than the usual "message" found in a play. It does not give us ready-made ideas, and therefore does not satisfy the average playgoer who is accustomed to having the intellect appeased. In a clever preface to the first volume of Ionesco's plays, Jacques Lemarchand describes such a spectator:

> There are people who are embarrassed by their intelligence. It is like a little Spartan fox, hungry, cruel, unsatiated; they must feed it constantly, and they tremble to think that it may some day die. . . . the day they find no answer to its maniacal question: "What is it about?" They are the people who hate photographs without captions, Japanese films

128

without subtitles, and eclipses of the moon when they are not visible from Paris.

The question of obscurity in the theater has been posed before, apropos of such writers as Giraudoux and Claudel. We may accept obscurity in poetry because we have the opportunity to return time and again to the poem in an attempt to comprehend. In the theater we should be able at least to come away from a first performance with some idea of what the author was attempting to say. Each time we return we may discover something new. It seems to me that in the kind of play we are discussing the dramatist must find a point between obscurity and the obvious, where he retains some of the sense of the mystery of life and is able to suggest more than appears on the surface, but at the same time meets the spectator on a ground where the latter may begin to understand what direction his thought must take. Just where this point is must be decided by each dramatist, and will depend to some extent upon the level of the public for which he is writing. I am convinced that both Beckett and Ionesco are much easier to understand, even upon first acquaintance, than many spectators are willing to admit. There are certainly obscurities in both authors, but they are balanced by the general intelligibility of each play, the impressively beautiful and moving passages in Beckett, the violently comical or terrifying ones in Ionesco, and the incontestable profundity of vision of both.

"If life is complicated further rather than clarified," declares Edward Wright, "the play has fallen down as a work of art." I am not so certain that the unique function of art is to clarify. Surely it must help us to understand life. But what if life cannot be understood in any clear and simple fashion? What if Bergson is right, and it is necessary to kill life in order to "understand" it? Then art should rather reveal life in all its chaos and complexity, and perhaps it can best do this

129

by an indirect method employing violence, magic, and incantation. "Who ever said the theater was created to analyze character, to resolve the conflicts of love and duty, to wrestle with all the problems of a topical and psychological nature that monopolize our contemporary stage?" demands Artaud. If this theater is to share the condition of poetry to any degree, as seems to be the case, then we cannot expect it to fulfill needs that are satisfied by a theater devoted to the logical exposition of a problem.

Romantic poetry envelops the reader and, using his emotions, carries him away. It is typical of symbolist poetry (and I am thinking of the major figures) that it leaves the reader in a more objective state; at the same time that it acts upon the unconscious through rhythm and association, it forces us to take a somewhat analytic attitude. Indeed, without assuming such an attitude the poetic worlds of Mallarmé and Valéry, at any rate, would be forever closed to us. Similarly, the theater of Beckett and Ionesco, at the same time that it works upon us by its "magic," keeps us at a distance. We are viewing our own world from the outside, or as Lebesque suggests, from above, a god's-eye view. Ionesco's exaggeration of character and Beckett's extremity of situation are largely responsible for keeping us at this distance. The very fact that these dramas elicit our laughter seems to indicate that we have kept ourselves detached. This does not mean that we remain cold during the entire performance, for the "magic" is there. But it does mean that we are aware of the play as a reflection or a refraction of our life rather than as a direct imitation, and the characters do not seem to deserve our sympathy in the way an Anna Christie might. The Brechtian feeling of distance is achieved, but we are not repulsed here by the too obvious preaching of a social gospel. Instead we are drawn into the play by the many exciting and subtle ways in which its themes are stated.

1. Samuel Beckett   2. Eugène Ionesco

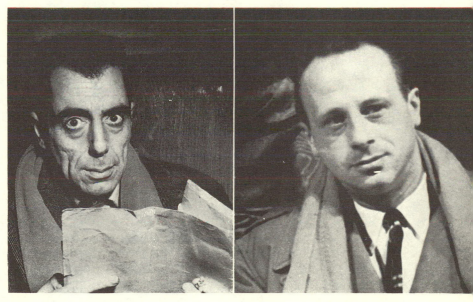

3. Arthur Adamov   4. Jean Vauthier

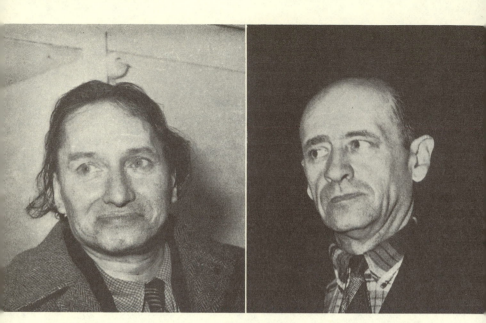

5. Michel de Ghelderode

6. Jacques Audiberti

7. Georges Schehadé

8. Père and Mère Ubu personally collect the taxes from the peasants of Warsaw in the Théâtre National Populaire production of Jarry's *Ubu roi*.

9. Gogo and Didi look on in astonishment as Lucky enters followed by his cruel master Pozzo, in the original production of Beckett's *Waiting for Godot* at the Théâtre Babylone.

10. Krapp listens to the tape recalling the sensual pleasures of his thirty-ninth year in Beckett's *Krapp's Last Tape* at the Théâtre Récamier.

11. Amédée and Madeleine are pushed out of their house and home by the mysterious and gigantic corpse whose feet and legs begin growing through their living room. Ionesco's *Amédée*, Théâtre d'Aujourd 'hui.

12. Béranger is dismayed by the metamorphosis of his friend before his very eyes in Ionesco's *Rhinoceros*, Théâtre de France.

13. Erna shows her compassion for The Mutilated One, now completely helpless in his cart, in Adamov's *La Grande et la petite maneouvre*.

14. Madame Irma in her role as Queen encounters the false Bishop in her house of illusions. Genêt's *The Balcony* at the Théâtre Gymnase.

15. Archibald, the master of ceremonies, prepares the encounter between the Black Queen and the White Queen in Genêt's *The Blacks* at the Théâtre de Lutèce.

16. Vauthier's egotistic monster, Capitaine Bada, wearing his crown of poetry, dominates his enslaved wife, Alice. *Le Capitaine Bada*, Théâtre de Poche.

17. The noble Lotvy and the evil Baron Massacre vie for the hand of the nature spirit, La Hobereaute, torn between her love for the former and her duty to the Druidic religion she serves. Audiberti's *La Hobereaute*, Théâtre du Vieux Colombier.

18. The insane, death-haunted king (Michel Vitold) in Ghelderode's one-act masterpiece, *Escurial,* at the Théâtre de l'Oeuvre.

19. Vasco innocently inquires his way of three soldiers dressed as soldiers masquerading as women, in Schehadé's *Histoire de Vasco.*

Arthur Adamov: Anti-Theater Triumphant

Arthur Adamov has recently turned his back upon the avant-garde and upon his early plays that embodied more than those of any other dramatist the revolutionary principles expressed by Artaud in *The Theater and Its Double*. Adamov's last play, *Paolo Paoli* (1956), indicates a turning to the drama of social implications with a message, written in a quasi-realistic style. A sympathetic critic has called this a "theatre of denunciation," a "theatre of critical truth," and a "demystifying theatre" (André Gisselbrecht). Robert Kemp, not to be hoodwinked by the "avant-garde" reputation of Adamov, claimed that in *Paolo Paoli* we can easily identify the ancient Théâtre Libre—"This is very old theatre." And he added skeptically, "as for the 'avant-garde' element, let us smile." Although Ionesco and the young critics do not usually admire Kemp's perspicacity, they would undoubtedly agree with him here, for Adamov's defection is not only evidenced by his last plays, but has been frankly announced by the dramatist.

The plays that interest us here were written between 1947 and 1953, some twenty years or more after the dramatist's arrival in France. Born in Russia in 1908, Adamov spent his childhood in Geneva, and settled in Paris in 1924. In 1946 he published a kind of psycho-analytic confession, entitled *L'Aveu*, which sheds considerable light upon his major obsessions and helps us to understand the wherefore of his early plays which are in great part an exorcism of private terrors. *La Parodie* (*The Parody*, 1947), *La Grande et la petite manoeuvre* (*The Great and the Small Maneuver*, 1950), *Le Sens de la marche* (*The Direction of the March*, 1951, virtually an untranslatable title since *sens* implies both physical direction and meaning, while *marche* refers to walking, marching, or some form of progression), and *Tous contre tous* (*All Against All,* 1952) are such plays, long, loosely constructed, almost episodic works revealing the nightmare existence within a frightening and incomprehensible police state.

In an effort to correct certain excesses of his first play, Adamov turned from *La Parodie* to a work on a more specific subject, with a small cast and a more controlled technique. The result was *L'Invasion* (1949), the first of four plays revealing an equally perplexing, but perhaps less frightening universe than the police state plays: *Le Professeur Taranne* (1951), *Comme nous avons été* (*As We Were,* 1952), and *Les Retrouvailles* (*The Recoveries,* 1953?).

Le Ping-Pong was written in late 1954 or early 1955 and is a transitional work pointing the way to the more conventional *Paolo Paoli.* In a 1958 interview Adamov stated that he was writing a second "historical" play, based this time upon the period of the Commune. Until now, however, he has produced no new original work, although he has made several translations of Russian dramatists.

Like Ionesco, Adamov came to the theater as a voice of protest, and his first play *La Parodie* is an attempt to embody in a crude and *visible* manner the themes of solitude and absence of communication suggested by the most common of everyday scenes. Like the other "police state" plays, *La Parodie* is an outgrowth of a close personal contact with Artaud the man and with his radical criticism of the conventional theater. In spite of Adamov's later skepticism regarding the value of Artaud's ideas, it is quite clear that the author of *The Theater and Its Double* has exercised an enormous influence on him. Adamov follows Artaud in his rejection of psychology, in his acceptance of the basic idea of a "theatre of cruelty," and in his utilization of the theater above all as a space to be occupied. "I propose a theater," Artaud had said, "in which violent physical images crush and hypnotize the sensibility of the spectator seized by the theater as by a whirlwind of higher forces." Adamov, it seems to me, has attempted to do this. Jean Vilar claims that he has stripped away the "lacework of dialogue and plot," and thus restored to his drama the *netteté,* or clarity of outline. A play of Adamov must be seen to be appreciated, for the text is only a scenario, describing in rather great detail the physical movement that is to take place, and will constitute the major impact and the principal means of communicating with the audience. Dialogue has been reduced to dry and frequently dull platitudes without any of the humor or verve of Ionesco, or the naked, suggestive poetry of Beckett. The characters are often ciphers, represented by letters ("N" in *La Parodie*) or by generic names (The Mother, The Sister, The Happiest Woman, and so on). It is only with difficulty that we become involved in their plight, for they are rarely alive enough to elicit pity or sympathy.

The treatment is episodic rather than linear, and we must sometimes follow many characters with various symbolic values through a series of short tableaux with little apparent connection. David Grossvogel is undoubtedly right when he speaks of Adamov's "plotless theatre," (although nothing could be further from the truth than the statement he makes next: that it "presents an appearance similar to that of Ionesco"), and if plot is, as Pierre-Aimé Touchard claims, "the skeleton of the action,"[11] then Adamov's is an exceedingly flabby theater whose flesh does not stand up because they depend too exclusively upon the visual ele- have furnished the necessary corrective to Artaud's too encompassing rejection of plot: "Just as a picture is a space to be moved (*émouvoir*), a play is a duration to be animated." Adamov's works tend to be stillborn because they depend too exclusively upon the visual element, they are moving pictures, but they do not move in any particular direction (and this is, of course, part of the point). *Le sens de la marche* is nowhere, and we have no sense of beginning, middle, or end. The theater is indeed a scenic space to be filled, but it is much more than that, and by doing away with what Vilar whimsically calls the "lacework of dialogue and plot," Adamov has done away with two essentials of any dramatic production.[12] That is why I said above that he *attempted* to follow Artaud's proposal to seize the spectator. As a matter of fact, however, the spectator is usually not seized by a play of Adamov: there is too great a distance between actor and spectator, no warmth is generated by the characters, no interest fostered by the episodic treatment which lacks the minimum plot required to give form to the action of the play. Although what I have said can be pretty well applied to most of Adamov's theater, it is particularly true of what I have called his police state plays, typifying most radically the anti-theatrical play which renounces traditional dramatic categories.

La Parodie attempts to show that both refusal of life and acceptance of life end in total destruction, and introduces a theme which runs through most of these plays. Through twelve brief tableaux we follow "N," the Employee, the Journalist, and various other characters as they wait for Lili, the eternal *femme fatale*, flirt with her, dance with her, attempt to find jobs, or simply lie about wallowing in self-torture. All this in a décor that is essentially the same, but from scene to scene is viewed from a different perspective, constantly giving us the feeling of being disoriented. The characters are mechanical, and the Employee, we are told, walks in all directions, even backwards. The nightmarish atmosphere recalls certain passages of *L'Aveu*, where Adamov describes "the cruel need to suffer, to fall down and grovel before everything." Lili undoubtedly is a projection of woman who, we read in *L'Aveu*, inevitably appeared to the author "in the guise of the eternal prostitute, her face painted, her eyes blank." Adamov goes on to describe scenes of sexual temptation in a

134

"leper-house of love," with the woman showing her most secret parts while "her face hardens into an indifferent mask of which the unspeakably vague smile plunges me into a dizzying abyss."

Such is the world that encloses, that imprisons my mind. Of course I have sometimes managed to believe in my deliverance from it. But I have quickly come to realize the illusory nature of such freedom.

Several years after writing these lines, Adamov was to exorcise such demons through his early plays, and it is in them that we see time and again the "sordid décor so dear to [his] dreams." The personal element no doubt gives a certain immediacy and pathos to these plays, but at the same time it fills them with private symbolism and meanings which are so highly particular that they are not always easily transferable to the majority of spectators. Like the nightmares of others, we can view them objectively without being gripped ourselves.

The dream atmosphere of *La Parodie* is further emphasized by the gratuitous change of one character into another. The newspaper director becomes at certain moments a cabaret manager, then once more is the director. One wonders what purpose all this serves aside from bewildering us further. The meaningless movements begin to annoy us rather than challenging us to discover their deeper meaning, and one would be tempted to dismiss them as survivals of a surrealist influence, had not Adamov admitted his admiration for Strindberg, and particularly for *The Dream Play*, which he had read and reread at this time. In *The Dream Play* we also see characters who are "split, doubled and multiplied." But Strindberg is trying to suggest the illogical and disjointed world of dream, and with a more obviously philosophical purpose: not simply to show that life is nightmarish and disjointed as a dream, but that all our existence is only a dream within the mind of God, an idea which Strindberg seems to have derived from his pursuit of oriental thought.

Strindberg is frequently considered the ancestor of expressionism. His "amorphous, rambling, and meaningless" fantasies prefigure what Eric Bentley calls the "bold, loose, unfinished, messy Expressionistic forms,"[13] and remind us that Adamov—to whose plays many of these adjectives might be applied with a fair degree of justice—follows the expressionists in structure, degree of abstraction, and use of the stage space as particularly important in itself.

The ten short tableaux of *La Grande et la petite manoeuvre* have profited, at least slightly, by the composition of *L'Invasion,* which separates it from Adamov's first play, for despite the episodic treatment, there is a certain tightening of structure. We follow The Mutilated One and The Militant (ciphers again) in their struggles against the enigmatic fatality which seems to weigh upon them, represented by the voices and the imperious whistles of The Monitors who must always be obeyed. The gradual destruction of The Mutilated One by incomprehensible forces is visibly represented by his loss of one limb after another, until finally he is only a limbless body in a wheelchair. The eternal woman, cold, cruel, and desirable, is still present, but more disturbing than Lili, because she is at first protective and maternal, attempting to shield The Mutilated One from his masochistic compulsions and obsessions, and then turns upon him, laughing heartlessly as she pushes the helpless victim to his destruction in the crowded streets.

The brief tableaux allow no time for building climaxes within scenes, in fact the espisodic nature of the play does not permit a real climax to be reached anywhere. One feels that the play could go on indefinitely, as long as the author could spin out his humorless flat style into vaguely dreamlike tableaux purporting to prove that "all human actions fail."

Le Sens de la marche and *Tous contre tous* are, like *La Grande et la petite manoeuvre* upon which they are modeled, allegorical works that Adamov has called "the monotonous demonstration of the fact that 'whatever you do, you are crushed.'" In the first the terrifying father figure represented by various characters, father, general, and pastor, dominate Henri in several situations, at home, in the army, at school, and so on, until he finally murders his dead father's friend who threatens to become a new father-image. *Tous contre tous*, in sixteen tableaux, recounts the wanderings of refugees and their persecutors, in a state whose policy is constantly shifting. In both plays visible elements again have a symbolic meaning: Henri's feverish walking back and forth, the refugees' pathetic limp which they vainly try to disguise.

In his evaluation of the plays written before *Le Ping-Pong*, Adamov points out certain characteristics which he came to consider too limiting: vagueness of setting, oversimplification of characters, symbolism of situation, and use of archetypes. He singles out *Le Professeur Taranne* as his only satisfactory play because it is the simple transcription of a dream, serving no allegorical ends. Instead, for the first time, he was forced to pay close attention to the details of his dream and to record them faithfully. As an evolved writer of social drama, it is natural that he should now look with approval upon a play in which for the first time, as he puts it, he "came out of the pseudopoetic *no man's land* and dared to call things by their names."[14] The police state plays, however, as the tag I have used suggests, already betray a social awareness and a political turn of mind. No matter how abstract they become, the characters are not inhabitants of the nonpolitical universe of Ionesco, or the asocial one of Beckett. On the contrary, they belong to a state that controls, dominates, and oppresses them, and they are aware of the social relationships existing between the people within the state, whether they be political leaders and refugees, or fathers and sons.

In *L'Invasion, Le Professeur Taranne* and *Comme nous avons été* we find with relief characters who seem

137

to be real people rather than algebraic figures, and in the first (the only long play of the three), something resembling a plot. *L'Invasion* is the story of Pierre who is attempting to decipher and put together the illegible manuscript left by his deceased friend. Discouraged by his colleague Tradel, misunderstood by his mother and his wife, Pierre retires to a mysterious retreat, a sort of hole in the attic, where he finally dies, never having discovered the meaning of the manuscript which he had at last torn into shreds. The mother, the wife, Tradel, and a mysterious stranger are summarily characterized, and The Woman Friend is a delightful social caricature who introduces a breath of humor into Adamov's rather humorless universe. An impressive use is made of visible elements once again, in the piles of paper which dominate the stage, and which finally almost drown Pierre as he tears them up, symbolizing of course not only the destruction of the work that was to give a meaning to his life, but the disappearance of Pierre beneath a work which was essentially another's. The title of the play refers to Pierre's life invaded by the apparently meaningless manuscript, just as his home was invaded by his assertive and possessive mother, forever present, enthroned in "her" armchair, and by The Stranger who arrives to seduce his wife. Social awareness is apparent in the satire of The Friend as well as in the depiction of the family relationships, and the political note is sounded briefly in the conversation criticizing the government for allowing immigrants to enter the country.

L'Invasion strikes me as one of Adamov's most satisfactory plays, because he has (Vilar notwithstanding) conserved here the minimal plot that the spectator seems to require, and presented characters who are able to interest us as human beings rather than simply as allegorical figures with no human warmth. At the same time Pierre and Agnès, The Mother and Tradel can stand for something which is beyond themselves, but

138

if the dramatist fails to interest us in the characters as characters, it is unlikely that we will attempt to go beyond and understand what further significance they can have. At the same time, *L'Invasion* does not reject the technique which is Adamov's most original contribution to the avant-garde theater: his preoccupation with the stage as a space to be occupied, filled with *visible* meaning. In this one long play it seems to me he has hit that happy middle ground where we are both interested and challenged, where there is enough of traditional dramatic technique to keep us going, and enough that is new, or that is mysterious or incomprehensible at first, to keep us from relaxing into a passive attitude.

The reviewer of *Tous contre tous* in *France Illustration* sums up quite well the theater of Adamov when he says, "Few dramatists have cared less about pleasing than has M. Adamov." For Adamov during his experimental period and before his defection to the social theater, in protesting against the conventional theater of psychology went so far in the other direction that it was often difficult to join him at any point. Particularly in the police state plays, but also to some extent in the others of the same period, he rejected plot more completely than have either Beckett or Ionesco, spurned characterization, and relegated dialogue to a minor role in his universe where characters rarely say what they mean, and never succeed in really communicating with each other. Instead of cracking and exploding dramatically, as does Ionesco's language, instead of dropping "like leaves, like sand," in an intense lyric overflow as does Beckett's, Adamov's dialogue simply drags along. Stressing the visible resources of the stage, he reminds us that drama is more than literature and that a play is only a play when it is presented on the boards before spectators. But the same may be said of ballet and pantomime, and it has been Adamov's error to deny certain essentials that distinguish drama from other genres in order to stress the importance of an element that is equally essential. Any theatrical revolution based uniquely upon the visible elements of theater will necessarily be a partial (and probably an abortive) revolution, for the simple reason that theater is a great deal more than a physical space to be filled. Beckett and Ionesco, as we have seen, have been keenly aware of the physical presence of both stage and actor, and have utilized them most effectively, but in their best plays they have not diminished the other requisite elements beyond the minimal limit. Their plays constitute a theatrical experience, and one that grips us either by laughter or by fear at the same time it involves us intellectually. Adamov may involve our intellect, never our emotions. The coldness of his early theater already betrays the future admirer of Brecht, and perhaps reveals better than the works of Brecht himself the famous alienation technique that the master of epic theater espoused.

Jean Genêt: Theater as Ritual

Like Adamov, Jean Genêt rejects the modern western theater that is, he claims, an amusement, whereas it should be a form of communion. Recalling Artaud without ever mentioning him, he evokes the oriental theater based upon ritual and ceremony, a theater of suggestion and symbols, where characters are metaphors rather than living people: what he calls an "allusive" theater. The actors in such a theater would be priests of a religion serving the "faithful" rather than exhibitionists strutting before an audience, and their school a seminary rather than a conservatory.

> Even the most beautiful occidental plays look like masquerades, not ceremonies. What happens on the stage is always puerile. The beauty of language sometimes deceives us about the profundity of theme. In the theatre everything happens in the visible world and nowhere else.[15]

Like Artaud, Genêt would restore myth and mystery to a theater from which gods have been too long absent. The prototype of such a theater in the modern world is that celebration which for the past two thousand years has reconstituted, in symbolic terms, the end of a supper: the Mass. "Theatrically speaking," says Genêt, "I know of nothing more effective than the elevation." Each of his plays is, in a certain sense, the religious celebration of an inverted rite in which Good is replaced by Evil and religious faith by love of beauty. In a closed world, which perhaps stands for the outside world, Genêt's characters perform their sacraments of love and hate, of identification and separation, and this closed world is always one of reprobates or outcasts, criminals, prostitutes, servants, Negroes, people who have been denied the sanction of the "virtuous" ruling caste, just as Genêt, thief and homosexual, has been denied it and branded an undesirable, a pariah. Rather than simply accepting the name "thief," when he was discovered stealing as a child of ten, Genêt, we are told by Sartre in his psychoanalytic study *Saint Genêt, Comédien et martyr* (*Saint Genêt Actor and Martyr*), decided to *become* what society wished to make of him, and to do so with a vengeance. His childhood was spent in reformatories, and his youth wandering about Europe where he served time in various prisons. In 1943 he began his first novel *Notre-Dame des Fleurs* (*Our Lady of the Flowers*) in prison, and during the following five years wrote the bulk of his work, including the two plays, *Deathwatch* (*Haute surveillance*) and *The Maids* (*Les Bonnes*). In all his writing his "essentially religious soul" (the phrase is Sartre's) is in evidence. Rejected by the world of the Good, Genêt turns to the world of Evil and attempts to reach the absolute through treason: just as a saint is beyond all written laws, the stool pigeon asserts his liberty and his "saintliness" doing what Good men require of him and against the very people with whom he associates himself.[16]

The world of criminals and pederasts into which the magic of Genêt's poetry plunges us is no anarchic state, but one as rigidly organized as the world most of us inhabit. At the top of the hierarchy stands the murderer, often an invisible godlike figure touched by the grace of crime: Harcamone, Boule-de-Neige. Somewhat lower are the *caïds*, hard and handsome leaders among the prisoners, perhaps only thieves, but set apart from the other thieves by their coldness and brutality, their virile beauty, their innate nobility, and almost mystic domination. Below them are the *durs* (toughs), the *cloches* (bums), and at the very bottom of the scale, the effeminate *lopes* (pansies), outcasts among outcasts.

This very personal system of values, and this highly subjective universe is reflected most clearly in Genêt's first play, *Deathwatch*,[17] which is to a great extent autobiographical, and represents the author's closest approximation to what is considered conventional theater. In *Deathwatch* there are three well-developed characters, a simple plot, language which satisfies reason, and a general meaning that the average audience can grasp if it is wakeful. But the allusive method is already apparent, for a great deal is hinted at which cannot be immediately understood. The major themes are two: the religion of evil, and the mystery of identity (illusion and reality), and they coalesce in the theme of metamorphosis.

Green Eyes is the pivotal character of the play, and the central figure in the lives of the other two prisoners who share his cell, the effeminate Maurice who is clearly in love with him, and the *dur* Lefranc who despite his pretended indifference to Green Eyes brings the play to its close by his murder of Maurice in a desperate effort to imitate, and therefore become, the murderer he so admires. Green Eyes, grandly handsome and indifferent, is the Christ figure of this perverted Mass in which Lefranc plays the role of priest and Maurice that of sacrificial victim. Beyond the closed cell, his presence powerfully evoked by Lefranc and by Green Eyes, is the invisible god: Snowball, the massive Negro condemned to death, black savage deity of Evil whose crime is greater than that of Green Eyes because it was more necessary and more clearly willed. Green Eyes stands apart from his two cell mates because he has separated himself from other men by his murder, has made himself "pure as divine injustice" (*Le Miracle de la rose*), for "blood purifies and raises him who has spilled it to uncommon heights" (*Notre-Dame des Fleurs*). The man condemned to death shines with a bright dark beauty, for he dares to go on living in this death-cell world whose only issue is imminent death, remembering the lost paradise of the outside world, and thus becomes a symbol of mankind. His life "has the beauty of great maledictions for it is worthy of what humanity, chased from the door of Heaven, has done through all the ages. Such is saintliness, to live according to heaven, despite God" (*Le Miracle de la Rose*).

As Lefranc chokes Maurice to death, Green Eyes stands on an inverted basin, like a god on a pedestal, and dominates the sacrificial act. It is an act without efficacy, for grace has had no part in it. "You thought you could become as great as me?" asks Green Eyes, with loathing.

> You poor fool, don't you realize it's impossible to overshadow me? I didn't want anything—you hear me?—I didn't want what happened to happen. It was all given to me. A gift from god or the devil, but something I didn't want.

Misfortune chose him, and now Green Eyes has made his paradise of that misery.

Lefranc, on the contrary, has chosen to murder in order to become like the criminals he admired. His role is that of imitator rather than free inventor, and through his imitation he does not succeed in becoming like his gods. The rite has failed in spite of elaborate preparations.

143

Lefranc represents, to a great extent, Genêt himself, and the abortive ritual suggests that the author, like Lefranc, has failed to identify himself completely with the men he so admired. The novels corroborate this. Lefranc's collection of photographs of criminals which he hides under his mattress reminds us of Genêt's gallery, which he describes in the opening pages of *Notre-Dame des Fleurs:* pictures of Pilorge, Weidemann, and other condemned murderers clipped from detective magazines and newspapers decorated the walls of the author's cell, surrounded by a whole court of lesser men, a Mexican mestizo, a cossack, a gaucho, athletes, all possessing the hard and empty look of the inflexible criminal. And at night Lefranc, like Genêt, prayed to his gods, said Mass to his saints. But for neither has the magical metamorphosis taken place. Despite his inked-on tattoo, his appropriation of Green Eyes' jacket, and his penetration into Green Eyes' private world by writing his letters for him, Lefranc remains what he is, a small time thief, and even his murder of Maurice only belittles him in his hero's eyes, and imparts to him no mystery or grandeur.

As the play ends Maurice is dead, Green Eyes condemned to death, and Lefranc will undoubtedly suffer the same fate. There is no salvation in the world of Genêt, unless it be through death, and only the saint-criminal touched by grace can attain it. Each of the plays is a ceremony ending in death, usually of an ignominious kind. "The scenarios," says a character in *The Balcony,* "are all reducible to a major theme . . . death." Perhaps this is because the criminal hero must die in order to retain his power, just as the religious hero becomes himself fully only through death. And the lesser mortals who remain behind, whether consciously or not, imitate the pattern he has set, and his life and death are re-enacted symbolically in the Mass or in the ceremonial theater.

Deathwatch shows us the life of three prisoners whose

actions have unconsciously become a ritual. In the world of the prison where everything is repeated from day to day, where variety and accident are reduced to a minimum, every act becomes a ceremony performed with almost religious devotion. Genêt's novels are heavy with religious, and particularly Christian, vocabulary, and it is difficult to find a page on which the rites or beliefs of the church are not evoked or suggested. In *The Maids* the ritual is no longer unwittingly performed. It is imposed upon the characters by themselves in an effort to give meaning and direction to their otherwise tawdry existence. Claire and Solange detest their mistress who is good to them, but for whom they are only objects, like the dainty seat of her bidet. To avenge themselves they have written letters to the police denouncing Madame's lover, and he has been imprisoned. When he is released and they fear their mistress will discover their duplicity, the maids attempt to poison her, but fail. Instead they kill themselves: Claire by drinking poison and Solange by accepting the responsibility for her death.

Sartre sees striking parallels between *The Maids* and *Deathwatch:* the absent Monsieur (the lover) would correspond to Snowball, Madame to Green Eyes, and the two maids to Maurice and Lefranc. These parallels strike me as false. Monsieur is only accused of petty thievery, he has none of the glamour or mystery of Snowball, none of his transcendent power. Madame is imitated by her maids, as Green Eyes is by Lefranc, but their purpose is not to become like her, for they do not love her (as is the case with Green Eyes); instead the end of their imitation is death. It is simply that they have never begun their ceremony early enough to reach the end. The purpose of the metamorphosis in this case is not self-identification, but vengeance.

As the curtain rises the two sisters are going through a scene they have obviously enacted often before, in which Claire plays the role of Madame and Solange

145

that of Claire. It is some time before we become aware of the real identity of the actresses. Indeed, Genêt wished to introduce a further complexity by having the parts played by young boys. Thus the maids who are pretending to be someone they are not, are themselves being portrayed not only by someone who is not they, but by actors whose very sex is different from theirs. *The Maids,* like *The Balcony* and *The Blacks,* contains a brilliant game of mirrors in which reflections play back and forth until we are dizzy and no longer know who is really who. In fact Genêt himself is not certain of his characters' identity. "My characters are all masks," he states. "How do you expect me to tell you whether they are true or false? I no longer know myself." Genêt's creatures share that taste for imposture and falseness which tempts their author to put on his calling cards, "Jean Genêt, false count of Tillancourt." Even in *Deathwatch* where identities are relatively clear, there are moments when we wonder whether Lefranc is really a tough, or Maurice really a homosexual, and just what the relationship of the men to one another is.

The Maids is really an interrupted ceremony. The dramatization of the maids' hatred for Madame is interrupted by the arrival of the real Madame. But when she leaves to join Monsieur, they resume their ceremony (it is they who give it this name), and Claire finally plays the role of Madame to the bitter end, drinking the poisoned tea they had prepared for her, while Solange describes the death of Madame. Just as the bread actually becomes the body of Christ in the Mass (for the believer), Claire has become Madame to the extent that Solange claims it is Madame who is really dead while the two maids are alive. As a matter of fact, of course, it is Claire who is dead, and Solange who will no doubt be condemned to death as her murderer, for she believes she has become herself through crime, has found at last her real identity: "Now, I have my own dress, and I'm your equal. I wear the red garb of criminals. . . . I'm the strangler. Mademoiselle Solange, the one who strangled her sister!" It is a false crime, only the appearance of a crime, just as Madame's death is only the appearance of her death. In his interesting commentary on *The Maids* Sartre stresses the "whirligigs of being and appearance, of the imaginary and the real," and sees them as an attempt on the part of Genêt to suggest the nothingness of a reality that is constantly revealing itself as unreal, as pure appearance. "In Genêt's plays every character must play the role of a character who plays a role." This is of course more than a simple game. It is the essence of ceremony in which all participants are transformed, or believe they are.

The whirligigs continue in the next play, *The Balcony*, written in 1956, several years after Genêt had announced he had given up writing plays.[18] The Balcony is the name of a famous house of prostitution. Its proprietress, Madame Irma, calls it her house of illusions, for here men from every walk of life may come and live out their dreams. The play opens with three glimpses of dreams come true: in one room a man dresses as a bishop and hears the confessions of one of Mme Irma's girls, while in the next a client in judge's robes weighs the feigned crimes of another, and in a third a "general" enacts a heroic death. Each of the men is wearing cothurns and has immensely padded shoulders so that, in his dream fulfillment, he is larger than life. And different from life too, for these men are essentially dead, and are bishop, judge, and general in appearance only. To become a true bishop, judge, or general, would have meant sacrificing a mode of being to the struggle to achieve that function in real life. In the closed world of Le Grand Balcon each man can regard himself in a mirror and see himself as the essence of his dreams. Distilled into himself, reflected in an eternity of mirrors, he has achieved his identity (and annihilation), and can even renounce life.

Outside Le Grand Balcon a revolution is raging. When the Queen and her entourage are presumed killed, Mme Irma is given the chance to play the role of the Queen, and the three Figures (bishop, judge and general) may now become in reality what they have always dreamed of being. But after assuming the real-life functions of their roles they discover that they no longer can dream. "Our ornamental purity," says the Bishop, "our luxurious and barren—and sublime—appearance has been eaten away." Reality lacks the value of lie, and it is only in dreams that we can drown ourselves.

Madame Irma's lover is the Chief of Police, who is also part owner of the bordello. His major concern is that he should be imitated by someone coming to the house of illusions. But his role in life has never been glamorous enough to inspire imitation. When Madame Irma becomes Queen, the Chief of Police becomes the National Hero, and finally at the end of the play he is impersonated by a defeated revolutionary who descends into a mock tomb that copies the monument built for the National Hero after his death.[19] Now the Chief may die himself, for he has found identity in his representation by others, and as the play ends he descends to his tomb where he too will be reflected endlessly by mirrors.

Like *The Maids, The Balcony* is an interrupted ceremonial. The play is divided into two parts by one scene which takes place outside the bordello. At the revolutionary headquarters we see a picture of reality which contrasts strongly with the illusions of Mme Irma's Balcony. The first half of the play shows a real ritual through which characters are momentarily transformed. The second half reveals a false ritual in which the imaginary world crumbles when forced to make contact with the real outside world. The second half of the play has been severely criticized as a "fog of symbolic rhetoric,"[20] and "a huge steaming muddle."[21] Brooks Atkinson strikes me as essentially fair when he writes:

> This is the part of *The Balcony* that becomes a riddle wrapped in an enigma. The double images acquire new significance. Everything means more than the author or the characters say. Only a mechanical computer could absorb all the meanings and tick out the correct answers.

"It's a true image, born of a false spectacle," says the Palace Envoy of a photograph of the Bishop taking communion with a monocle for holy wafer. The statement applies pretty well to most of the play (and perhaps to most ritual, religious or theatrical), a true image of what Mr. Atkinson calls "a withering of dreams," but riddled through with pretense and play. As the curtain falls Mme Irma, no longer Queen, turns out the lights in her brothel and tells the audience to go home, "where everything will be even falser than here." Tomorrow illusions will begin again at Le Grand Balcon, but in the meantime we must recognize that even our life outside the theater is an illusion.

By addressing the audience directly Mme Irma prepares us for Genêt's last play, *The Blacks* (*Les Nègres*), 1958, which is no longer a fictional story presented by characters who are maids, prisoners, prostitutes, or revolutionaries. It is frankly a ceremony presented before us by a troupe of Negroes who are acting out a ritual killing that takes place every day, and is in fact taking place somewhere off stage at the very moment we are witnessing the pageant. For as usual there are several levels of appearance and reality. The most "real" of these levels is that at which we are the audience and the Negroes actors on a stage before us. On this level we are addressed directly as an audience, and even invited to the stage at one point. At one remove from this is a "real" action which is taking place off stage and which is only suggested by the actors: a Negro, traitor

149

to his race, is being judged and executed, and a new Hero acclaimed so that he may destroy the enemy. The white audience is not permitted to see this true action, for as one actor points out, this play is both Greek tragedy and modest: "the ultimate gesture is performed off stage." What we are allowed to witness is the third level, that of parade, masks, and ceremony.

Genêt specifies that *The Blacks* is meant to be performed before whites, but if it should be presented for a colored audience, there must always be present one white person, who dressed in ceremonial robes, occupies a prominent seat. For the spectators are as integral a part of this work as the congregation in a church service. The Negroes enacting the murder of a white woman whose catafalque we see draped in white at the center of the stage, are observed and judged by a court of whites who sit on a gallery at the back of the stage: the Queen, the Judge, the Missionary, the Governor, and the Valet, playing card characters, or chess pieces who are in reality Negroes themselves wearing exaggerated white masks that, however, permit their brown skin to show at the edges. After the troupe has re-enacted the crime, the members of the Court descend from their gallery and make an imaginary trip deep into the African jungle where they intend to punish the Blacks. Instead the Black Queen Felicity vanquishes the White Queen, and the play ends as the entire cast, including the Court now rid of their masks, joins in a minuet, the same dance with which the play began.

Appearance and reality flash back and forth as in *The Balcony*, and we are often not sure whether the actors are themselves or playing a role. The levels of reality multiply, shifting from real life to ceremony, from black to black masked as white. When the sheet is finally removed from the catafalque, it is revealed to be only two chairs.

The Negroes clearly represent another world of outcasts for Genêt, and reflect the same hatred of the "good" people whose way of life is something foreign imposed from without upon the noble African whose praises are sung in outbursts of violent lyricism. The members of the white court play their roles to the teeth, underlining the self-righteousness and superiority of the white, their insidious piety, the hypocrisy and blindness of their attitudes to the Negro. The ceremony of magic and incantation, concerted laughter and ritual movement, is nothing less than a Mass celebrating the liberty of man and the glory of revolt against the ruling caste. The fact that there is no corpse after all only heightens the meaning of the ritual, for the killing was something more than a physical act. It was a symbolic vengeance upon the entire white race, upon those who are good and kind, like Madame in *The Maids,* but deny the humanity of all that is different.

> The time has not yet come [says Archibald, the Master of Ceremonies] for presenting dramas about noble matters. But perhaps they suspect what lies behind this architecture of emptiness and words. We are what they want us to be. We shall therefore be it to the very end, absurdly.

This statement, made during the last few moments of the play, sums up rather neatly the meaning of the play, the method employed, and the very personal involvement of Genêt in it. According to the author, western society is not yet ready for that noble and ceremonious theater that depicts gods rather than men and is a religious experience rather than a simple amusement. In *The Blacks* he has attempted to approach this kind of theater, suggesting a kind of absolute of beauty and hate behind this "architecture of emptiness," a world in which the Negro is no longer the negation of white but a total universe. In the words of the Black Queen:

> Beyond that shattered darkness, which was splintered into millions of Blacks who dropped to the jungle, we were Darkness in person. Not the dark-

ness which is absence of light, but the kindly and terrible Mother who contains light and deeds.

The Negro in this play, like the criminals in Genêt's novels, like Genêt himself, has decided to play out the stereotyped role assigned him by society, but to play it out to the end, even absurdly, choosing freely to become what he is condemned to be. It becomes clear at this point that, as Pierre Marcabru points out, "these Negroes are only allegories, only phantoms born from a scorn, a rage, a repulsion which is that of Jean Genêt before an order which his whole being refuses."

The theater of Jean Genêt is a theater of revolt expressed in ceremonial terms in which death plays a predominant role, not only in the obvious use of death cells, murder, tombs, and catafalques, but in the annihilating effect of his game of mirrors in which reality is reflected back and forth until it almost reaches the point of invisibility. His revolt is not only against ordered society, it is against life itself, a life which refuses man the satisfactions of an absolute purity. Diving into the inverted world of dark and evil, Genêt adopts an essentially religious attitude, attempting to reach the absolute through his inverted religion. His theater is a Mass celebrating that religion. Despite the quasi-realistic atmosphere of *Deathwatch,* a ritual underlies it, and the author reminds us at the start that "We are playing tragically, but we are playing." With *The Maids* the ritual aspect becomes explicit as the maids invent a ceremony for their lives. In *The Balcony* the ritual is played at first voluntarily and then imposed from without, and an impossible synthesis is attempted with reality. In Genêt's latest play there is no pretense at realism, no plot or fixed characters. With it we have arrived at a theater that is almost pure ceremony, a theater that "shakes the rules of the stage and defies judgement," just as any religious ceremony would do. Like the Catholic Mass, like the Voodoo ceremonies of Haiti, and like the Dionysian celebrations that undoubtedly preceded the flowering of tragedy in Greece, this ritual theater speaks a language which has not been heard for many hundreds of years on the European stage.

5

From Babel to Eden

THE POETIC LANDSCAPE, David Gascoyne suggests,[1] is Eden: man, a totality in which conscious and unconscious fuse, in a décor which forms a meaningful part of his experience and is even a part of man himself. Nature becomes a temple, where Baudelaire's "living pillars" speak to us a mysterious language, that language "of the soul and for the soul," evoked by Rimbaud. Man is at harmony with things. We have seen in the plays of Beckett and Ionesco that man is often at loggerheads with the world of things, that he seems a misfit in a universe that has become uncomfortable and has even dispossessed him. At the same time there is an awareness, vague and tormenting, of a lost paradise now forever unattainable. As in the Baudelairian experience of spleen, things fall apart and man is imprisoned under "a low heavy sky which weighs like a cover," he is overcome by terrifying visions, and by the gray of the city with its constant suffering, poverty, and death. The horror of the present reality but points up the pathos of man's dereliction as he attempts to retrieve a rag of the lost "green paradise," through dream and fantasy, or imaginary voyages, only to be cast back upon the rough stony beach of reality. Reality is chaos, a world which conforms to no pattern, which refuses consolation, and in which man, far from being able to communicate with others, frequently may not even be certain of his own identity or meaning. In short, a world of Babel.

Such is the name which Lou Bruder, writing in *Thé-âtre de France,* (Vol. IV) gives to the avant-garde theater: "Le Théâtre de Babel." It is, he claims, a theater of confusion and linguistic disintegration, revealing a pathological obsession with chaos. Monsieur Bruder is preoccupied chiefly with Beckett, Ionesco, Adamov, and Vauthier. But there are other experimental dramatists writing in French today who reveal a vision closer to that of Baudelaire's more happy poems, and give us at least a glimpse of the Eden that we, now grown old, have lost. Dramatists and poets, who cling to a vivid if imaginary childhood world and who, like Audiberti, can dedicate a play "To the dogs and the fir-trees of the district of Lozère."

If we traced an imaginary line leading from our modern Babel back to a happy Eden, we might place at one extreme the names of Ionesco, Adamov, Beckett, Tardieu, and Vauthier; at the other, that of Schehadé. Somewhere in between we would locate Genêt (who by his annihilating play of mirrors would seem to belong to the former, but whose faith—or hope—in the magic and ritual of a perverted religion seems to pull him in the other direction), Pichette, Ghelderode, and Audiberti.

The Babel of Jean Tardieu and Jean Vauthier

Jean Tardieu, the author of several volumes of poetry and prose and of translations of Goethe and Hölderlin, has published two volumes of plays, entitled *Théâtre de Chambre* and *Poèmes à Jouer.* Like chamber music, this chamber theater is made up chiefly of short works for small ensembles, usually developing a single theme. Several of the plays are experiments in musical forms, in which notes are replaced by words. *Conversation-Sinfonietta* employs phrases of everyday conversation, spoken in varying patterns by two basses, two contral-

155

tos and a soprano, and tenor, moving through an *allegro ma non troppo* movement, to an *andante sostenuto*, and ending with a *scherzo vivace*. *La Sonate* (*The Sonata*) shows us three gentlemen recalling "what happened" in a piece of music they heard at a concert. Through three movements the themes are presented, interwoven, varied, and finally end in a Beethoven-like cadence in which "matin" (morning) is repeated some fourteen times. The most ambitious of these compositions, *L'A.B.C. de notre vie* (*The ABC of Our Life*), again presents themes which are associated in various ways: the illusion of man's individuality, the ever-present influence of others, the splendid isolation of love, the grandeur and futility of human words.

Aside from these works, which reveal Tardieu's interest in language as such (one critic has called him a "profound philologist"), the plays in these volumes fall into two groups: what one might call plays of parody, and plays of anguish. The parodies sometimes mock real-life situations, as in *La Société Apollon ou Comment parler des arts* (*The Apollo Society or How to Speak of the Arts*), in which an officious and affected directress of art lecture tours takes her group to the studio of "the master," and during his absence explains his highly abstract work of art, which, upon his return, we discover to be nothing more than his latest invention: a grinder and cutter for the kitchen. Or the delightful "Comic Ballet without dance or music," *Les Amants du Métro* (*The Lovers of the Subway*), in which the strangers we briefly encounter in the subway are sharply presented through a few inane sentences and several well-chosen attitudes.

More frequently the parodies take some form of theater as their point of departure and we see Tardieu making fun of the overuse of asides (*Oswald et Zénaïde*), the artificiality of monologues (*Il y avait foule au manoir*), and the "realistic" theater in which the characters are oblivious to the audience and never allow us to know just what they are talking about (*Eux seuls le savent*). These are among the most successful of Tardieu's plays and reveal his fine sense of humor, turned toward the absurd and exaggerated.

The humorous note is sustained again in what I have called the plays of anguish, works that, usually through a comic incident, reveal man's unpleasant situation in a world not made for him. A feeling of guilt dominates him (*Monsieur Moi, Le Guichet*), an awareness of a mysterious inimical presence which kills (*Qui est là?, Le Meuble*), or humiliates (*La Politesse inutile*). Death is frequently evoked, but it is never looked upon as a restful conclusion; rather it is the last absurd silence which constantly threatens us, and finally annihilates existence, reducing it to that silence which was always its essence. In *La Serrure* (*The Keyhole*) the voyeur client at the bordello looks through a gigantic keyhole to watch the woman of his dreams undress. She removes not only her clothes, but her entire skin and finally appears as a death figure to which the client cries out, "I'm coming to you, love of my life!" The *reductio ad absurdum* of this kind of theater is found in *Une Voix sans personne* (*A Voice with Nobody*), in which we watch a completely empty stage, under changing lights, while a voice evokes the past.

In the Kafka-like *Le Guichet* (*The Information Window*) the timid client attempts to inquire about train schedules, but is not allowed to pose his questions until the official has filled out an exceedingly detailed form. Undecided as to which train to take, the client asks the opinion of the official, who finally casts his horoscope and tells him that he will die within a few minutes, upon leaving the information room. Any other questions—how will he die?—become superfluous. This little play, one of Tardieu's best, presents in miniature a picture of life, as we follow the client's birth, marriage, and family life given in statistical form to the official, his experience with the red tape of officialdom, the frustrations of the little man in contact with the monstrous machine, and finally the reduction of the apparently sensible to simple nonsense in the light of death.

Ce que parler veut dire (*What Speaking Means*) carries these ideas into the field of linguistics, as a professor lectures on the deformations of language within social groups. After attempting to illustrate his lecture by means of a record which becomes independent and begins to insult him, the professor questions his students in the audience, and presents a family scene, finally concluding:

> Thus, Ladies and Gentlemen, ends our little walk through the social curiosities of contemporary language. It has scarcely been reassuring! We have everywhere seen *imprecision* replace the precise word, *gestures* fill the yawning void of vocabulary, and *childish babbling* invade the language of adults! . . . (*He suddenly changes his tone.*) And now, let's go *bye-bye!*

Even the linguistic expert, when he becomes a simple human being, reverts to the imprecise babbling he had criticized and which is apparently the most frequent (if not the only) means of communication among men. His identity as linguist is lost, and ultimately Babel triumphs as both living and speaking end in silence: death and incomprehensibility.

Jean Vauthier's plays, by contrast, are extremely verbal, and the luxuriance of lyricism, the obsession with words, make one wonder whether one is in the presence of a play, or perhaps of a poem or an opera. But beneath the language, once again, lies emptiness, noncommunication, and defeat. Setting aside his new treatment of Machiavelli's *Mandragola* (directed by Gérard Philipe for the TNP in 1952), each of Vauthier's three published plays might be called a duel which results in the annihilation of both parties involved. They are a duel first of all between two characters (for never are there more than two important characters in Vauthier's plays), and secondly, as Marc Beigbeder has pointed out, between the inner character and his outer utterances. Ultimately both inner and outer man, both protagonist and antagonist, are frustrated in their attempts to give meaning to themselves, their lives or their relationships. In the final analysis, they are useless beings engaged in a losing combat. Like the titular character of Vauthier's best-known (if not best) play, all his people are "Fighting Personages."

Le Capitaine Bada (*Captain Bada*, performed in 1952 by André Raybaz) introduces us to Vauthier's vigorous theater, with its combination of earthy realism and exaggerated lyricism which give it a kind of Renaissance *élan*, an alternance between beauty and brutality which seizes and twists the spectator, leaving him finally bruised and worn out. Throughout three acts and four scenes we see the struggle between Bada, a would-be poet, and his sweetheart (then spouse) Alice. The first act shows the pursuit of Bada by Alice. The young man finally acquiesces, and the second act is made up chiefly of the pursuit of Alice by Bada, for now that she is his, Alice refuses to be possessed. Joined by two dancers, Bada and Alice perform a kind of farcical ballet, a buffoonish duel between man and woman, satyr and nymph. The two scenes of the last act take place years later, but the fight has not ended, and the married life of the couple has been a protracted agony during which the shiftless husband claims to have been harassed and distracted from his work by his irresponsible and light-headed wife, who only longs to escape from her dictatorial and terrifying keeper. The dialogue of the act is not an amusing exaggeration of the clichés and boredom of married life, in the style of Ionesco, but a frightening paroxysm of recriminations and accusations. "Two beings, four ears, twenty toes trampling the ground of this paradise!" cries Bada ironically; "You and me, me and you, O hymenea!"

Finally an angel from the funeral parlor comes

through the window to take Bada off to heaven, but not before the old poet has cast off his plumed (and slightly flea-bitten) helmet of poetry, thus accomplishing a symbolic renunciation. Nonetheless, his widow, turning to the audience, declares that Bada was a worthy man, and pointing to the piles of unfinished papers and manuscripts, assures us that he will soon receive his due.

We know better, of course, for Bada was a failure as a poet just as he was a failure as a husband. His disappearance leaves not a trace behind him, except in the deluded heart of Alice who will herself, no doubt, soon disappear. Like all of Vauthier's heroes, Bada is engaged in a search for an absolute, whether it be beauty, God, poetry, or simply *the* word of all words. And like the other heroes he is doomed to failure.

Le Personnage combattant (*The Fighting Personage*) was accepted by Jean-Louis Barrault for performance in his experimental theater, Le Petit Marigny, in 1956. It is Vauthier's most widely known play, and the one that brought his name before a large public, simply by association with Barrault. It is, if nothing else, a tour de force, for the play has only two characters, one of which is on stage for only a few minutes. It is virtually a one-man play lasting a full evening, what Lou Bruder called a "frantic and baroque one-voiced oratorio."[2] The major difficulty posed by the play, the dramatist tells us in one of his copious and sometimes irritating notes, was to "make dramatic something which was anti-theatrical; life on the stage must arise from a reading made to the public." In effect, a large part of the play consists of a rereading of a manuscript written years ago by a now successful novelist who returns to the squalid hotel room where he lived as a struggling but sincere young artist, in an attempt to recapture the truth and vitality of his youth. Through encounters with the objects of the room, the sounds of neighbors, the trains entering and leaving the nearby station, the hotel boy, his typewriter and manuscript, the Personage struggles through to what Barrault describes thus:

> a kind of ransom and individual redemption through the total giving of the self. The man, after a night of suffering, finds again the faculty of transfiguring life. He finds the poetic gift of metamorphosing things.[3]

I am not so sure that it is a clear victory won by the Personage. A few minutes before the end of the play the curtain begins to fall (an outworn device since Giraudoux's *La Guerre de Troie n'aura pas lieu*), but rises again as the Personage hears the sound of the train he had believed nonexistent. It is a whole new revelation for him and opens up the way to the metamorphosis mentioned by Barrault. But at this moment of realization, the Personage is brutally—and one is tempted to say justifiably, for this "hero" is an insufferable cad—struck down by the hotel boy. After a brief return to his feet, during which he does a *danse noble* declaiming, "Oh, my life, you are worth being lived!!!" he falls to the ground again and is dragged off by the hotel boy. The ending is ambiguous, for, curiously enough in a work which abounds in explicative notes, the stress is laid nowhere. Are we to understand that the individual is redeemed, and the fact that no one else cares or is capable of appreciating his redemption does not matter a whit? Or is the implication that the artist may think he has found truth, but it is inconsequential because his truth and his very life are denied by all other men? This is no longer the "savory ambiguity" of a *Godot*, in which essential meanings shine through. It is the annoying fuzziness of what should be a clear denouement.

It would be unfair to say that, in spite of his claims to the contrary, Barrault was attracted to *Le Personnage combattant* by the personal challenge of holding an audience by himself for two and a half hours. Certainly this may have been one of his reasons for doing the work, but he has shown himself too sincere a partisan of experimental theater to be accused of any purely selfish interest in the new plays he presents. Furthermore, *Le Personnage combattant*, despite its rather constant ambiguity, its disturbing mingling of extreme realism in setting and manners with highly literary lyric flights, despite its frequent nondramatic, static quality, and the annoyingly coquettish variety and size of type for the voluminous notes, which make the book read more like a novel or poem than a play, and cause one to wonder whether it is really capable of standing on the dialogue (or rather, the monologue) alone—despite these weaknesses, the play does have positive merits: it is vigorous and strong, courageously experimental, and completely original. Originality is no recommendation in itself, but Vauthier's originality is a positive contribution to modern dramaturgy because he has succeeded—or come closer to succeeding than have his predecessors—in putting on the boards in a virile and striking way (although there are long moments) a rich, symphonically structured poem in which a number of suggestive themes weave a complex whole. Occasionally one has the impression in this and other of Vauthier's plays that Rimbaud is being "performed."

Vauthier, like the other avant-garde writers, lays great stress upon the visible and nonverbal aspects of his play, and the notes which form a veritable orchestration of each text, describe in minute and sometimes picturesque detail not only the intonation and timbre of the actor's voice, but his precise dance-like movements upon the stage, the nuances of his gestures, grimaces, and poses, as well as the smallest particulars of the décor, the sumptuous off-stage sounds, and many of the psychological and philosophical subleties related to actor, sound, or set. Unlike Beckett and Ionesco, however, one does not feel a richness of connotation or a profound symbolism behind these visible or aural effects. They seem, rather, the precisions of an author

162

who is his own *metteur en scène,* and knows exactly what effect he wishes to produce and by what means.

Vauthier's third play, *Les Prodiges* (*The Wonders*), returns us again to the problem of the couple. Through forty-two "sequences" we follow the misunderstandings of Marc and his mistress Gilly, the former a romantic, deceitful aspirant of the absolute, the latter a selfish, avaricious, and shallow sensualist. At the end Gilly leaves Marc, as she had intended to do from the beginning.

Of Vauthier's three published plays, *Les Prodiges* seems to me the least satisfactory, the most obscure, the most static, the most trivial, while his early play, *Bada* seems the best, for it is immediately comprehensible on one level, possesses more color, more fire and movement than the other two, and finds a happier blend of realism and lyricism. Jean Vauthier has chosen an extremely difficult way, for he refuses any compromise with his liberty and individuality as an author, and never adopts the facile formula. He has reduced action and intrigue to a minimum—and beyond, has stripped the stage bare of any superfluous characters, rendering to it an Aeschylian simplicity abounding in long monologues and duos. In return, the one or two characters at the core of each play are complex and solid beings who, through their desperate search of an absolute, grotesquely aware of themselves playing out their lives, reveal ironically, and sometimes even comically, the despair of a young author who knows man as irrevocably divorced from his dreams.

The Limbo of Henri Pichette, Michel de Ghelderode, and Jacques Audiberti

About midway between the poles of Babel and Eden stand three writers, Henri Pichette, Michel de Ghelderode, and Jacques Audiberti. The first two, strictly speaking, perhaps do not belong to the dramatic avant-garde of the 1950's. Pichette, because he is first of all a poet and his two incursions into the theatrical field have only shown up his shortcomings as a dramatist. Ghelderode, because the bulk of his theater writing lies between the dates 1918–1937, and he has added virtually nothing since then. But his popularity in France dates from that of the avant-garde writers we have been discussing, and his independent spirit gives him a kinship with men like Ionesco, Beckett, and Adamov. Audiberti has written most of his plays since 1946, and despite his denial of ties with Beckett and Ionesco, he has caused conservative critics similar headaches because of his disregard for current dramatic modes. Not so hopelessly pessimistic as the authors at the Babel pole of our imaginary line, these dramatists tend to see man divided between good and evil, light and darkness, pleasure and torment.

Henri Pichette's *Les Epiphanies* (*The Epiphanies*) was presented in 1947 with a cast boasting Gérard Philips, Roger Blin, and Maria Casarès. It was, in Roger Shattuck's words, "the most promising poetic event of the post war decade."[4] The play is divided into five sections: Genesis, Love, War, Delirium, and The State. The Poet—whose monologue forms the play, interrupted by various other characters, chiefly the Devil and the Loving Woman—comes into being, falls in love, is overwhelmed by the Devil and war, and finally is shot, but resuscitates to claim his central position. Just as he had stated at the beginning: "From the first pulsation of the world I turned upon myself I thought like a circumference," at the end he announces, "So I am equinoctial: . . . till the last pulsation of the world." There is no real drama in this play, only words, conversation, lyricism; no true conflict, no action, no intrigue, no movement. It would probably have been intolerable without the talents of Philipe, Blin, and Casarès, who made of it a brilliant poetic recital, for the verbal brilliance and invention is undeniable.

The published version of the play seems to render impossible any further presentation: it is printed in a manner highly reminiscent of Mallarmé's *Un Coup de dés*, but gone mad on a surrealist jag with Victorian printer's figures. How, for example, to represent on the stage five dotted lines at the bottom of a page, or a black page covered with "R's" in various type faces, or a white page covered with large black dots, or two full pages printed vertically in capital letters. Such tricks, smacking of surrealist exuberance, are amusing to the reader, but have nothing whatsoever to do with drama, experimental or otherwise.

Pichette's second play, *Nucléa,* acted by Philipe and Vilar at the TNP in 1952 with sets by Alexander Calder, is somewhat more conventional. It is divided into two sections: The Infernals, a nightmare; and The Human Heaven, a dream. Once again the dramatic struggle between good and evil, love and hate, is presented in a nondramatic way. Shattuck rightly observes that "by dividing *Nucléa* into two halves representing war and love, Pichette vitiates the dramatic effect which might have resulted from a closer confrontation." And he concludes:

> Pichette and his fellow poets want to write poetry to be seen and heard. The great risk they run is that of lacking a sure dramatic sense, for the theatre cannot content itself with mere declamation of resonant lines.[5]

Michel de Ghelderode, with his supernatural, metaphysical, baroque theater, runs no such risk, for through his original and vibrant language shines a sure feeling for the theater. Dramatic conflict is the very essence of his plays, as it is of his attitude toward life. This modern romantic with a Medieval and Renaissance soul, sees man in Manichaean terms of dark and light, good and evil, flesh and spirit. "I have an angel on my shoulder and a devil in my pocket," he has said, and surely most of his theater bears witness to the conflict, or sometimes to the blending, of the diabolical and the mystical. As a Fleming, Ghelderode falls heir not only to the traditionally rowdy and worldly spirit of the Flemish as it is immortalized in those large and detailed festive scenes of Breughel, but he also inherits the medieval, tortured, metaphysical fantasies of a Bosch, and the mystical temperament of the Spanish invader at the twilight of Spanish greatness. And Michel de Ghelderode is Flemish to the core, assimilating these characteristics to the point that they are not only highly personal, but have become obsessive. Sequestered in his home since 1939 by asthmatic attacks, the recluse has plunged more deeply into the supernatural world he loves and feels is more real than the world most of us inhabit. Dolls, puppets, mannequins, clutter his study, reminding him that inanimate objects too are alive and sensible, possessing their own individualities and attitudes—and reminding him also of ever-present Death, and of the enigma of man's life: a marionette who knows neither who is pulling his strings nor the meaning of the play he is acting.

"I discovered the world of shapes before discovering the world of ideas," Ghelderode tells us in the *Ostend Interviews*. In stressing the sensuous aspects of his plays, all that is not dialogue, Ghelderode reminds us of a similar emphasis in other dramatists of the avant-garde. In his rejection of ideologies he tempts us to describe him as a Parnassian of the theater, for he is concerned neither with edifying, corrupting, nor convincing. More than any other dramatist we have discussed, Ghelderode is an instinctive writer, exorcising through his dramas his personal obsessions and fears. Hence the profound feeling of anguish and anxiety which pervades most of his plays. He has cared less than most other dramatists to expound upon his dramatic theories, and in the *Ostend Interviews* he bluntly refuses to answer certain questions put to him, while underlining the complete liberty of the dramatist, and affirming at the end, in no uncertain terms: "I do in the

theatre only what it pleases me to do, and I have no accounts to render to anyone."

The formal variety of Ghelderode's work bears witness to the sincerity of this statement. He writes for no
one but himself, and if his plays are performed, that is
an accident to which he remains indifferent. Unhamp-
ered by the formal requirements of a stage, he may
write something as free and unmountable as *Sire Halewyn,* with rapidly shifting scenes and horseback rides
across a snowy plain. On the other hand, he will produce
a short play with the unity and tightness of *Escurial.*
Taking his inspiration where he finds it, Ghelderode has
dipped deep into the resources of the popular theater:
fair, circus, music hall, and guignol. A number of his
plays were originally intended for performance by mar-
ionettes. Others show the influences of expressionism
and surrealism, the spirit of *Ubu,* or that of Apollinaire
and Cocteau. Structure tends to be loose, characters farcical or exaggerated, but the only rule is complete
liberty, and no single generalization applies strictly to
all the plays.

Jean Francis, in his study of Ghelderode, has pointed
out that one of the playwright's contributions has been
"to remind our contemporaries brutally that there are
eternal things which cannot be classified, dessicated,
demonstrated, and that humanity continues to walk
midst mystery, fear and the unexplained. Where most
authors—our contemporaries—attempt to discover rational explanations, Ghelderode discovers the demon."[6]
The rational man is much in the position of the author
Jean-Jacques in *Sortie de l'acteur* (*Actor's Exit*) who
at the end of the play, as he contemplates the sky, turns
to the old mime Fagot, and asks, "If you looked at it till
the end of time . . . would you ever find the key to the
mystery?" The wise old Fagot replies: "The key to the
mystery? . . . But don't you realize that mystery has
no door? . . ."

Rather than giving us answers and adages, Ghelde-

167

rode presents us with a motley, living world of animated figures in a variety of surroundings ranging from bars and brothels to palaces and disaffected convents. And through this vast fresco, willingly or not, like the author in *Sortie de l'acteur*, he discloses his vision of the human predicament:

> I was a wretch like you [complains the actor Renatus] and you snatched me away from my ignorance of my human condition; you revealed it to me! . . .
>
> *Jean-Jacques.* How could I know? I've never wanted to reveal or demonstrate, and since men have been speechifying, has the theatre ever revealed or explained anything? . . .

This passage stresses not only the nondidactic ends of Ghelderode's drama; it underlines his dislike of overemphasis on dialogue and harangues, and suggests that whatever vision may be revealed must be revealed only indirectly, through the incantatory power of words and moods, for Ghelderode is not only a poet in his use of language, he is a poet in the creation of that aura which exists before language or dialogue begins, and which will encompass the characters once they are placed in movement. Rephrasing Gautier's famous statement, one might say the Belgian poet is a man for whom the *invisible* world exists; but, in the theater at least, the invisible world can only be manifested through the visible, or through that which appeals to the senses. Hence a play by Ghelderode usually surrounds us, as if by magic, in a dozen sensuous ways, through the chiaroscuro of the set, the richness of colors, the profusion of sounds, and even the odors which the author evokes. Lights, shadows, textures, music of bells, bagpipes, horns, barbary organs, the baying of hounds, all tend to draw us into the strange world created by the author, in which we see kings and buffoons, witches and necromancers, burghers and monks, men of yesterday and today, men of all ages, performing grotesquely, seriously, tragically, and comically, the ugly acts that make them men, half demon and half angel—although in Ghelderode's drama the proportions tend to run four fifths demon and one-fifth angel. The Devil is always just around the corner, and Death peeking in at the window.

The early plays, those written between 1918 and 1921 (*Piet Bouteille, Les Vieillards, Le Cavalier bizzare, Un Soir de pitié*), are short scenes centering about a single, simple incident, containing little development either of character or plot. But whether set in Brabant farmhouse, old folks home, hospital for the poor, or bar, these four little plays bear many of the marks which will come to be associated with Ghelderode. Any of them might have been inspired by a painting: the death of the drunk Piet Bouteille, the misery of the grumbling old folks waiting for charity, or the terror of the aged sick expecting death, recall certain Breughel canvases, while the bar of Bacchus in *Un Soir de pitié*, invaded by the masked carnival crowd, suggests, like the pantomime *Masques ostendais* of 1930, the uncanny masks and carnival scenes of James Ensor. Music, bells and other sounds play an important role, there is an implicit criticism of human hypocrisy, bigotry, and selfishness (including that of the clergy); supernatural elements are not lacking, and we are constantly made aware of old age, corruption, and death.

Four years later Ghelderode wrote *La Mort du docteur Faust* (*The Death of Doctor Faust*), his first long play. Doctor Faust, living in his medieval study, emerges into a modern world at carnival time, and attends a performance of *Faust* in a tavern. There he encounters a working girl, Marguerite, whom he takes to a hotel. Afterwards he refuses to marry her as he had promised, explaining rather naïvely, "I'm an old man, . . . and besides I exist in another epoch." An enraged crowd is about to tear him to pieces when the devil Diamotoruscant saves him by making the entire scene appear as an advertisement for the *Faust* performances

169

at the tavern. When Marguerite kills herself the actors in the tavern drama are held responsible and pursued. They seek refuge, by chance, in the real Faust's home, where the two Fausts come face to face and interchange identities. The actor playing the role of Faust gives himself up to the crowd, while the real Faust, attempting to kill his impersonator, who has fused with him, kills himself.

This "music hall tragedy" is somewhat in the experimental tradition of Apollinaire and Cocteau, and takes advantage of the expressionistic techniques then in their heyday. In several scenes the stage is divided into two areas with simultaneous dialogues taking place in each, projections are used, titles flashed on a screen, and at one point a puzzled character enters topped by a gigantic question mark. The temporal division between 16th century study and 20th century city not only gives rise to some amusing incidents and dialogue, but almost forms a summing up of the periods which are to preoccupy Ghelderode during his theatrical career. Most of his plays either form part of a vast fresco of the Middle Ages and Renaissance, or contribute to a picture of the modern world, particularly the world of the theater, the circus, and the fair, a world of performers who, representing what they are not, pose in a tantalizing way the question of reality and illusion, the problem of man's identity and his true meaning. Time and again Ghelderode will return to this theme, but in *La Mort du docteur Faust* it is already amusingly outlined in the perplexing scenes between the actor Faust and the real Faust, and those between the actor Devil and Diamotoruscant, and is tersely exposed by Faust as a vicious circle when he says, "To live is to continue to betray myself, for I am someone superior to myself."

The carnival atmosphere with its strange masks (again Ensor inspired) and frenzied crowds establishes this period of gaiety and liberty, when no one is quite what he seems, as the Ghelderodian period par excellence. Whether the play be medieval, modern, or Biblical, whether centered about entirely original characters, or about legendary or quasi-legendary ones, the sounds of carousing, singing, dancing, parades, and celebrations are almost invariably heard in the background. Against this lively backdrop the death theme emerges as even grimmer by contrast, despite its frequent comic treatment, as in the case of the coquettish death figure with gigantic scythe that comes skipping across the stage just in time to pass Faust's door as he puts a bullet through his breast.

In this theater tragic and burlesque constantly meet as the serious and frightening themes of death, corruption, and evil are treated in a comic manner and juxtaposed to that other favorite Ghelderodian theme of appearance and reality.

It would be convenient to divide the thirty-odd plays of Ghelderode according to theme, setting, length, or techniques employed. But no such division seems justifiable. We can, however, note that, after the four brief plays of 1918–1921 and the seminal *Mort du docteur Faust* (1925), Ghelderode tends to stress in the five years from 1926 through 1930, the appearance-reality dichotomy in plays with a modern setting: *Trois acteurs, un drame* (1926), *Don Juan* (1928), *Pantagleize* (1929), *Le Club des menteurs, Le Ménage de Caroline, Masques ostendais,* and *Sortie de l'acteur* (1930).

In *Trois acteurs, un drame* (*Three actors and their drama*), three discouraged actors decide actually to kill themselves during the performance. As it turns out, however, they are too accustomed to dying on-stage, and fail in their attempt. It is, instead, the despairing author who commits suicide in the wings. *Sortie de l'acteur* (*Actor's Exit*) is also laid in a theater setting and has, along with the earlier play, been placed in the Pirandello tradition despite Ghelderode's insistence that he had never read or seen the works of the Sicilian dramatist at that time. Surely his own profound convictions that "No one is certain of reality," that "we are victims of phantoms," and that "we live in the midst of magic," are sufficient to account for the theater-as-life and life-as-theater aspect of his works. *Sortie de l'acteur* traces, in that rather loose fashion which is typical of much expressionism, the sickness (Act I: Cold Behind the Curtain), death (Act II: Illusions still Posted), and ascension (Act III: Twilight Comedy) of the actor, more spirit than flesh, Renatus (= Reborn). Before disappearing up the ladder, carried off by angel policemen, the spirit of Renatus has time to identify himself to the author Jean-Jacques and point out his abiding truth: "My name is specter. I know, specters are undesirable and outmoded, although the theater once used them in great quantities. It will come back to them, Sir. Fashions die, specters do not."

The three short works, *Club des menteurs* (*Liar's Club*), *Ménage de Caroline* (*Caroline's Place*), and *Masques ostendais* (*Ostend Masks*, a pantomime), show neither reality nor illusion victorious. In none of them does Ghelderode attempt an answer to the question, which is more real? He is content to pose the problem, revealing life as an eternal enigma. "Nature," says Charles V in *Le Soleil se couche* some years later, "remains this secret book, illegible forever."

The two long plays, *Don Juan* and *Pantagleize* are modern morality plays, morality plays which, like Ghelderode's other dramas, do not preach, but simply reveal the anguish and idiocy of man's predicament, forever frustrated in his desires, forever the butt of an indifferent or inimical universe.

Don Juan is dedicated to Charlie Chaplin, and it is apparent that Ghelderode had him in mind as he created the titular character of his play, for unlike the Don Juan of legend, the protagonist of the Belgian play is a thin, pale, nervous little man who at carnival time decks himself out as the Spanish roué. He is lured into a bar-fronted brothel by the barker who, as so often in

172

Ghelderode's theater, serves as chorus and commentator:

> You did well to rig yourself out in those old things.
> Wearing a mask, you're true. Never show your
> face, if men like you ever have one! Your adven-
> ture could be incomparable. From the moment
> you stop before this shop of love, a supernatural
> melodrama begins, the likes of which you dare
> not dream. . . . Don't turn aside from the evil
> path; don't be troubled by the prestige of the name
> and identity which your costume confers upon
> you. . . . You're as good as the original! . . . Fol-
> low your destiny.

And indeed, Don Juan follows his destiny, attempting
to live his legend so completely that he feels he has become Don Juan. Like the King in *Escurial*, like Barabbas, he feels he must invent a character, or adopt one,
in order to feel alive, to become someone recognizable.
But all men are Don Juan, or would like to be, and the
Chaplinesque hero discovers that he has competitors
for the love of Olympia, the eternal woman of the
Babylon Bar. When he passes beyond the bar, behind
the décor, and experiences love, Don Juan is disillusioned, and finally horrified, for he discovers that love
and death are one and the same thing, and the woman
he has adored is a hideous, bald, syphilitic hag, now
become a corpse. As he flees, he is followed by a little
old man in green, the original Don Juan, once Olympia's
lover, now the demon who will torment the new Don
Juan, revealing to him his future as he lifts the handkerchief from his face disclosing a spongy, gray visage,
the nose decayed with disease, the mouth a bleeding
sore: Don Juan, wounded in the service of Venus.

Pantagleize, equally as grim in its implications, but
much gayer on the surface, is subtitled a "depressing
vaudeville," and shows most fully the comic inclina-
tions of our author. Somewhat ominously the play is
set "in a city in Europe, after one war, and before an-

other." The hero, a philosopher who attempts to remain detached in his observation of the antics of the strange human animal, is another Chaplinesque figure who unwittingly walks into a trap: having decided to adopt as his cliché of the day the apparently innocent remark, "What a beautiful day!" he becomes the unconscious catalyst of a revolution, for his little phrase was the signal the revolutionaries were awaiting. From the heights of philosophical detachment he tumbles into a central position in the revolt, but remains completely unaware of the role he is playing. Through meetings with the insurgents, a comic love scene with the heroic Jewess Rachel, encounters with police disguised as palm trees or corpses, or on a difficult mission to obtain the national treasury, he walks untouched. Still completely innocent of what is happening, he is judged, condemned, and sent before a firing squad. The pathetic humor of Pantagleize's situation, the verbal wit of his philosophizing, the absurdity of his pursuers' antics, and the satire of the revolutionaries and their powerful opponents in the military, cannot blind us to the fact that *Pantagleize* is essentially a serious play that offers a rather hapless commentary on man's position: commitment and noncommitment are equally futile, and in the last analysis it is the strong and powerful who are right. Whether we choose our identity, as did Don Juan, or remain apart, like Pantagleize, the end is the same—down the big black hole.

In addition to the modern dress plays, the 1926–1930 period witnessed the composition of five other works. Two are Biblical dramas which offer a grossly human picture of the events and characters centered about the Crucifixion: the one-act *Les Femmes au tombeau* (1928, *The Women at the Tomb*), with its evocation of Flemish primitive paintings, and the three-act *Barabbas* (1928) which presents the events of Holy Week from the viewpoint of the rabble, recalling at times the Crucifixion painting of Breughel in which the Christ figure is all but lost among the crowds of eager spectators who fill the countryside. A hypocritical Caiphas, a sick and vicious Herod, a weak Pilate, and a group of terrified disciples, contrast starkly with the forceful (and forced) Barabbas who, playing the role of cutthroat, exults in evil and declares that criminals will render justice and avenge the death of Jesus. Ironically, however, Barabbas is cut down by the just of the earth, the very priests who had contrived his release in place of Jesus.

Christophe Colomb and *Escurial* (1927), are two of Ghelderode's most successful dramas. The first, loosely constructed in the expressionistic fashion, recounts amusingly, imaginatively, and anachronistically, the adventures of Columbus as he seeks not so much a new world as forgetfulness and adventure with its "adorable anguish." "Farewell, America," he cries to the newly-discovered continent. "You were too easy to discover." And he sails off finally to the last great adventure, death, ending as a statue who is nonetheless touched at the homage rendered by such a character as Buffalo Bill.

Escurial, the first of the large group of plays dealing with the Middle Ages and the Renaissance, blends in a brief, tense dialogue between the King (presumably Philippe II) and his buffoon, the themes of death, appearance, and reality, with a creation of mood through color and sound unsurpassed in the modern theater. As usual the enigma is not solved, and the game of identities ends in death.

Fastes d'enfer (*Chronicles of Hell*, 1929), the first of the violently demonic plays, shows with a scabrous, Rabelaisian verve, the hypocrisy and profligacy of the clergy of Lapideopolis after the death of their heretical bishop who rises from his bier to pursue his murderers and only returns to it when his sorceress mother commands him to do so. In a decaying palace, already familiar to the reader of *Escurial,* surrounded by the supernatural and the vague rumbling of the restless crowds outside, the vicious clergy scuttle about like monsters of vice from a Bosch canvas, their ugly exteriors an authentic representation of their corrupt souls.

All the plays written since 1931—that is to say, until 1937 when Ghelderode stopped writing for the theater, with the sole published exception of a lengthy mystery play written in 1952—deal with the Medieval and Renaissance periods and continue the demonic strain of *Festes d'enfer* without relinquishing any of the themes of the earlier works. These are, if anything, emphasized by the deep shadows and bright colors of the period, and we enter more fully into the fantastic and popular Breughel and Bosch worlds in which devils and angels rub shoulders with tradesmen, hangmen, and burghers, and the noise of peasant bagpipes and carnival dances is vaguely heard in the background. Some of the plays are directly inspired by Breughel: *Les Aveugles* (*The Blind Men,* 1933) and *La Pie sur le gibet* (*The Magpie on the Gibbet,* 1935) are brief, cruel, sometimes comical sketches, and bear the titles of actual paintings.

Mademoiselle Jaïre (1934), returning to the Biblical themes, presents a piquant transposition of the Miracle of Jairus' Daughter to a 16th century Flanders. The Christ figure, Le Roux (Red), is taken during Holy Week and crucified on Good Friday on a hill outside the Flemish town. With his death, Mademoiselle Jaïre may also die and return once again to the grave she so desires.

Other plays continue the Spanish strain noted already in *Escurial*. *Le Soleil se couche* (*The Sun Sets,* 1933) shows the last days of the Emperor Charles V at the Monastary of Yuste, contrasting the Emperor's Flemish earthiness to the Spanish religiosity of his son Philippe, and revealing life's strong grip on him despite his decision to celebrate his funeral while still alive. The grim atmosphere of the play is accentuated by the presence of the fanatic Fray Ramon, the shadow of Philippe and his Inquisition, and the persistent hammering we hear in the background, which we finally discover to be the sound of the carpenters fashioning Charles' coffin. A contrast is offered by the Fleming Fray Pascual, the mysterious Messer Ignotus (= Unknown), and his puppet theater which poses once again the question of identity, and by the Emperor himself in whom the earthy and the mystical contend with one another.

L'École des bouffons (*The School for Buffoons,* 1937) returns to the stage the jester of *Escurial,* Folial, now become master of a school for buffoons in a crumbling convent. Before his students leave their school to face the world Folial is to reveal to them the secret of their art. "The secret of our art," he whispers, "of art, of great art, of all art which wishes to endure? . . . is cruelty! . . ." Superfluous lesson, for the deformed outcasts who fill Folial's school knew it instinctively. Indeed few are the characters of the Ghelderodian universe who are not cruel, and few are the plays which do not reveal the cruelty of the poet himself as he exposes pitilessly the ugliness of man to our gaze, and inexorably suggests the futility of all effort.

It seems apposite to recall here the name of Antonin Artaud, and to remember that he advocated a theater of cruelty. Ghelderode was writing at the same time as Artaud and probably was unfamiliar with his essays, but, in the spirit of the great surrealist, the Belgian poet also makes us aware that "the sky can still fall on our heads." He catches us through our skin and our viscera rather than through our minds, using a kind of "total theatre" that would have pleased Artaud.

The disquieting *Hop Signor!* (1935) adds the elements of perversity and sadism to the earlier picture, and in Marguerite Harstein love is equated not only to death, but to sterility and pain as she looks forward lustily to dying at the hands of the gentle headsman with the paradoxical name, Larose.

But the theater of Ghelderode is not all hell-fire and

brimstone, suffering, and cruelty. The devil wields power not only in hell, he contributes as well to a great deal of pleasure on earth, and in the remaining plays we see the bouncing Rabelaisian verve of the author at its highest peak. In countries with such significant names as Brugelmonde and Breugellande, lust, gluttony, greed, all forms of corruption, the seven capital sins and pleasant minor variations run wild. The good citizens of Brugelmonde (*D'un Diable qui prêcha merveilles*, 1934, *Of a Devil Who Preached Marvels*) are panic-stricken when they discover that a zealous monk from Rome is on his way toward their modern Sodom where he will expose their vicious behavior. They are saved, however, by the good devil Capricante who sends the preacher Bashuiljus down the wrong road, and preaches in his place, praising the sinful citizens to the skies. When the enlightened Bashuiljus returns seeking just one honest man in order to save Brugelmonde from destruction, Capricante plays to perfection the role of the innocent young Christian too good for this world, thereby saving the town; and the two "monks" set off for Rome, singing *Te Deum laudamus*.

La Balade du Grand Macabre (*The Grand Macabre's Stroll*, 1934) shows Breugellande in danger, for Nekrozotar—Death, or an imposter who seriously believes himself to be Death—announces the end of the world. After the passing of a comet and a catastrophic night, the spurious Death, his drunkard friend Porpenaz (= Purplenose), and the philosopher Videbolle (= Emptyhead), waken in Breugellande instead of in heaven, and resume the enjoyable task of living, loving, and drinking.

In Magie rouge (*Red Magic*, 1931), an earthy medieval farce built upon cuckoldry, avidity, sensuality, and alchemy, the miser Hieronymus, so stingy he has not even given himself to his wife, is duped by the young woman and her lover, who introduces himself into the house as an alchemist prepared to manufacture gold for the old man. Hieronymus—an impressive figure, even next to Harpagon—loses not only his wife, but his money as well, and is accused of black magic and murder to boot. The passionate young blood of the lovers wins, and there is absolutely no tone of condemnation in this amoral, "Parnassian" theater.

La Farce des Ténébreux (*The Farce of the Dark Band*, 1936), whose chief character is treated much like the central figure in a Molière farce, is once again earthy and medieval in flavor, dealing with the "deflowering" of the town "virgin," Fernand d'Abcaude (= De la Queue) who at first wishes to remain chaste and faithful to the memory of his dead Azurine. At a fancy brothel where Fernand's doctor has taken him for a "cure," we discover that Azurine was none other than Putrégina (= Queen of Whores), the ablest woman in town whose exploits are described in glowing terms. The play ends with a paean to life and pleasure as Fernand is initiated into the joys of the flesh. As the bed crashes to the ground under the impact of such genial activity, the room is invaded by Fernand's friends who pronounce the moral of the piece: "During the day, be as you wish to appear. Our wisdom is only illumined in darkness. At night become human!"

The crude and ribald element of the farces, present to a lesser degree in the other plays, restores the balance in this theater that might easily incline to somber pessimism. Despite the conclusion that all effort is futile (*Pantagleize*, for example), Ghelderode constantly returns to life as a vital force that is sufficient in itself. Despite the metaphysical yearning inherent in the problem of appearance and reality, despite the terror which lies behind the death figure, present even in the wildest of farces, Ghelderode manages to establish an equilibrium by his instinctive faith in nature and in life. This busy world of lecherous creatures, accepted, entered into, invites man also to accept himself, and to

179

accept life not only as pleasure, but as suffering; not only as ennobling, but frequently as degrading.

"I love this Flemish laughter which contains a grating of teeth," says the King in *Escurial*. Ghelderode's humor is seldom divorced from cruelty, and rarely reflects a rosy outlook; it is instead, as one might expect, the result of lucidity, and arises most frequently from an awareness of man's weaknesses, vices, his ugliness, and stupidity. This is the reason for our laughter at the behavior of such characters as Fernand or Hieronymus, our amusement at the predicament of the bigoted lechers and thieves of Brugelmonde, our delight when a person's name so perfectly embodies his characters: Putrégina, Visquosine, Salivaine, Sodomati, Carnibos. Whether the humor arises from character, situation, or language, we react as observers of the absurd human comedy which, as one of the dwarfs in *Hop, Signor!* observes, "even when it makes us shudder, contains something to make us laugh!"

The same healthy breath of humanism we see in Ghelderode, blows strong in Audiberti's world, a world that, like that of the Belgian author, is poised dramatically between good and evil. Here, however, evil is seen not as the work of the devil, but as the result of the whims of some malevolent deity, or of man's constant frustration in his human condition. It is a world of creatures tormented by love and a vague metaphysical yearning that goes beyond love, but which cannot be satisfied.

Good, on the other hand, is usually expressed in terms of that which is natural. Audiberti is fond of mountains and forests, trees and lakes, peasants and provincials, all that which is part of, or has remained closest to, nature. But man must sooner or later awaken to the realization that he is now separated from his natural realm and dwells outside the Eden that was once his. The peasant Garon in *La Hobereaute*, disguised as a bear with a troupe of itinerant players, describes the history of the human race in his own life:

> At first I was a bear, the animal. Then I became a man. Being man, I let myself be devoured by humanity. I desired money. I bowed to the Cross. I worked for the duke, for the state. Paying diggers and woodsmen, I built the road. . . . Once the road was finished, I wanted to become a bear in the forest, as before. But I had become man. I had become the vassal of God. My bear's head is a wooden head. My claws were made by the shoemaker. I can no longer understand the reeds, the firs.

All men, the dramatist suggests more than once, are more or less God, and if they but knew how, might tap the supernatural that surrounds them. The world we enter here is a magic one in which wonderful transformations, strange metamorphoses, and frightening creations are possible. It is very unlike the world we usually inhabit, and completely dissimilar to that one we see in the drama of the so-called realists, for Audiberti attempts to give a new kind of realism to the theater—or rather a very old kind of realism: the realism of the theater which is, of course, nonrealism, for the theater is not reality. It is what the author calls an "accepted delirium," an "authorized oasis of lies." Upon this oasis, working with themes rather than clear-cut ideas, spinning out brilliant and imaginative dialogue, creating thick-blooded characters, Audiberti builds his amusing, frightening, disconcerting, and not infrequently thought-provoking plays. The danger is that vigor, imagination, lyricism, and rhetoric may take over. On occasion they lead the dramatist to embroider at length upon inessentials, to create superfluous characters or scenes for the pure joy of invention. His too full-blooded creative imagination is perhaps responsible for certain *longueurs* and for the diffuseness of some of his later plays (like *Les Naturels du Bordelais*). Audiberti, like the other avant-garde writers, knows no rules, and although he is generally faithful to such basic tenets of dramatic writing as plot and character, he restricts himself to no genre, and claims that his inspiration has come more from opera than from drama. This can be seen in the lyricism of his works, in the musicality of his dialogue (where interior rhymes are not infrequent), and in his use of song or verse. Indeed, *La Hobereaute* was first published under the title *Opéra parlé* (*Spoken Opera*), and was followed by an opera libretto, *Altanima*.

Audiberti is least successful in plays with a modern setting, for the period pieces are more richly suggestive and possess that poetic aura that only time can give, and which helps us suspend our disbelief, thereby rendering more acceptable the stage magic we witness. *L'Effet Glapion* (*The Glapion Effect*, 1959), admittedly a "vaudeville," borders on the trivial, while the cruel *Les Naturels du Bordelais* (*The Bordelais Natives*, 1953), modern murder mystery of a sadistic Don Juan, falls apart as the puzzling characters are metamorphosed into crickets, hoping thus to escape the pain of being men; but here there is none of that almost tragic inevitability which we feel in *Rhinoceros*, and the metamorphosis seems more a fantastic intrusion than a realistic conclusion. *La Logeuse* (*The Boardinghouse Keeper*, 1954?), is saved by its energetic creation of the title character, Madame Cirqué, mature, strong-willed, intense, mettlesome, animal, yearning to be dominated by a man's will, but apparently condemned to remain unsatisfied. Every male who comes within range, falls under her charm, and finally grovelling at the feet of this modern-day Circe, assumes the role of wife or mistress.

The male counterpart to Mme Cirqué, and perhaps the very man she needs, is found in Audiberti's most successful one-act play *Les Femme du Boeuf* (*The Ox's Women*, played at the Comédie Francaise in 1948).

The prosperous butcher of a town in southern France houses no less than thirty women in his home—daughters, nieces, maids, and so on—and yet he is lonely and unsatisfied, for to come near him is certain death. The Ox, as he is called, weighs 144 kilos, and has killed three wives by sheer force of his being alive. When he goes outside, the sun itself perspires. This man's son, by some ironic twist, is a gentle, effeminate, poetic soul who has gone to live in the mountains as a shepherd, and there, while his father tosses alone in his gigantic bed at night, the son is visited by fairies: all the women of the Ox.

Audiberti's earliest long plays, *Quoat-Quoat* (1946) and *Le Mal court* (*Evil is Abroad,* 1947), are among his most appealing, for despite their bitterness, they are well larded with humor, and possess a unity and a tidiness rarely found in this author. *Quoat-Quoat* is to some extent a satire of 19th century melodrama. In an atmosphere somewhat reminiscent of *H.M.S. Pinafore,* the youthful Amédée sets off on a dangerous governmental mission to Mexico. Before long he has fallen in love with the captain's daughter (against the governmental restrictions controling the actions of secret agents), has stepped outside time for a moment to live his future exploits, and is arrested by the captain for his infringement of the ruling, and condemned to death. The action is incongruous and nightmarish, and we are convinced by the generally farcical treatment of the play that all will end well. Indeed, at the last moment, a mysterious woman passenger reveals that Amédée is not the real secret agent but a decoy, and he is therefore pardoned. But Amédée refuses to live, believing that he must face his own death, because to survive now would be to become someone else; and he runs up on deck before the firing squad. The play does not end here. The good but grim captain, we begin to suspect, is someone more than the captain of a ship —he is perhaps God himself, and his ship a grotesque representation of life's voyage. As the curtain falls, the good Lord raises his hand to annihilate ship and all, returning the universe to primeval emptiness.

Quoat-Quoat combines fantasy and farce with serious issues like death, identity, good, and evil. It is a distant relative of *Godot*, amusing, suggestive, ambiguous, although less so than Beckett's masterpiece.

Le Mal court, first performed in 1947, and revived with Suzanne Flon in 1955, is Audiberti's greatest commercial success. During three rapid acts, in a glittering conventional 18th century atmosphere, the author recounts the awakening of innocence to an awareness of evil. Princess Alarica, about to cross the border of Occident, whose king she is to marry the following day, learns that for political reasons the King has cancelled his marriage contract. After giving herself to a hired agent who had earlier attempted to seduce her in order to give the King an excuse for breaking, Alarica discovers that the night has been a mere diversion for the man. Her trusted governess, she further learns, is a spy for the government of Occident. Antigone-like, she cries out bitterly, "People are tricking everywhere! . . . The world is ignoble." As the play ends, the Princess has learned her lesson and adapts herself to the world, becoming hard and ruthless in order to cope with life and with her role as ruler of the miserable kingdom of Courtelande.

The plays that follow, *La Fête noire* (1948, *Black Feast*, originally published as *La Bête noire, The Black Beast*), and *La Pucelle* (1950, *The Maid*), are already blemished by that diffuseness which is Audiberti's greatest flaw. But they are vigorous, intense, earthy pieces in which the Audibertian preoccupations with good and evil, metamorphosis and identity, reality and illusion, are exposed in a colorful avalanche of words.

La Pucelle is a highly original treatment of the Joan of Arc story, dealing not with the oft-described battles, victories, and trial, but with the identity of Joan as she discovers her role as heroine. At the same time that the tomboyish Joannine leaves home for war, she leaves behind her colorless double Jeannette who marries the boy next door. As the play closes, ten years later, an itinerant theater is presenting a play based upon the events of Joan's life. But their principal actress has defected to a neighboring troupe, and Jeannette is pressed into the role of Jeanne. As she is "burned" at the stake, a strong wind catches fire to her dress, and the peasant Jeannette, like her heroic double Joannine, is burned to death. The theater, we are told, is like a Mass which re-enacts what actually happened and thereby gives it a new reality. Lest we be puzzled by this interplay of identities and realities, the Duchess, herself (like us) a part of life's mystery, warns us that "it isn't the world's business to furnish us answers, but enigmas." Clarity and explanations are not part of life, nor are they part of Audiberti's theater. Only the vitality and mystery of life persist.

In *La Fête noire* the frustrated desire of the strangely attractive but mysteriously unlovable Félicien gives birth to a horrible monster that ravages the countryside, violating and killing young women. Men and the Church (amusingly satirized in the person of Monseigneur Morvellon) join to destroy the beast, but none can face the truth that the beast is a part of man himself, and they kill a goat thinking they have thereby annihilated evil. Félicien, renowned throughout the civilized world for his studies of the monster, is finally destroyed by the monster itself, in the shape of the jealous and angered Lou Desterrat who finds his niece in Félicien's arms, and shoots the couple.

La Fête noire is a difficult play, and its obscurity cannot be ascribed only to the richness with which the characters express themselves. The author fails to make clear the precise origin of his monster, and even leads one to assume that Félicien himself is the beast, while later he allows the pretty young Alice, perhaps more lucid than the others, to assert that all women are the monster. Félicien's error, at any rate, seems to have been that he idolized women, making them something inhumanly perfect and desirable, whereas they are real beings that must be accepted as they are. "Imagination dominates all natures," he claims, "and nothing exists, after all, but useless immensity." The disappointed idealist become monster and nihilist is a familiar figure here, reappearing in the godlike captain of *Quoat-Quoat*, the embittered Princess of *Le Mal court*, the sadistic Don Juan of *Les Naturels du Bordelais*, and the renegade Christian, Lotvy, in *La Hobereaute*. All these characters betray a metaphysical preoccupation, an effort to discover a meaning behind apparent meaninglessness.

Audiberti has stated that, while theater may be both reflection and diversion, it is the former that interests him particularly[7]—which is not to say that his theater is not diverting. But the reflection here, as elsewhere in the avant-garde theater, remains germinal, it is not developed logically, but is expressed thematically with variations and *fioriture* (and one recalls again that Audiberti recognizes the importance of opera in his inspiration). Such obscurity, and the author's reluctance to deliver a message, of course inspire ire in more conservative critics, who say to themselves, like Robert Kemp in his review of *La Hobereaute*, "A respectable effort, but to tell us what?" The critic today, like the public, sits in the theater waiting to be told. The unfortunate Kemp left the performance, his "ears sick from the shouting, and [his] brain in a pulp."[8]

La Hobereaute (1956?; the title refers to a kind of small falcon, *The Hobby*) is one of Audiberti's most ambitious and richly suggestive works, in which the struggle between good and evil is depicted in terms of the conflict between nature and the Church. In a highly flavored Middle Ages (9th century Burgundy) the dying druidic religion, the cult of the oak and the mistletoe, makes a desperate attack on the new religion. La

Hobereaute, a spirit of nature who flies through the air and slips to the bottom of the lake where she sees enthroned "the silence of motionless, dazzling truth," is ordered by the druid priest to marry the hideous and criminal Baron Massacre, rather than the upright, noble, and sensitive warrior Lotvy, whom she loves. Such an unjust marriage, between utter natural purity and absolute corruption, can only bring discredit to the church that sanctions it. Lotvy swears eternal war on such a religion, and turns to burning convents and violating nuns. When he comes to the monastery near the Baron's chateau, where he hopes to fight his enemy and win La Hobereaute for himself, he is captured by the Baron and bound to a tree. There he is killed by one of his own followers who believes he has gone over to the nobles' faction. La Hobereaute, embracing him, is strangled by the jealous Massacre, who then kills himself. Amidst the litter of corpses wanders the spirit of Aldine, Lotvy's sister and La Hobereaute's serving woman, who has drowned herself.

The familiar theme of the obsession with love or desire which renders monstrous, personified by Massacre, is here contrasted to the more idealized love of Lotvy and La Hobereaute. Lotvy, Kemp suggests, may be understood to represent Roman wisdom, a lay wisdom —perhaps wiser than that restrictive sagacity of the Church. Even the Prior of Mont-Wimer is a victim of the struggle between nature and Christianity, and as he sits before his monastery he composes love poems to the woman he left behind.

The precise meaning of *La Hobereaute* is not always clear, but in its total impact it surely suggests that man, torn between good and evil (Lotvy), persecuted in his natural feelings by a malevolent deity or some unjust earthly rule (Massacre, the Church), can now find happiness and unity (union with the nature goddess) only through death. Bound to the tree (the tree of life, the cross of man's suffering), Lotvy can at last be united

with La Hobereaute, for death has released the sprite
and returned her to her former supernatural condition.
She is, in fact, the spirit of the universe, nature personified, and man is her child. Looking at Lotvy dying upon
the tree, La Hobereaute sees both Father and Son, Man
the only measure of the universe: "He is the living,
shrieking tree," she cries, "forever disputed by good and
evil. He personifies man divided."

Audiberti's humanism and pantheism reach full flower
in this play that, in many ways, embodies the virtues
and defects of his theater: a vigor that gives dramatic
accent, but sometimes distracts; an inventiveness that
enriches, colors, and amuses, but not infrequently dif-
fuses; and an ambiguity that is both suggestive and ob-
scuring.

In Audiberti's world we are far indeed from the
"corpsed" universe of Beckett in which "there is no
more nature." If evil and anguish persist, at least Babel
lies some distance down the plain, and we have almost
reached the doors of Eden.

The Threshold of Eden: Georges Schehadé

Even the most optimistic of the experimental playwrights in France today cannot take us into the Garden
of Eden. But Georges Schehadé places us at the thresh-
old, and allows us a glimpse within, for at least some
of his characters are living the innocent existence of
prelapsarian man. His plays have been enthusiastically
greeted by such poets as Supervielle, Michaux, Pichette,
Char, and Breton, and as enthusiastically anathematized
by such reactionary critics as Jean-Jacques Gautier.
They are generally of a loosely-structured, episodic nature, with large groups of characters occupying the
stage in succession. The first three of Schehadé's plays
are constructed in the form of a search, while the fourth
breaks away from the search pattern, but retains other
major characteristics.

Monsieur Bob'le (1936?) is the story of a gentle,

saintly man who must leave his village of Paola Scala to be about his business on some mysterious island. As he returns home finally, he falls ill, and dies in a distant port.

La Soirée des proverbes (1953?, *The Soirée of Proverbs*) recounts the adventures of young Argengeorge who, hearing of a marvellous *soirée* to be held in the middle of the forest at the Quatre-Diamants, follows the guests and seeks admission. But all the guests are aged and have gathered in memory of a night long ago when they were young and idealistic. They fear Argengeorge, his eyes still bright with youth, and it is only with difficulty that he gains admission. He soon realizes that his hopes for a brilliant evening are to be disappointed, for the guests are only caricatures of what they once were, and can never find their real selves again: there will be no *soirée des proverbes*. Suddenly the hunter Alexis arrives. He is none other than Argengeorge when old. Argengeorge, who in this single night has tasted of old age, of life and the disappointments it contains, who knows that faith and hope must die, prefers to die himself. As though they understood each other without speaking, Alexis raises his gun and shoots his young self. And now the *soirée des proverbes* can indeed take place, for Argengeorge has found the secret of remaining young and pure.

Histoire de Vasco (1956?) tells of a timorous barber who is chosen by the General Mirador to carry a message into enemy territory. The General believes a frightened man will succeed because he has a feeling for nuances. Vasco is captured, however, and because he refuses to give correct information, he is killed. He is mourned by Marguerite, an extravagant young girl who had dreamed of a barber hero, and set out in search of him, but failed to recognize him when she came face to face with Vasco.

Les Violettes (1959?) is the tale of Madame Boromée's pension, and how its order is upset by the arrival of the diabolical Professor Kufman who, using the violets that grow in profusion there, carries on scientific experiments aimed at blowing up the world. The professor, however, elopes with a romantic young lady and his work is carried on by Baron Fernagut and the other pensioners, who had originally opposed the mistreatment of the violets, and it is they who in the last scene blow themselves up.

We might say that Schehadé's theater is a theater of seekers, for aside from the peripheral characters like Lieutenant Septembre (*Vasco*) and the Diacre Constantin (*Soirée*), who are seeking other persons, there lies at the center of Schehadé's theater a search for purity which forms his major theme. The protagonist is the hero-saint-poet, whether he be the middle-aged Bob'le, the youthful Argengeorge, or the innocent Vasco, who attempts to find and keep his purity, even in contact with life. In his latest play, the most bitter and at the same time the most comical of his works, Schehadé shows us the charming Baron Fernagut swayed from his innocent love of hens and violets by the sinister Kufman.

The early Monsieur Bob'le is the prototype of the saint, simple, unassuming, confident, otherworldly. When he prays he reveals himself a poet as well:

> Oh my Father! You who are Brightness . . . Memory . . . Intelligence . . . You who are grain and granary . . . rose and gardener . . . You who are seated at Your own right hand! . . . The rose at Your feet is a nocturnal beast . . . the air is Your path.

The poet is he who touches the sources of life and is capable of communicating his feelings to the common man. Monsieur Bob'le's very life has become a poem which is full of meaning and comfort for those with whom he comes in contact—and no one may know him without feeling that he is an unusual being. Only the egotistic, the blind, seem to miss the real meaning of

Monsieur Bob'le. The head doctor in the hospital where he lies dying is so impressed with his own role that he is incapable of seeing anyone else, as, puppet-like, he repeats time and again his pet phrase, "My presence is necessary."

If Monsieur Bob'le's life is a poem, he has not failed to leave a written message also in the form of a little gray notebook called the *Trémandour*. It is a book of proverbs, vague and beautiful, which the people of Paola Scala consult for the answers to their problems, and which they quote to one another.

> He who wears a hat must be more just than other men, for, a priori, he is sinning against the sun and moon.

> Sleep is not only a respite and a pasture for our bodies, it is the perfection of life because it is full of dreams . . . and ageless!

> Sorrow is a blue eye like a grandmother's, that is to say, without youth!

> I would like children to be stubborn, just enough not to be too mobile.

The themes of innocence, purity, youth, and the ideal are implicit in these proverbs, and they are the favorite themes not only of Monsieur Bob'le, but of Georges Schehadé.

Argengeorge in *La Soirée des proverbes* is also the poet who seeks the ideal in life, and desires the diamond-bright purity of youth to endure even in old age, free from distortion or compromise. At the Quatre-Diamants he hopes to find the secret of eternal youth, for he believes he will see there, "figures of life, moving with their keys! . . . With their bones, their mouths, and the bells of good and evil at their ankles. For they are living. . . . Gypsies following forever a profound image." And this profound image is that of themselves when young, an ideal uncorrupted self, which they wish to recapture. One of the old guests explains to Argengeorge how, many years ago, the people now gathered at the Quatre-Diamants had received a letter: "We will meet at Mion, at mid-February, if it snows . . . There will be no *soirée* if there is no snow." Since then they have gathered many times at the same place, now but the shadows of that first night, for they have lost their faith, and their hearts are closed. Only the memory of that night brings them back; they are in search of a dream.

But, Schehadé seems to say, it is only through death that we can return to the first *soirée des proverbes*. As the curtain falls we see this symbolized: "We see through the windows, several drops, then the heavy snowfall of a mysterious winter." Because Argengeorge has chosen death rather than compromise with life, there will be a snowfall, and the *soirée* may take place.

Histoire de Vasco, like *La Soirée des proverbes,* intimates that innocence and youth cannot easily be maintained in contact with life. Vasco is once again the poet, young, innocent, and imaginative. Sergeant Paraz, one of the enemy disguised as a chestnut tree who captures Vasco, gives us his portrait: "Eyes of a child who believes in the wolf, that basket, and then that umbrella to situate him in the zone of innocence. Next to him a loaf of white bread looks like a lamb's turd." Vasco's fear is the symbol of his innocence. Lieutenant Septembre, as he wandered in the forest looking for Vasco, had longed for his youth in similar terms: "How I would like to be afraid, to be emptied of sorrow and disgust." Vasco dies before he can become the hero the General Mirador would make of him, for he must die in order to preserve his innocence, his awareness of nuances. Only those who are on the margin of sanity, like Marguerite's father César or the Diacre Constantin, can preserve their innocence in life. The ideal dog, César reminds us (for he is a dealer in stuffed dogs as well as a savant), is not the frisking beast that gets his paws on everything, but the dead, stuffed animal that is kept stored away in a box and brought out each evening for a stroll.

The world of Schehadé, a world of wonder, of innocence, of poetry and fairy tale, contrasts the pure and young in spirit with the old and corrupt who have lost touch with the poetic truth of childhood. We are far from the colorless, disintegrating universe of Beckett, or the absurd exaggeration of the quotidian we find in Ionesco. Nor does this world resemble the realistic one of Anouilh's *Pièces noires,* or the frothy fantasy of his *Pièces roses.* Anouilh shares the theme of the quest for purity with Schehadé, but Anouilh's heroes and heroines usually assert themselves noisily, shout their message to the uncomprehending members of the facile race, and if they die, they do so willfully, arrogantly. Schehadé's calm heroes are almost overtaken by death. Or rather, their search for purity is a search for death, but the hero is unaware of this until death is imminent.

Contrasting with seriousness of theme is a lightness of tone, for despite the presence of death and disillusionment, Schehadé's characters are intensely comical, because they are transparently human, illogical, and picturesquely exaggerated. Their improbable speech betrays their vices and manias, and almost every peripheral character constitutes a satire of some human foible: avarice, stupidity, prudery, or pride. Each character is clear-cut, well defined, simple, vivid, and intense, a highly theatrical creation which comes forcefully across the footlights.

Each play has a large cast; in *Monsieur Bob'le* there are more than thirty characters. Certain types recur. Next to the innocent hero is the half-mad man who feels at home with nature. Contrasted to them are the self-important, the blind, the cruel, and thoughtless. But the emphasis is always on the poetic world of youth and innocence which we have lost, and which the author would reveal to us subtly through his symbols, always beautiful, often vague, suggesting but the shadow of a lost reality.

This world is a fanciful one, unlike our own, but not unfamiliar—a world similar to that of childhood in which generals and lieutenants strut about in colorful costumes with clanking swords and spurs, where trees move and talk, where a man has conversations with ravens, and where old ladies foretell the future by looking into a well. It is a world in which the brotherhood of men with animals and objects is more than once suggested. César is on good terms with turkeys but has been insulted by a sly rooster; and he is as careful of his stuffed dogs as if they were alive. Madame Hilboom, an old peasant from Vasco's village, has frightened the apricots of Père Rondu, and after eating them she regrets it: "I shouldn't have eaten the apricots . . . but pray for the rotting fruit . . . an oremus for each apricot . . . like at church on Sunday." Vasco, searching for Monsieur Bertrand, fears that he has missed the river during the night: "Perhaps the river crossed me . . . and went on its way." There is life and personality in nature breathing about us at all times, if we can but perceive it. Schehadé has a decided preference for outdoor settings, and particularly for woods and forests. Even when the characters are inside, the outdoors is evoked. *La Soirée des proverbes* opens with a reference to night and day appearing in the fields together, and closes with a magic snowfall.

The dramatic quality of Schehadé's plays largely lies in their appeal to our inborn desire to imitate what we once did intuitively. Moreover, they reveal to us the drama of our own struggle with life—compromise opposed to integrity. The search for the ideal is one of the basic myths of mankind, and Schehadé has succeeded in presenting it in an original way. A metamorphosis has taken place, and the myth is turned into what Barrault calls "palpable poetry."

194

In addition to such palpable poetry, or rather integrated with it, is the poetry of language. Schehadé's language is particularly rich in imagery and personification, through which the poet gives us a fresh perception of reality, suggests new dimensions, reveals new relationships of man to man and man to things. Animals and objects form one brotherhood with man. The poetry of these plays frequently combines clarity of image and originality of expression with a certain ambiguity. Like the other authors we have studied, Schehadé prefers to suggest rather than state outright. Through words which, as T. S. Eliot has said in another context, "strain, / Crack and sometimes break under the burden, / Under the tension, slip, slide, perish, / Decay with imprecision," he attempts to reveal the core of life. We are expected to absorb this poetry through some non-rational process, for Schehadé gives scant credit to ideas, and would agree with Giraudoux that "those who wish to understand in the theatre, are those who do not understand the theatre." Argengeorge, seated at the inn in the first act of *La Soirée des proverbes*, is reading a huge book entitled *The Grammatical Fountain*. When President Domino inquires as to its contents, Argengeorge replies:

> *Argengeorge.* A treatise on the emancipation of words. Ever since people have been marrying them, at church or at the courthouse, by pen or pencil, they have been aspiring to more consciousness, to the happy life of birds and lions.
> *President Domino.* And ideas, what becomes of them in this . . . revolution?
> *Argengeorge.* They drag behind like muzzled animals.
> *President Domino.* Then ideas are . . . little poodles?
> *Argengeorge.* In my opinion, less than that, sir.

We see in the plays of Schehadé this emancipation of words. The poet attempts to give new meanings and a new consciousness to them by divorcing them from old contexts and giving them their liberty. If ideas then become difficult to grasp, it is unimportant to the poet, for he feels that truth and life are to be found through some intuitive process, in the immediate perception of beauty and of the relationship of ourselves to the world, to life, to that very beauty we perceive.

This nonrational approach is of course at the base of the criticism of such reviewers as Jean-Jacques Gautier, who, reviewing *La Soirée des proverbes* in *Le Figaro* (Feb. 1, 1954), allowed himself this fanciful comment: "It's clear as a bucket of dust poured into a tub of India ink on a moonless night, in the middle of an endless tunnel whose lights have gone out as the result of a short circuit." To which Max-Pol Fouchet supplies a reply in *Carrefour* (Feb. 3): "We understand *La Soirée des proverbes*. Here, upon the stage, is the inner gesture by which the poet brings up to daylight the fruit of his deep sea fishing. It is a question of a *mystery*." And this is precisely the reason that the plays of Schehadé cannot be seized in their entirety by the rational faculties. Their chief appeal is to that part of the personality to which myths speak their universal language, and where to appeal to reason is to reduce the myth to dust.

Our so-called dramatists of Babel also approach reality in a nonrational manner, but their disintegrating universe, where men can no longer communicate and are dominated by lifeless objects, is very different from the Eden glimpsed in Schehadé's theater, which suggests that life is more than mere appearance, that it may be for everyone, as it is for his heroes, a constant if desperate search for truth, for innocence, for youth, and for the ideal.

6

Conclusion

"Nothing changes less than the avant-garde," Anouilh has said, expressing at the same time surprise at the originality of *Godot* and *The Chairs*.[1] In a certain sense, of course, he is right, for since its beginnings the avant-garde has constituted a revolt against bourgeois ways of thinking and living, and has sought means of expression that are original, surprising, and amusing. Today's avant-garde broadens that revolt by refusing not only the bourgeois world, but the entire bourgeois cosmos, and it enriches theatrical expression by introducing various imaginative new devices into its plays. But such is the variety among the writers themselves, that it is difficult to speak of them as a group. Gradual dehumanization in Beckett's theater is matched by the slow humanization of Ionesco's, verbal aridity in Adamov by verbal brilliance in Audiberti, excessive pessimism in Beckett by gentle optimism in Schehadé, reduction of plot in Beckett or Ionesco by diffuseness of plot in Audiberti, complexity of very few characters in Vauthier by simplicity of very many characters in Schehadé, emphasis of cliché in Ionesco by lyricism in Genêt. But while there are profound differences among these writers, at the same time there is a certain common purpose which unites them spiritually.

This purpose has been to destroy the now decadent forms of realism and naturalism which, despite the rebellions of earlier vanguards (Maeterlinck, Strindberg, Yeats, O'Neill, the Expressionists, etc.), continue to dominate our commercial, and in some instances our art, theater. In their place the avant-garde of 1950–60 would place something more vital which, like the great drama of the past (be it realistic or not), attempts to reveal man's situation both as a member of society and as an inhabitant of a universe. Naturalistic theater is based upon the assumption that the theater should imitate life. Our authors feel that the theater should reveal life, but that it can do this best by some indirect method rather than by slavish imitation. Occasionally we may have the impression we are witnessing a photographically real scene, for example, some of the clichés of *The Bald Soprano*. A few moments of attention, however, convince us that this is indeed far from realism, and that the author has employed a gross exaggeration of reality that amuses us and reveals some truth about people and society.

In moving away from realism, most of our authors have moved toward some primitive kind of spectacle, adopting the form or spirit of some nonliterary theater, medieval farce, circus, music hall in the case of Beckett or Ghelderode, the guignol with Ionesco, ceremony in the theater of Genêt, and ballet or pantomime in Adamov's. The result has been a theater that reaches us largely through our senses. And even when the drama is still literary to a marked degree, as is the case with Audiberti and Schehadé, words are used in a manner far different from that of the realistic theater, and they hit us at a level deeper than that of waking consciousness and logic. At the same time that these plays carry an emotional impact, they seem, if not inarticulate, at least frequently obscure. This very obscurity, resulting now from form, now from language, now from the nature of the material involved, causes us to ask questions. Unlike the realistic theater, which may leave us intellectually satisfied, the avant-garde theater tends to

198

stimulate thought. Whether we have what Walter Kerr calls "busy minds," or not, it is difficult to leave a performance of *Endgame, Escurial,* or *The Balcony* without wondering what the author was attempting to say. In a naturalistic play it is usually quite clear, and the lazy playgoer is often satisfied simply to pronounce it a good or bad performance, an interesting or dull play, and let it go at that. But even the lazy playgoer cannot dismiss *Godot* as an interesting or tedious play without wondering what there is that does not meet the eye on first contact. The reason for this is that a realistic play usually tells a story, or investigates a situation, using characters which are recognizable, and when we come away we feel we have witnessed a "slice of life," or have been told a suspenseful story, or have learned that birth control is good or bad, or education is necessary for the masses, or that money is evil. But when we leave *Godot* (or almost any play of Beckett, Ionesco, Adamov, Genêt, Tardieu, or Vauthier) we may very well ask ourselves: Have we seen a slice of life? Obviously not. Have we been told a story? Frequently not. Have we learned a lesson? Hardly. If none of this has happened in the theater, then what has happened? If the theater is to have any dimension at all, certainly the simple theatrical experience, the thrilling of our viscera, is not enough. There must be something beyond it. In most serious theater there is. In the avant-garde plays it is not always so easy to find. Because of this, we assume, not necessarily during the performance, but almost inevitably after it, a somewhat analytic attitude that gives us coolness and distance. If the play has failed to move us, to dominate us with its magic to the extent that even during the performance we remain absolutely cold, then, it seems to me, it has failed, no matter how good it may be as philosophy, poetry, or literature. The theater, as Ionesco has remarked, is the theater, and the avant-garde drama marks a return to the theater as theater, in which the nontheatrical elements are secondary to the wound inflicted by the drama itself. This drama is composed of characters representative of, but not necessarily imitating, real men, in a situation that is real but not necessarily realistic, presented on a stage frankly accepted as such and aware of its generic peculiarities. Such a definition might well apply to other ages of world drama, but it does not apply to post-Ibsen drama in the West, and stresses the fact that the avant-garde has not completely rejected earlier conceptions of theater, and is in some regards more radical (in the etymological sense of return to roots) than the more conventional dramatists.

If this drama keeps us at some distance by its obscurity and promise of a deeper meaning lying below the surface, it draws us to it because it forms, however exaggerated or farfetched, a picture of our own human situation. Despite the nihilism of such plays as *Endgame* or *Krapp's Last Tape*—which after all forms the backbone of a great deal of the literature and philosophy of our day—the avant-garde dramatists have won a relatively large audience throughout the world. They have succeeded in their most effective plays, in embodying their ideas in a piece of dramatic writing without employing the explicit method of the pulpit or the platform.

If a writer sets out to reveal "Man's Condition," he seriously risks ending up with a dead abstraction. The avant-garde dramatists have not always successfully avoided the trap. The early Adamov plays are dry, lifeless productions in which The Man and The Mother, for example, go through the meaningless motions of life. Most of the authors we have discussed, however, avoid the pitfall because their ends are not didactic, and their method is not an explicit one. Hamm and Clov are no more specifically Man than they are God and Christ, or simply two derelicts, Hamm and Clov. Because of their actions, because of their words, the ambiguity of their situation, we are tempted to think of

200

them as representing something more than they appear to be. The same is true of most of the plays at what I have called the Babel pole, although none of them, it seems to me, have achieved the rich suggestiveness of Beckett's works or of those of the later Ionesco.

It is well to remember that French drama has been more turned toward the abstract than has the English. The great age of English drama gave birth to works with a popular appeal characterized by vigor, color, and variety of characters. The great age of French theater was the age of Racine, a patrician theater characterized by restraint, balance, a noticeable lack of color, and few but exemplary characters.[2] The avant-garde theater continues such a tradition, using, of course, many new techniques, and presupposing an entirely different world from that ordered one for which Racine was writing. It is natural then to expect the lack of order to be reflected in the form of the play itself. It is no longer the rational world of Descartes and Louis XIV that we see reflected, but the irrational world of Freud, Hitler, existentialism, and the atom bomb.

It seems significant that the writers we have placed closest to Babel are not only most pessimistic, they are the most unconventional of the avant-garde writers. It would appear that the further we get from Babel, and the closer we come to Eden, the more traditional the form of the play becomes. Ghelderode's dramas already have more shape than those of Beckett, Ionesco, or Tardieu, his approach to plot and character is more like what we are accustomed to. By the time we reach Audiberti and Schehadé the major obstacle to popular acceptance seems to lie not so much in their abject pessimism or in peculiarities of structure, characterization, or plot, as it does in language. The obscurity of Ionesco and Beckett may be partly ascribed to their rejection of the common dramatic categories, but with Schehadé and Audiberti obscurity often arises from an overexuberance of language. One is, as sometimes with the exuberant Christopher Fry, overcome by the richness and profusion of verbal invention, and it is this, as well as the subtlety or ineffability of the ideas treated, which impedes understanding.

Language is, of course, our principal means of communication, and by attacking and undermining it as they have, the Babel-writers of the avant-garde remain faithful to their convictions regarding the meaninglessness of man's place in an empty universe and the lack of any rationale in life or in the theater. Just as there are no rules governing existence or semantics, there are no rules governing the making of a play.

This tends to confirm what I said earlier: that the unconventional shape taken by the majority of avantgarde plays is a result of attempting to find a more faithful reflection of the content in the form itself. It is not, as some critics would like to believe, a simple avidity for novelty.

Of the various techniques employed by the avantgarde, the most striking is perhaps that of using concrete visual elements to suggest a metaphysical bias. Anything visible on the stage may be pressed into service, from the décor (the tree in *Godot*, the two windows in *Endgame*, the many doors in *The Chairs*, the handless clock in *La Parodie*) and costumes (the hats in *Godot*, shoddy old-fashioned clothes in *Jacques*, Lili's changes of costume in *La Parodie*), to the hand props (Lucky's suitcase, Pozzo's whip, the Fighting Personage's typewriter, the messy piles of paper in *L'Invasion*), and the very movements of the characters (the dance in *Bada*, the stiffness in *La Parodie*, the position of Yeux Verts on the inverted basin at the end of *Deathwatch*).

Color, light, and shadow also aid in establishing the mood of the play; grayness in *Endgame*, the black and white of *La Parodie*, dark shadows in *Escurial*, décor of light in *The Killer*. Sound seconds the other concrete devices: whistles in *La Grande et la petite manoeuvre*,

Act without words I, and *Endgame;* bells, bagpipes, and music throughout the plays of Ghelderode; sounds of machinery and life in *Le Personnage combattant.*

Again Audiberti and Schehadé do not employ such devices with such frequency as the Babel-writers. The use of sound, color, light, props, and décor, are of course common in realistic drama, but there their purpose is most frequently to mirror life, to give a more real feeling to setting or movement. Occasionally an object will be used symbolically. In the avant-garde theater these techniques have almost become a new convention, so frequently are they employed. The concrete object has to some extent replaced the audible word as a means of communication, for where one language has broken down a new one has been devised to take its place. Again, the Eden-oriented writers, not having renounced language, do not need to depend so strongly upon the visible. As a matter of fact, the Babel-oriented writers have not entirely renounced language either. It is one of the elements of the dramatist's trade, and they could not do without it. But they do attempt to call our attention to the weaknesses and inadequacies of our language, and in doing so depend upon it for many of their comic effects, as well as for the connotative power of words so important in poetry. But their use of words is often a nonlogical, associative one, in which ideas reach us not as clearly-organized propositions, but as suggestive clusters in a sort of thematic arrangement, somewhat similar to a musical composition. This is most obviously true in the works of Tardieu and Vauthier, but the method is employed by most of the other avant-garde dramatists as well. Such a method tacitly criticizes language for a lack of precision and at the same time concedes to it a certain subversive power.

The refusal to use words as a logical instrument tends to restore the play to its place in the theater: as a theatrical experience that reflects or reveals life but cannot either define or explain it as, say philosophy might attempt to do. Words can neither sum up life, nor can they successfully sum up the meaning of a poem or a myth, because that meaning is inherent in the structure of the totality and the relationship of components. As a play approaches poetry and myth, and the substrata of life itself, it becomes more difficult to say exactly what it is about. The critic can only attempt to elucidate some of the problems involved, offer a partial interpretation, and then send his reader back to the theater, which is the only place that the play can have its full meaning. This is particularly true of the avant-garde drama, since it is largely nonliterary and depends not infrequently upon the strictly theatrical aspects of drama.

Character and plot are usually simplified and sometimes even overlooked. But the characters range from the cold abstractions of Adamov, through the elemental figures of the early Ionesco, to the caricatures of Schehadé and the many-dimensioned creation in Vauthier's *Personnage combattant*. Plot may be reduced to a simple situation, as in many of the Babel-oriented plays, which are generally short, or it may be developed more conventionally as in the longer works of Ghelderode, Audiberti, and Schehadé. Circularity of plot is used notably by Beckett, Ionesco, and Genêt with specific intent, and sometimes for comic effect. The most experimental in this respect, as in others, are the dramatists clustered about the Tower of Babel. The experimentation of those writers who hover near the gates of Eden has been largely confined to linguistic audacity and rejection of the "message" as part of a serious play.

Perhaps what is most characteristic of all the writers we have discussed, whether from one extreme or the other, is their mingling of the serious and the comic. Almost half a century ago Apollinaire pointed out that henceforth it would be impossible to bear a play which did not oppose the tragic to the comic.

For there is such energy in humanity today and in contemporary letters, that the greatest misfortune appears to have a *raison d'être*, and may be seen not only from the viewpoint of benevolent irony which allows us to laugh, but even from the viewpoint of true optimism which consoles us and allows hope to grow.[3]

Such a mingling of the tragic and comic may also very well be a reflection of the nondogmatic stand taken by the writers of the avant-garde, typified so well by Ionesco's rejection of all tyrannies, whether they be of the spirit or of the body. In a universe without absolutes tragedy is impossible. In such a universe pure comedy is no longer possible either, for man seems to belong nowhere, is the constituent of no hierarchy, either divine or social. Man examines himself as a peculiar, suffering animal in the zoölogical garden of the world, and the result is often amusing. But when he turns to the infinities that surround him, the result is disquieting. Precisely because the dramatists of the avant-garde usually see man not only in a horizontal context, but in a vertical one as well, they blend the amusing with the disquieting. Those who are the most hopelessly pessimistic and the most clearly "meta-physical" are often the most laughable, perhaps because their pessimism leaves them no recourse but laughter. Pessimism, like a double negative, can after all negate itself into something resembling an affirmative: if everything is so futile and meaningless, and yet life is all we have, we may as well make the best of it we can, laughing not only at the ridiculous spirit of seriousness of others, but at our own disillusionment.

Obviously this bitter, if diverting, lucidity is not every man's cup of tea. It is doubtful that the avant-garde theater will ever become a popular theater in the sense that Broadway shows and the French boulevard theater are popular. It is no more the "theater of our times" than musical comedy is. Its audience is relatively small, but extremely wide-awake, and is growing at a rather surprising rate. Where ten years ago Ionesco could not find more than a few stragglers to play to for several evenings, he is now performed in one of the French national theaters, and in New York, both on and off Broadway, as well as in little theaters across the country. Genêt has become a box office success in Paris and New York, and Beckett draws favorable comment on both sides of the Atlantic. In Washington, Theater Arts Research, Inc., and its Market Playhouse have been founded to study methods of acting and production suitable to the plays of the avant-garde. One begins to wonder whether a theater that has become so respectable, and has been sanctioned by satire from the pen of Anouilh, deserves any longer to be called avant-garde!

Lou Bruder calls the avant-garde a "swansong of bourgeois society."[4] If this is so, it is a song which has lasted for at least a decade, and if we count its roots in the anti-bourgeois theater of Jarry, it has gone on for a good sixty years or more. But the bourgeois are hard to kill, and their spirit may well outlast (by several millennia) the avant-garde theater, which rather than a swansong is a savage attack on the eternal bourgeois spirit.

It seems sensible to look upon the avant-garde theater not as the answer to all the ills of modern drama, but as another adventure in the theater, a new effort to revitalize a theater largely dominated for over sixty years by realism, naturalism and the thesis play: a return to primitive sources, a search for new techniques, a challenge to contemporary drama to examine itself, to seek new frontiers. The influence of these writers can be felt already in the young dramatists writing today, a Gatti or an Arrabal in France, Gelber and Albee in the United States, Pinter in England. Whether the avant-garde drama survives in its present form for many years or not, it will have played an important role in renewing western drama at mid-twentieth century. And we may

206

be sure that, within another generation or two a new courageous and outrageous drama will spring up to replace it, rebelling against whatever new conventions it may have created.

Appendix A:
Metteurs en Scène
of the Avant-Garde

THE FOLLOWING directors contributed greatly to the success of the avant-garde theater by their courageous devotion to its ideals, and their skill and imagination in mounting the plays mentioned after their names.

Roger Blin. *La Parodie* (1952), *En attendant Godot* (1953), *Fin de partie* (1957), *Les Nègres* (1959), *La Dernière bande* (1959).

Jean-Louis Barrault. *La Soirée des proverbes* (1954), *Histoire de Vasco* (1956), *Le Personnage combattant* (1956), *Rhinocéros.* (1960).

Roger Planchon. *Le Professeur Taranne* (1953), *Le Sens de la marche* (1953), *Paolo Paoli* (1957).

Jacques Polieri. *La Jeune fille à marier* (1953), *Une Voix sans personne* (1956), *L'A.B.C. de notre vie* (1959), *Rhythme à trois temps* (1959).

Jean Le Poulain. *Barabbas* (1950), *Magie rouge* (1951), *La Hobereaute* (1958).

Andre Reybaz. *Quoat-Quoat* (1946), *Fastes d'enfer* (1949), *Le Capitaine Bada* (1952), *Mademoiselle Jaïre* (1953).

Jean-Marie Serreau. *La Grande et la petite manoeuvre* (1950), *Tous contre tous* (1953), *Amédée* (1954).

Jean Vilar. *L'Invasion* (1950), *Nucléa* (1952), *La Nouvelle Mandragore* (1952).

Georges Vitaly. *Les Epiphanies* (1947), *Le Mal court* (1947), *La Fête noire* (1948), *Pucelle* (1950), *Monsieur Bob'le* (1951), *Les Naturels du Bordelais* (1953).

Appendix B:
Avant-Garde Dramatists in English

ADAMOV, ARTHUR

As We Were. In *Evergreen Review,* Vol. I, No. 4. Grove
Press, 1957.
Paolo Paoli. London: Calder, 1960.
Ping-Pong. Grove Press, 1959.
Taranne. In *Four French Comedies,* Putnam, 1960.

BECKETT, SAMUEL

Endgame. Grove Press, 1958.
Krapp's Last Tape and Other Dramatic Pieces. Grove
Press, 1960. (Contains: *Krapp's Last Tape, All That
Fall, Embers, Act Without Words I* and *II.*)
Waiting for Godot. Grove Press, 1954.

GENÊT, JEAN

The Balcony. Grove Press, 1958.
The Blacks. Grove Press, 1960.
The Maids and Deathwatch. Grove Press, 1954.

GHELDERODE, MICHEL DE

Christopher Columbus. In *Tulane Drama Review,* March,
1959.
Escurial. In *From the Modern Repertoire,* Vol. V (edited
by Eric Bentley), Doubleday, 1957.
Seven Plays. Hill and Wang, 1960. (Contains: *The Women
at the Tomb, Barrabas, Three Actors and Their Drama,*

Pantagleize, The Blind Men, Chronicles of Hell, Lord Halewyn.)

IONESCO, EUGÈNE

Four Plays. Grove Press, 1958. (Contains: *The Bald Soprano, The Lesson, Jack, The Chairs.*)

The Killer and Other Plays. Grove Press, 1960. (Contains: *Improvisation or The Shepherd's Chameleon, Maid to Marry, The Killer.*)

The Rhinoceros. Grove Press, 1960.

Three Plays. Grove Press, 1958. (Contains: *Amédée, The New Tenant, Victims of Duty.*)

Notes

Chapter 1.

[1] Roger Shattuck, *The Banquet Years* (New York: Harcourt, Brace & Co., 1958), p. 19.

[2] *Théâtre Populaire*, May 1, 1956, p. 41.

[3] *Evergreen Review*, Vol. I, No. 4.

[4] Eric Bentley, *The Playwright as Thinker* (New York: Meridian Books, 1955), p. 208.

[5] Georges Pillement, *Anthologie du Théâtre Francais Contemporain* (Paris: Le Bélier, 1945), Vol. I, p. 22.

[6] Script of an interview, "Art-Anti-Art," for the BBC Third Programme, Jan. 5, 1960.

[7] Mr. Brunius speaks of "Two by Ribemont-Dessaignes, four by Tzara, two by Breton and Soupault . . . two by Aragon, one by Aragon and Breton, and two by Vitrac." To these we may add the plays of Raymond Roussel, Picasso's *Desire Caught by the Tail*, and several impressive works by Georges Neveux, which have never received the recognition they deserve. Many of the plays of the dada and surrealist writers are impossible to come by, and for discussion of them I am indebted to Mr. Brunius' script as well as to the introduction to M. Pillement's *Anthologie*.

[8] *Cahiers de la Compagnie Madeleine Renaud Jean-Louis Barrault*, nos. 22–23, p. 47.

Chapter 2.

[1] "The Point is Irrelevance," *Nation*, April 14, 1956.

[2] "Siete Notas sobre *Esperando a Godot*," *Primer Acto*, no. 1, April, 1957.

[3] "*Waiting for Godot*: A Biblical Appraisal," *Religion in Life*, Fall, 1959.

[4] "Beckett's Letters on *Endgame*," *Village Voice*, March 19, 1958.

[5] J. C. Trewin in *Illustrated London News*, April 20, 1957.

[6] "Beckett and Ionesco," *Hudson Review*, Summer, 1958.

213

[7] *Saturday Review,* Oct. 27, 1956.
[8] Georges Belmont, *Arts,* April 1, 1957.
[9] "Beckett: Style and Desire," *Nation,* Nov. 10, 1956.
[10] "Beckett's Dying Gladiators," *Commonweal,* Oct. 26, 1956.
[11] "The Comedy of Samuel Beckett: 'Something old, something new . . .'" *Yale French Studies,* No. 23.
[12] *Village Voice,* March 19, 1958.
[13] *Le Figaro,* April 23, 1956.

CHAPTER 3.

[1] Jacques Brenner, "La vie est un songe," *Cahiers des Saisons,* No. 15.
[2] Georges Lerminier, "Clés pour Ionesco," *Théâtre d'aujourd'hui,* Sept.–Oct., 1957.
[3] "The Metaphysical Farce: Beckett and Ionesco," *French Review,* Feb., 1959.
[4] *Hudson Review,* Summer, 1958.
[5] "The Tragedy of Language," *Tulane Drama Review,* Spring, 1960.
[6] "Ionesco and the Comic of Absurdity," *Yale French Studies,* No. 23.

CHAPTER 4.

[1] *Arts,* Jan. 20, 1960.
[2] "Le Théâtre aux Enfers," *Cahiers de la Compagnie Madeleine Renaud Jean-Louis Barrault,* nos. 22–23, May, 1958.
[3] *Philosophy in a New Key,* pp. 152–153.
[4] See, for example, Eric Fromm, *The Forgotten Language.*
[5] *The Burning Fountain,* p. 159.
[6] Ruby Cohn, *op. cit.*
[7] J. Doubrovsky, *op. cit.*
[8] Rosette Lamont, *op. cit.*
[9] Edward A. Wright, *Understanding Today's Theatre* (Englewood Cliffs, N.J.: Prentice-Hall, Inc., 1959). Throughout this chapter Professor Wright's excellent handbook to the theater serves as a guide to the traditional ideas of what theater should or should not be.
[10] *New York Times,* June 1, 1958.
[11] Quoted in Gouhier, *L'Oeuvre Théâtrale,* p. 64.
[12] I am essentially in agreement here with John Gassner, as he expresses himself in *Form and Idea in Modern Theatre* (New York: Dryden Press, 1956), pp. 190–191: "However greatly indebted the playwright . . . may be to his own theatrical imagination and that of his stage director, he will need language. The art of the mime, the subtleties of stage movement, the most expressive scenery and stage lighting, all technical and histrionic skills, may well be deplored if they should tend to reduce the artist of words to a cipher in the theater."
[13] *The Playwright as Thinker* (New York: Meridian Books, 1955), p. 262. The preceding brief quote is also from Bentley, describing Diebold's attitude, *Ibid.,* p. 173.

[14] *Théâtre*, Vol. II, Gallimard. This volume contains an enlightening discussion of his theater by Adamov.

[15] *Les Bonnes, Introduction*, pp. 12–13. (A Sceaux, chez J.-J. Pauvert, 1954)

[16] See Sartre's discussion of this problem in *Saint Genêt*, p. 172, *passim.*

[17] The chronology of *Deathwatch* and *The Maids* is pointed out in a note of the Evergreen edition, p. 101.

[18] Roderick MacArthur, "Kaleidoscope," *Theatre Arts*, Jan., 1950.

[19] This tomb, we are told, is built in La Vallée de los Caïdos, obviously a reference to Franco's monument. In *Arts* (May 1, 1957) Genêt tells us: "My point of departure was situated in Spain, the Spain of Franco, and the revolutionary who castrates himself is all the republicans when they admitted their defeat."

[20] Colin Mason, *Spectator*, May 3, 1957.

[21] T. C. Worsley, *New Statesman and Nation*, April 27, 1957.

CHAPTER 5.

[1] Quoted by Robin Skelton, *The Poetic Pattern* (Berkeley: University of California Press, 1956), p. 172.

[2] "Le Théâtre de Babel," *Théâtre de France*, No. IV, p. 25.

[3] Preface to *Le Personnage combattant*, p. 11.

[4] "A Poet's Progress: Henri Pichette," *French Review*, Dec., 1958, p. 111.

[5] *Ibid.*, p. 119.

[6] Jean Francis, *Michel de Ghelderode, dramaturge des pays de par deça* (Brussels: Labor, 1949), p. 112.

[7] *Arts*, 24–30, June, 1959.

[8] *Le Monde*, Sept. 25–Oct. 1, 1958.

CHAPTER 6.

[1] "Du Chapitre des *Chaises*," *Le Figaro*, April 23, 1956.

[2] This is, of course, an oversimplification, but in its general lines what I have said is true. There are certainly colorful passages in Racine, and great individual characters, just as there are some dead abstractions and dry spots in Elizabethan drama.

[3] Preface to *Les Mamelles de Tirésias* (Paris: Editions du Bélier, 1946), p. 15.

[4] "Le Théâtre de Babel," *Théâtre de France*, Vol. VI.

Selected Bibliography

For avant-garde plays in English, consult Appendix B. The following bibliography is not exhaustive, but includes works consulted, works quoted, and works considered most valuable. Entries are numbered for the purpose of cross referencing within the bibliography.

GENERAL

1. Albérès, René-Marill. *L'Aventure intellectuelle du XXe siècle*. Paris, Albin Michel, 1959.
2. Anouilh, Jean. "Du chaptire des *Chaises*," *Le Figaro*, April 23, 1956.
3. Apollinaire, Guillaume. *Les Mamelles de Tirésias*. Paris, Editions du Bélier, 1946.
4. Artaud, Antonin. *The Theater and Its Double*. New York, Grove Press, 1958.
5. Balakian, Anna. *Surrealism: The Road to the Absolute*. New York, Noonday Press, 1959.
6. Beigbeder, Marc. *Le Théâtre en France depuis la libération*. Paris, Bordas, 1959.
7. Bentley, Eric. *The Playwright as Thinker*. New York, Meridian Books, 1955.
8. Bishop, Thomas. *Pirandello and the French Theater*. New York, New York University Press, 1960.
9. Blau, Herbert. "Meanwhile Follow the Bright Angels," *Tulane Drama Review*, Sept., 1960.
10. Bruder, Lou. "Le Théâtre de Babel," *Théâtre de France*, Vol. VI.
11. Brunius, Jacques. "We Called our Hippopotamus 'It's

Toasted,' " BBC script, broadcast Wednesday, January 6, 1960.

12. *Cahiers de la Compagnie Madeleine Renaud Jean-Louis Barrault*, vols. 22–23: "Antonin Artaud et le théâtre de notre temps."

13. Chiari, Joseph. *The Contemporary French Theatre, The Flight From Naturalism.* New York, Macmillan Co., 1959.

14. Cocteau, Jean. *Théâtre*, vols. I, II. Paris, Grasset, 1957.

15. Dort, Bernard. "Sur une avante-garde: Adamov et quelques autres," *Théâtre d'aujourd'hui*, Sept.–Oct., 1957.

16. Dumur, Guy. "Les Poètes au théâtre," *Théâtre de France*, IV.

17. Duvignaud, Jean. "Au-delà du langage," *Théâtre de France*, IV.

18. Esslin, Martin. "The Theatre of the Absurd," Garden City, N.Y., Anchor Books, 1961.

19. Fergusson, Francis. *The Idea of a Theater.* Garden City, N.Y., Doubleday, 1953.

20. Fowlie, Wallace. *Age of Surrealism.* n.p., Swallow Press, and William Morrow and Co., Inc., 1950.

21. ———. *Dionysus in Paris.* New York, Rinehart, 1951.

22. Fromm, Eric. *The Forgotten Language.* New York, Rinehart, 1951.

23. Gassner, John. *Form and Idea in Modern Theatre.* New York, Dryden Press, 1956.

24. ———. *The Theatre in Our Times.* New York, Crown Publishers, Inc., 1954.

25. Gouhier, Henri. *L'Oeuvre théâtrale.* Paris, Flammarion, 1958.

26. Grossvogel, David. *The Self-Conscious Stage in Modern French Drama.* New York, Columbia University Press, 1958.

27. Guicharnaud, Jacques. *Modern French Theatre From Giraudoux to Beckett.* New Haven, Yale University Press, 1961.

28. Hobson, Harold. *The French Theatre of Today.* London, Harrap, 1953.

29. Ionesco, Eugène. "There is no Avant-garde Theatre." *Evergreen Review*, Vol. 1, No. 4.

30. Jarry, Alfred. *Ubu enchaîné.* Paris, Fasquelle Editeurs, 1953.

31. ———. *Ubu roi*. Paris, Fasquelles Editeurs, 1958.
32. Kerr, Walter. *How Not to Write a Play*. New York, Simon and Schuster, 1955.
33. Langer, Susanne K. *Philosophy in a New Key*. Cambridge, Mass., Harvard University Press, 1942.
34. Lalou, René. *Le Théâtre en France depuis 1900*. Paris, Presses Universitaires de France, 1951.
35. Lumley, Frederick. *Trends in Twentieth Century Drama*. Fair Lawn, N.J., Essential Books, 1956.
36. MacArthur, Roderick. "Kaleidoscope," *Theatre Arts*, Jan., 1950.
37. Mauriac, Claude. *L'Alittérature contemporaine*. Paris, Albin Michel, 1958.
38. Murdoch, Iris. *Sartre, Romantic Rationalist*. New Haven, Yale University Press, 1959.
39. Neveux, Georges. *Théâtre*. Paris, Julliard, 1946.
40. ———. *Zamore, suivi de Plainte contre inconnu*. Paris, La Table Ronde, 1953.
41. Oxenhandler, Neal. *Scandal and Parade, the Theater of Jean Cocteau*. New Brunswick, N.Y., Rutgers University Press, 1957.
42. Paris, Jean. "The Clock Struck Twenty-Nine," *Reporter*, Oct. 4, 1956.
43. Picasso, Pablo. *Desire Caught by the Tail*. New York, Philosophical Library, 1948.
44. Pillement, Georges. *Anthologie du théâtre français contemporain*, Vol. I. Paris, Le Bélier, 1945.
45. Raglan, Fitz Roy Richard Somerset. *The Hero*. London, Watts and Co., 1949.
46. Roussel, Raymond. *La Poussière de soleils*. Paris, Alphonse Lemerre, 1927.
47. Shattuck, Roger. *The Banquet Years*. New York, Harcourt, Brace and Co., 1958.
48. Skelton, Robin. *The Poetic Pattern*. Berkeley and Los Angeles, University of California Press, 1956.
49. *Théâtre de France*, vols. IV, VI.
50. *Théâtre populaire*, No. 18 (May 1, 1956), "Du côté de l'avant-garde."
51. Tzara, Tristan. *La Fuite*. Paris, Gallimard, 1947.
52. Valency, Maurice. "Flight into Lunacy," *Theatre Arts*, Aug., 1960.
53. Vitrac, Roger. *Théâtre*, I, II. Paris, Gallimard, 1948.

54. Wheelwright, Philip. *The Burning Fountain*. Bloomington, Indiana University Press, 1954.
55. Wright, Edward A. *Understanding Today's Theatre*. Englewood Cliffs, N.J., Prentice-Hall, Inc., 1959.

BECKETT

WORKS BY BECKETT

En attendant Godot. Paris, Editions de Minuit, 1952.
Fin de partie. Paris, Editions de Minuit, 1957.
Tous Ceux qui tombent. Paris, Editions de Minuit, 1957.
La Dernière bande. Paris, Editions de Minuit, 1960.

STUDIES AND INTERVIEWS

1. Beckett, Samuel. "Letters on *Endgame*," *Village Voice*, March 19, 1958.
2. Belmont, Georges. "*Fin de partie*," *Arts*, April 10–16, 1957.
3. Champigny, Robert. "Interprétation de *En attendant Godot*," *PMLA*, June, 1960.
4. Cohn, Ruby (editor). *Perspective*, "Samuel Beckett Issue," Autumn, 1959, including an excellent introductory study by Professor Cohn, and a fine bibliography on Beckett.
5. ———. "Something Old, Something New . . ." *Yale French Studies*, Vol. 23.
6. ———. "Waiting is All." *Modern Drama*, Sept., 1960.
7. Barbour, Thomas. "Beckett and Ionesco," *Hudson Review*, Summer, 1958.
8. Eastman, Richard M. "The Strategy of Samuel Beckett's *Endgame*," *Modern Drama*, May, 1959.
9. Gold, Herbert. "Beckett: Style and Desire," *Nation*, Nov. 10, 1956.
10. Gregory, Horace. "Beckett's Dying Gladiators," *Commonweal*, Oct. 26, 1956.
11. Harvey, Lawrence E. "Art and the Existential in *En attendant Godot*," *PMLA*, March, 1960.
12. Kern, Edith G. "Drama Stripped for Inaction: Beckett's *Godot*," *Yale French Studies*, Vol. 14.
13. Lamont, Rosette C. "The Metaphysical Farce: Beckett and Ionesco," *French Review*, Feb., 1959.
14. Mayoux, Jean-Jacques. "The Theatre of Samuel Beckett," *Perspective*, Autumn, 1959.

15. McCoy, Charles S. *"Waiting for Godot:* A Biblical Appraisal," *Religion in Life,* Fall, 1959.
16. Moore, John R. "A Farewell to Something," *Tulane Drama Review,* Sept., 1960.
17. Nores, Dominique. "La Condition humaine selon Beckett," *Théâtre d'aujourd'hui,* Sept.–Oct., 1957.
18. Rexroth, Kenneth. "The Point is Irrelevance," *Nation,* April 14, 1956.
19. Sastre, Alfonso. "Siete notas sobre *Esperando a Godot,*" *Primer Acto,* No. 1, April, 1957.
20. Shenker, Israel. "Moody Man of Letters," (Interview), *New York Times,* May 6, 1956, II, 1:6.
21. Stone, Jerome. "Malone Dies," *Saturday Review of Literature,* Oct. 27, 1956.
22. Trewin, J. C. "The End Crowns All," *Illustrated London News,* April 20, 1957.

See also the "General Bibliography," nos. 2, 6, 9, 10, 15, 16, 17, 18, 21, 26, 27, 35, 37, 42, 49, 50, 52.

IONESCO

WORKS BY IONESCO

Théâtre I. Paris Gallimard, 1954. Contains: *La Cantatrice chauve, La Leçon, Jacques, ou la soumission, Les Chaises, Victimes du devoir, Amédée, ou comment s'en débarasser.*

Théâtre II. Paris, Gallimard, 1958. Contains: *L'Impromptu de l'Alma, ou le caméléon du berger, Tueur sans gages, Le Nouveau locataire, L'Avenir est dans les oeufs, ou il faut de tout pour faire un monde, Le Maître, La Jeune Fille à marier.*

Rhinocéros. Paris, Gallimard, 1959.

STUDIES AND INTERVIEWS

1. *Cahiers de la Saison,* "Portrait d'Eugène Ionesco," No. 15, Winter, 1959. A wealth of articles by and about Ionesco.
2. *Cahiers de la Compagnie Madeleine Renaud Jean-Louis Barrault,* No. 29, "Les Rhinocéros au théâtre."
3. Doubrovsky, J. S. "Ionesco and the Comedy of Absurdity," *Yale French Studies,* No. 23.
4. Dumur, Guy. "Ionesco des pieds à la tête," *Arts,* Jan. 20–26, 1960.
5. Fowlie, Wallace. "New Plays of Ionesco and Genêt," *Tulane Drama Review,* Sept., 1960.

6. Ionesco, Eugène. "Art-Anti-Art" (Interview), BBC Broadcast, Jan. 6, 1960.

7. ———. "Depuis dix ans je me bats contre l'esprit bourgeois et les tyrannies politiques," *Arts*, Jan. 20–26, 1950.

8. ———. "Expérience du théâtre," *Nouvelle Nouvelle Revue Française*, Feb., 1958. (Translated as "Discovering the Theatre," in *Tulane Drama Review*, Autumn, 1959.)

9. ———. "Le Point de départ," *Cahiers des Quatre Saisons*, No. 1, Aug., 1955. (Translated as "The Point of Departure," in *Theatre Arts*, June, 1958.)

10. ———. "Théâtre et anti-théâtre," *Cahiers des Saisons*, No. 2, Oct., 1955. (Translated as "Theatre and Anti-Theatre," in *Theatre Arts*, June, 1958.)

11. ———. "La Tragédie du langage," *Spectacles*, No. 2, July, 1958. (Translated as "The Tragedy of Language," in *Tulane Drama Review*, Spring, 1960.)

12. ———. "The World of Ionesco," *Tulane Drama Review*, Oct., 1958.

13. Lerminier, Georges, "Clés pour Ionesco," *Théâtre d'aujourd'hui*, Sept.–Oct., 1957.

14. Pronko, Leonard. "The Anti-Spiritual Victory in the Theatre of Ionesco," *Modern Drama*, May, 1959.

15. Reed, Muriel. "Ionesco," *Réalités* (English language edition), Dec., 1957.

16. Touchard, Pierre-Aimé. "Eugène Ionesco a renouvellé les mythes du théâtre," *Arts*, Feb. 27–March 5, 1957.

17. Watson, Donald. "The Plays of Ionesco," *Tulane Drama Review*, Oct., 1958.

18. Wilbur, Robert H. "Ionesco in Paris: Sopranos to Rhinoceroses," *Northwest Review*, Spring, 1960.

See also "General Bibliography" nos. 2, 6, 10, 12, 15, 16, 17, 18, 21, 26, 29, 35, 42, 49, 50, 52. And "Beckett Bibliography," nos. 7 and 13.

ADAMOV

WORKS BY ADAMOV

Théâtre I. Paris Gallimard, 1953. Contains: *La Parodie, L'Invasion, La grande et la petite manoeuvre, Le Professeur Taranne, Tous contre tous.*

Théâtre II. Paris, Gallimard, 1955. Contains: *Le Sens de la marche, Les Retrouvailles, Le Ping-Pong,* a preface by Adamov.

Paolo Paoli. Paris, Gallimard, 1957.
"The Endless Humiliation," from *l'Aveu, Evergreen Review,*
Spring, 1959.

STUDIES

1. Gandon, Yves. "Tous contre tous," *France Illustration,*
May 16, 1953.
2. Lynes, Jr., Carlos. "Adamov and 'le sens littéral' in the
Theatre," *Yale French Studies,* No. 14.

See also "General Bibliography," nos. 6, 10, 12, 15, 18, 21,
26, 27, 49, 50.

GENÊT

WORKS BY GENÊT

Haute surveillance. Paris, Gallimard, 1949.
Les Bonnes. Sceau, Jean-Jacques Pauvert, 1954, with an
introduction by the author.
Le Balcon. Décines, l'Arbalète.
Les Nègres. Décines, l'Arbalète.

STUDIES

1. Clark, Eleanor. "The World of Jean Genêt," *Partisan
Review,* April, 1949.
2. Clurman, Harold. "Theatre," *Nation,* July 6, 1957.
3. Genêt, Jean. "J'ai été victime d'une tentative d'assassinat,"
Arts, May 1–7, 1957.
4. Marcabru, Pierre. "Les Nègres," *Arts,* Nov. 11–17, 1959.
5. Mason, Colin. "Contemporary Arts," *The Spectator,* May
3, 1957.
6. Sartre, Jean-Paul. *Saint Genêt, Comédien et martyr.* Paris,
Gallimard, 1952.
7. Worsley, T. C. "*The Balcony* at the Arts," *New Statesman
and Nation,* April 27, 1957.

See also "General Bibliography," nos. 6, 21, 27, 28, 36, and
"Ionesco Bibliography," No. 5.

TARDIEU

WORKS BY TARDIEU

Théâtre de Chambre. Paris, Gallimard, 1955.
Poèmes à jouer (Théâtre II). Paris, Gallimard, 1960.

STUDIES

See "General Bibliography," nos. 6, 49, 50.

VAUTHIER

WORKS BY VAUTHIER

Théâtre. Paris, l'Arche, 1953. Contains: *Le Capitaine Bada, La Nouvelle mandragore.*
Le Personnage combattant. Paris, Gallimard, 1955.
Les Prodiges. Paris, Gallimard, 1958.

STUDIES

See "General Bibliography," nos. 6, 10, 49, 50.

PICHETTE

WORKS BY PICHETTE

Les Ephiphanies. Paris, K Editeur, 1948.
Nucléa. Paris, l'Arche, 1952.

STUDIES

1. Shattuck, Roger. "A Poet's Progress: Henri Pichette," *French Review,* Dec., 1958.
See also "General Bibliography," nos. 6, 21, 27, 49, 50.

GHELDERODE

WORKS BY GHELDERODE

Théâtre I. Paris, Gallimard, 1950. Contains: *Hop Signor!, Escurial, Sire Halewyn, Magie rouge, Mademoiselle Jaïre, Fastes d'enfer.*
Théâtre II. Paris, Gallimard, 1952. Contains: *Le Cavalier bizarre, La Balade du Grand Macabre, Trois acteurs, un drame, Christophe Colomb, Les Femmes au tombeau, La Farce des ténébreux.*
Théâtre III. Paris, Gallimard, 1953. Contains: *La Pie sur le gibet, Pantagleize, D'un Diable qui prêcha merveilles, Sortie de l'acteur, L'Ecole des bouffons.*
Théâtre IV. Paris, Gallimard, 1955. Contains: *Un soir de pitié, Don Juan, Le Club des menteurs, Les Vieillards, Marie la Misérable, Masques ostendais.*
Théâtre V. Paris, Gallimard, 1957. Contains: *Le Soleil se couche, Les Aveugles, Barabbas, Le Ménage de Caroline, La Mort du docteur Faust, Adrian et Jusémina, Piet Bouteille.*

STUDIES AND INTERVIEWS

1. Francis, Jean. *Michel de Ghelderode, dramaturge des pays de par-deça.* Brussels, Labor, 1949.
2. Hauger, George. "The Plays of Ghelderode," *Tulane Drama Review,* Autumn, 1959.

3. Iglesis, R., and A. Trutat, *Les Entretiens d'Ostende*. (Interviews) Paris, l'Arche, 1956.
See also "General Bibliography," nos. 6, 26, 27, 49, 50.

AUDIBERTI

WORKS BY AUDIBERTI

Théâtre I. Paris, Gallimard, 1948. Contains: *Quoat-Quoat, L'Ampélour, Les Femmes du Boeuf, Le Mal court.*
Théâtre II. Paris, Gallimard, 1952. Contains: *Pucelle, La Fête noire, Les Naturels du Bordelais.*
Théâtre III. Paris, Gallimard, 1956. Contains: *La Logeuse, Opéra parlé, Le Ouallou, Altanima.*
Le Cavalier seul. Paris, Gallimard, 1955.
La Hobereaute. In *Paris-Théâtre*, No. 146.
L'Effet Glapion. In *l'Avant-Scène*, No. 205.

STUDIES

1. Cornell, Kenneth. "Audiberti and Obscurity," *Yale French Studies*, No. 4.
2. Damiens, Claude. "Jacques Audiberti: un surréaliste dompté," *Paris-Théâtre*, No. 146.
3. Dumur, Guy. "Audiberti, ou le Théâtre en liberté," *Thèâtre Populaire*, No. 31.
4. Kempt, Robert. "La Hobereaute," *Le Monde*, Sept. 25–Oct. 1, 1958.
See also "General Bibliography," nos. 6, 27, 49, 50.

SCHEHADÉ

WORKS BY SCHEHADÉ

Monsieur Bob'le. Paris, Gallimard, 1951.
La Soirée des proverbes. Paris, Gallimard, 1954.
Histoire de Vasco. Paris, Gallimard, 1956.
Les Violettes. Paris, Gallimard, 1960.

STUDIES

1. *Cahiers de la Compagnie Madeleine Renaud Jean-Louis Barrault*, No. 4: "Le Petit théâtre" (articles on *La Soirée des proverbes*).
2. ————, No. 17: "Georges Schehadé et l'*Histoire de Vasco*."
See also "General Bibliography," nos. 6, 21, 27, 49.

225